MW00387092

PERSIAN FEASTS

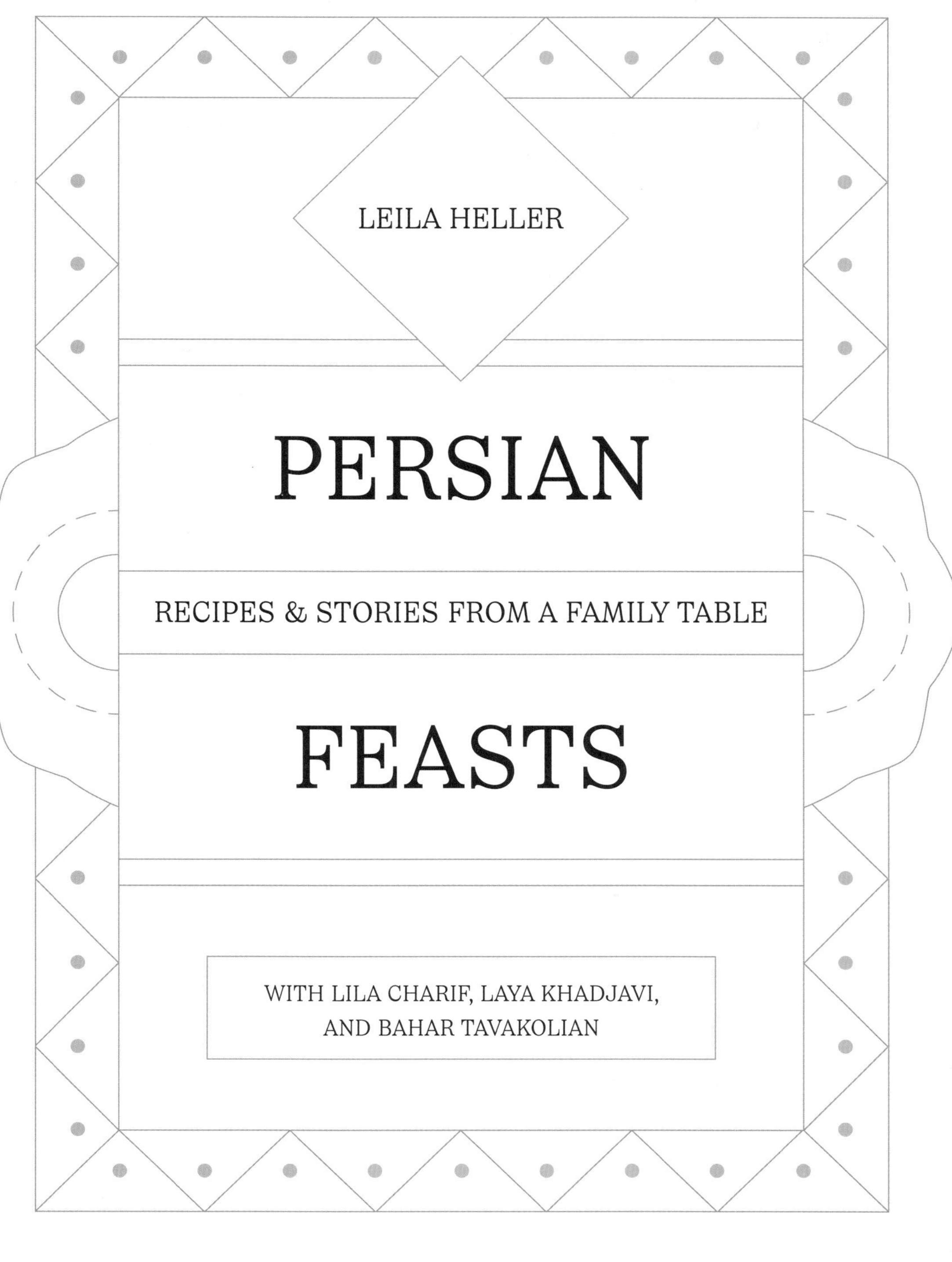

LEILA HELLER

PERSIAN FEASTS

RECIPES & STORIES FROM A FAMILY TABLE

WITH LILA CHARIF, LAYA KHADJAVI,
AND BAHAR TAVAKOLIAN

THIS BOOK IS DEDICATED TO MY MOTHER

NAHID BAYAT MAKU TAGHINIA-MILANI,

A *SHIRZAN* (LION LADY), AND THE BRILLIANT,

COURAGEOUS, AND BRAVE WOMEN OF IRAN,

WHO INSPIRE ALL OF US.

Vegetarian

Vegan

Dairy-free

Gluten-free

Nut-free

5 ingredients or less

30 min or less

SCENTS OF A DISTANT LAND

Tehran, 1979.

She felt the front wheels slowly lift off the ground. My grandmother's heart skipped a beat and, as she grasped my grandfather's hand, a bead of sweat dripped down her forehead.

The back wheels teetered back and forth.

My grandmother clutched my grandfather's hand between hers. She closed her eyes, hoping this was a bad dream. She wished she could wake up and smell the orange blossom tree outside her window. She wanted to feel the steam from the fresh bread baking downstairs. More than anything, she wanted the feeling of carrying her famous cherry rice into the dining room, where her family would be gathered around the table.

Nahid Joon with her children Leila (right) and Mamady (left)

However, it was not meant to be. And as the back wheels finally lifted off the ground, the last of her hopes began to evaporate along with the view of her beloved home.

As she looked back, she saw the distant turquoise domes and minarets, and the streets she had walked for the past forty-three years.

The seatbelt sign was turned off.

She peered through the window at the snow-capped mountains, overlapping all the way up to the Caspian Sea. She was overcome with emotion:

joy in thinking back on her happy times, but mostly a deep sadness that would stay with her for many years to come.

She took one long last look at Iran.

My grandmother closed her eyes and sat back, not knowing if she would ever see her home again.

New York City, Thanksgiving Day, 2010.

The waft of Persian cherry rice and oven-roasted turkey drifted into the hallway outside my grandmother's New York apartment. As I walked toward her door, I was intoxicated by the bewitching aroma of saffron, cumin, turmeric, and cloves. I was immediately transported to my Iranian home, a colorful Persian-styled oasis, reminiscent of a souk, in the middle of New York City.

After dinner, I sank deep into the turquoise silk cushions next to my grandma. I listened to stories of Iran and of her native Azerbaijan, where her ancestors had lived for over one thousand years. I relished these moments, as she rarely spoke about her life in Iran before the revolution.

She told me about the orange blossom trees, the rose gardens, and her home in the hills below the Alborz Mountains. I was always overjoyed to hear about my heritage, my Zoroastrian ancestry, and the meaning behind the traditions we celebrate. My grandma, however, was left teary-eyed. I realized that after thirty-three years in the United States, she was still a Persian at heart. The memories of her life in Iran still played an integral part in her daily life in her adopted country.

Through her recollections, I feel tenderness in my heart for Iran, despite the fact that I have never set foot in that distant land. I know that my grandmother will never have the sense of security that I feel as an American, even though she is a proud, naturalized citizen.

The ups and downs of my grandmother's life have been my greatest source of inspiration. I have learned that material possessions are not important, as they can always be taken away from you. Like my grandmother, I know that no matter what the future holds, no one can ever rob me of my education, traditions, friendships, and, most importantly, values. I can survive and thrive anywhere in the world with the strength of character I have developed through having her as my role model.

—Philip Salar Heller

INTRODUCTION

My mother, Nahid Taghinia-Milani, known as Nahid Joon, celebrated Persian cuisine and culture in every aspect of her life. For her, cooking was the art of transforming an everyday necessity into a feast. It was an act of love. I always had a sense of this growing up, but it was much later that I realized my mother's passion manifested in creating timeless culinary masterpieces. It was a meditative and therapeutic experience, defining her identity and essence.

I grew up in Tehran in the 1960s in the foothills of the splendidly snow-capped Alborz Mountains. While Iran was developing into a modern society, it still maintained many enchanting traditions from its 5,000-year-old culture. For my mother, this culture was embodied in the stories of food that passed from generation to generation. She felt the responsibility to share these ancestral stories and recipes with me, my children, and all of our friends and family. Whenever I reminisce about our family life in Tehran, our meals at home still conjure vivid memories of the flavors and textures of her signature dishes.

My brother and I loved to accompany my mother shopping at Tajrish Bazaar, near our home. Everyone—from the butcher and fishmonger to the fruit vendor and spice merchant—was always happy to see her and show off the best produce in their stands. I learned from her how to choose the best melons and fragrant spices and smell everything I buy.

Although she never returned to Iran after the revolution in 1979, my mother loved her country fervently. The alienation from her homeland prompted a more profound attachment to her heritage and its preservation. She spent her life in the United States, longing for a country where she had her roots, where her ancestors had lived for over a thousand years.

My mother's legacy was her cooking. She was a true artist. The abundant spices, fresh herbs, and myriad ingredients were her paints; her sense of smell and taste were her paintbrushes.

Her elaborate dishes were defined by the rich traditions of her exotic past and the modern influences of her present life. Her cuisine combined classic, sophisticated Persian cuisine with contemporary inspirations from great Western chefs. The vibrant colors, the irresistible fragrances, and the exceptional flavors created extraordinary sensations with every bite. My mother eschewed conventional cooking guidelines and never followed recipes; instead, she was guided by her instincts and senses. She composed, experimented, and tasted as she went along. She was audacious in her bold use of unusual ingredients.

Her cooking often reflected her mood, whether she added Persian lime juice or pomegranate molasses for a sour note or infused a dish with honey for something sweet. When she craved warmth, she'd include cinnamon, nutmeg, or cardamom. Her finishing touches would include a sprinkle of fresh herbs or a splash of rose water or orange blossom water.

During our travels every summer—where we visited impressive food halls and markets to discover local flavors and ingredients—my mother sought out new ideas for her dishes. I recall her fascination with the spice markets in Istanbul, Marrakesh, and Dubai, the open-air food and cheese markets in Paris, the fish market in Barcelona, and the Munich fruit market with its sixty-five varieties of berries.

My mother had an innate talent for entertaining, and her dinners were magical. She was the most gracious and enchanting hostess. She shared her table with those she loved and mesmerized her guests with her well-orchestrated menus and innovative and creative cuisine. The floral displays on her tables demonstrated her skills as an ikebana master. The choice of classical or Persian music and the selection of china, silverware, and antique embroidered tablecloths were always perfectly curated.

Her life's journey took her from Tehran to Geneva, London, Nice, and finally New York. In the United States, she brought the same sophistication and elegance to her hospitality and became the de facto ambassador for her beloved homeland. She raised her children in a warm and happy home, nurtured her many friendships, and lived a highly refined life.

Nahid Joon's favorite room in her New York apartment was her kitchen. It was designed by the renowned architect Nasser Ahari, our late cousin, who added beautiful sculptural details throughout. Her exquisite food was prepared in this very kitchen, and these dishes are now recorded through the many recipes and stories in this book.

All my life, I have been my mother's daughter. As I built my career as an art gallerist, my mother was by my side every step of the way. She raised me and gave me an appreciation for different cultures and a truly international perspective, which influenced my approach to art and life. The countless hours we spent together in the kitchen have informed my cooking today—I have fond memories of the meals we prepared together for my gallery events.

My mother had always wanted me to write a Persian cookbook, but I believed it was an endeavor that belonged to her—a project she had worked on all her life. When she passed away unexpectedly in 2018, I wished to continue her legacy. Encouraged by my coauthors Lila Charif, Laya Khadjavi, and Bahar Tavakolian, who were like daughters to my mother and are like sisters to me, I decided to fulfill her dream.

This cookbook is a love letter—from a daughter to a mother, and from all the people who loved Nahid Joon and her food. My mother would have been delighted to share her life's work with you. This book illuminates her extraordinary life's journey; it's her legacy and final gift of love for all who cherish Persian cuisine.

—Leila Heller

FAMILY HISTORY

My mother, née Nahid Khanom Bayat Maku, traced her heritage to a long line of Persian rulers and military leaders. Her ancestors were from the Bayat tribe and descendants of Oghuz Turks who migrated from the Aral steppes in Central Asia, arriving in Persia from Turkey before the eleventh century. Over the following centuries, the Bayat clan migrated to different regions in Persia and settled in Azerbaijan. They were strategic allies for early Persian leaders, including the rulers of the Safavid Empire during the sixteenth century. As a feudal family, they controlled a tribal kingdom within Azerbaijan with their own army, owning land and villages and playing a crucial role in the agricultural development and economic prosperity of Azerbaijan.

The family was also influential in international politics. When the Treaty of Gulistan was signed in 1813, a peace treaty between Russia and Persia that concluded the first Russo-Persian War, parts of Azerbaijan were ceded to Russia. However, one of Nahid Joon's ancestors, her great-uncle Teymour Pasha Khan (Amir Toman), played an instrumental role in the diplomatic negotiations to maintain Maku and the surrounding region of Azerbaijan as a province of Persia. In recognition for brokering this successful agreement with the Russians, the Bayat family was gifted a principality in Azerbaijan by Nasseredin Shah, the most important king of the Qajar dynasty.

The Maku Khanate witnessed numerous battles during World War I, as it was located at the intersection of various frontiers. (A khanate was a political territory ruled by a khan and equivalent to a kingdom or empire.) Struggles in the aftermath of the war between Turkey, Russia, England, and Armenia gave rise to heated events in the Maku Khanate. Azerbaijan was also at a junction between East and West. Because of its location along the Silk Road, its geographic position was strategic in terms of trade and geopolitical importance.

The Maku Khanate was a melting pot of cultures, religions, and ethnicities, which contributed to the inherent diversity of this independent principality. Maku also played a predominant role in the political, trade, and religious history of the Armenians. It had been a region of the old Armenia, previously known as Artaz, and had become part of Persia in 521 BCE. Some of the most important Armenian churches, such as the Church of Tatavous (also known as Ghara Kelissa), were built in the vicinity of Maku. To this day, Armenians from all over the world make annual pilgrimages to Maku to visit this church.

In 1920, Maku played another major role in the international arena when the territory took in Armenian refugees who were being persecuted by the Turks. Along with the khanate's support of anti-Bolshevik forces in Russia, these actions drew the ire of neighboring states. Russian and Turkish forces invaded, but neither country could conquer Maku because its army was so powerful. My grandfather, Hamdollah Pasha Khan, fought valiantly in this war and led the Maku army to its victory.

In order to consolidate their power and influence over the territory that they controlled, the family constructed the famous Baghcheh Joogh Palace,

which eventually became a national heritage site. (*Baghcheh* is the Farsi and Turkish word for "garden," and *joogh* is the Armenian word for "village.") The palace was built at the end of the Qajar dynasty by Teymour Pasha Khan (Amir Toman), the sixth khan of the Maku Khanate and Nahid Joon's great-great-uncle, and completed by his son Eghbalolsaltaneh, Sardar of Persia's northwest territories and one of the commanders for the Persian shah, Mozaffaredin Shah Qajar. Eghbalolsaltaneh married Anali Khanom, the daughter of the Khan of Yerevan. Nahid Joon told me on many occasions that Eghbalolsaltaneh went on hunting trips to Russia with Nicolai, the last czar of Russia, and he admired his hunting palace. Nicolai accommodated him by sending forty architects, builders, and craftsmen to Maku, who, with their Persian counterparts, built the Baghcheh Joogh Palace.

The palace was a combination of traditional Persian and nineteenth-century European, Russian, and Persian architecture. The stucco reliefs, the mirror work, and the stained-glass windows were the creation of talented Persian and Russian craftsmen. Eghbalolsaltaneh traveled to Paris and other European cities and purchased the furniture, sculptures, and paintings for the palace (including the first gramophone imported to Persia). The Bayat Maku family and the descendants of Eghbalolsaltaneh continued to live in the palace until they donated it to the State in 1974, when it was transformed into a museum that still exists today. It is visited by thousands of tourists annually.

One of the highlights of the palace is its dining room ceiling, which has a fresco depicting the dinner following the signing of the Treaty of Gulistan. Two dining scenes are portrayed in the fresco. The table at the right is Persian, with men in traditional attire around a Persian *sofreh* (a traditional tablecloth) and eating meat kebabs, Persian stews, and naan (Persian bread) with their hands. The table at the left is Russian, decorated with silver candelabra and wine goblets, with the men elegantly dressed and women in ball gowns seated at a long banquet table. The shared ceiling is adorned with rows of fruits, which highlight the abundance of produce grown in the fertile lands of Azerbaijan. The contrast between both tables is remarkable and illustrates the different cultural traditions of both empires.

In 1925, Reza Shah Pahlavi integrated Azerbaijan along with other provinces into modern-day Iran. To consolidate his new Iran, Reza Shah moved my immediate family from Maku to Tehran, merging the army of the Bayat family with his own army. He made my grandfather a minister of parliament and assigned him the title of *Salar Lashkar* (Commander of the army). Thereafter, he was called Salar Pasha Khan Salar Lashkar.

My mother was born in Tehran in 1933, the daughter of Hamdollah Pasha Khan Bayat Maku, the commander-in-chief of the Azerbaijan army (*Salar Lashkar*) and Nosrat Khanom Majdolmolk Amin Afshar. On her father's side, she was a descendant of Ahmad Sultan, the founder of the Maku Khanate, and of Hossein Khan Sardar and Ali Khan Sardar, two of the first rulers of Maku. She was a great-granddaughter of Sadighdolleh, the first son of Ali Khan Sardar, and Sadighnezam. She was a granddaughter of Amir Amjad, the third son of Ali Khan Sardar.

Ahmad Sultan was a general for Nader Shah, founder of the Afsharid dynasty that ruled Persia during the eighteenth century. When Nader Shah was murdered, Ahmad Sultan fled to Maku with one of the wives of Nader Shah, taking with him part of Nader Shah's jewelry collection, which he brought from his conquests of India. These jewels were taken from the

Bayat Maku family to Tehran when Reza Shah consolidated Iran. They are currently in Bank Meli in Tehran and are the backing for the Iranian currency. The collection includes the largest known pearls in the world and were, at one point, the worry beads of my great-grandfather.

On her mother's side, Nahid Joon also was a descendant of Nader Shah. Her maternal grandfather, Majdolmolk Amin Afshar, was the Minister of the Court during the reign of Mohammad Ali Shah Qajar in the early twentieth century.

My father, Parviz Taghinia-Milani (née Taghiof), was born in Samarkand, Uzbekistan, to Mohammad Hossein Taghiof and Leila Oskoui Taghiof. My grandfather owned the largest tea factories in all of Russia. When the Bolsheviks took power, they confiscated the Taghiof estate and the factories. My grandfather fled to Shanghai, where one of his brothers had a tea business that supplied the tea leaves that were traded on the Silk Road to Samarkand. My grandfather's other brother was in charge of their office in Bombay, where they packaged the leaves and exported them to Samarkand.

During the Bolshevik Revolution, my grandmother Leila and her six children (including my father) went into hiding to escape from the Bolsheviks and waited for my grandfather to return. My grandfather died in Kandahar, Afghanistan, while traveling to pick up his family to move them to Shanghai. The family then moved to Mashad in the Khorasan province of Iran, where another uncle lived.

When he was eighteen, my father traveled for nine months via Bombay to the United States to continue his studies. He attended Cornell University and subsequently moved to Los Angeles, where he received his degree in business administration from UCLA while working at the War Office during World War II. He then moved to New York City and received another degree from New York University's business school. With his brother Nader, he started an office in New York, trading cotton and jute with his other brother Jaffar in Tehran. At thirty-two years old, he traveled to Iran on a summer vacation to visit his brother and sisters. Upon his arrival, his sisters arranged for him to meet my mother, Nahid Joon, and he was spellbound by her grace and beauty. He then requested her hand in marriage, but my grandfather Salar forbade her to move to the United States. He asked my father to return to Iran if he wished to marry her. My father returned to Iran within months and, in 1952, he and Nahid Joon married.

At the beginning of their fifty-year marriage, Nahid Joon's sisters-in-law worried that their brother would go hungry because his Azerbaijani-Persian bride did not know how to cook Russian food. Like most Persian women, Nahid Joon had learned the art of cooking from her mother, using the fabulous ingredients that came from the Bayat family's fertile lands in Azerbaijan. Nahid Joon quickly learned recipes originating from Uzbekistan and southern Russia. She integrated these influences into her cooking, which can be appreciated in many of the recipes in this cookbook.

On our visits to Baghcheh Joogh Palace, my mother always acknowledged the frescoes on the dining room ceiling. The sofreh was covered with flowers, pomegranates, grapes, pears, and apples, and the ceiling was adorned with frescoes of gourds, eggplants (aubergines), melons, watermelons, quince, and other fruits. These frescoes illustrated a Persian feast enjoyed by both the Persians and the Russians and inspired her as a symbolic fusion of East and West in Iran. They also captured the essence of her cooking.

REGIONAL CUISINES OF IRAN

The cuisine of Iran, with origins dating back centuries, is arguably one of the most sophisticated in the world, offering an incredible array of dishes. This cuisine hails from the lands of ancient Persia and has evolved through the ages to what comprises the myriad and distinct regional cuisines in present-day Iran. Also shaping this cuisine is the variety of climes in Iran, the country's terrain and geography, with rich soil and plentiful sunshine, as well as the ethnocultural diversity of the country. Seasonal ingredients, fresh herbs, fragrant spices, fruits, nuts, and aromatic rice are the staples of Persian cuisine.

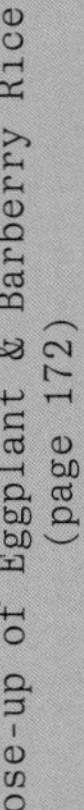

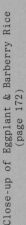

Close-up of Eggplant & Barberry Rice (page 172)

Recipes, passed down through generations, are refined with time. The most delicious and elegant meals can only really be enjoyed in private homes of Iranians, where centuries-old traditions and know-how are kept alive and continuously perfected. The result is a richly layered cuisine with complex yet subtle flavors.

The population of Iran comprises Persians, who make up the majority of the country, Turks, Kurds, Baloch, Bakhtiari, Lur, and Arabs. It also includes minorities such as Armenians and Assyrians.

Iran has always been at the crossroads of East and West, dating back to when it was a trading hub along caravan routes that made up the ancient Silk Road. Marco Polo would have traversed these routes in the thirteenth century, passing through date palm groves and fragrant citrus orchards and feasting on wild fowl and game. This strategic positioning introduced exotic spices, teas, fruits, and culinary traditions from far-flung countries, including China, India, Greece, and Italy.

Iran is a large country of over 630,000 square miles (about one-sixth of the size of the United States). Its geography ranges from the mountainous (Kurdistan and Azerbaijan in the west and northwest, Khorasan in the northeast) to the lush, forested regions of Gilan and Mazandaran bordering the Caspian Sea. The foothills of the Alborz and Zagros mountain ranges have a dry temperate climate, and south and east to the central desert plains form the country's hot heartland. Further south are the hot and humid provinces and marshlands bordering the Persian Gulf.

Below are some notable regions and dishes that inspired Nahid Joon's artful creations in this book.

Dried rosebuds

AZERBAIJAN

The Azerbaijan provinces in northwest Iran, from where Nahid Joon's paternal and maternal families hail, border Armenia and Azerbaijan to the north and Turkey to the west. The mountainous region enjoys all four seasons: fragrant springs, hot and dry summers, crisp autumns, and cold snowy winters. Its refined cuisine is characterized by elaborate cooking techniques and the use of herb and spice blends to impart complex flavors to the food.

The widely popular Iranian thick soup (*aash*) come in various forms in Azerbaijan. Nahid Joon's legendary creations, inspired by Azerbaijani cuisine, were brought to new heights of culinary sophistication. This includes Pomegranate & Herb Potage (page 78) and Barley & Herb Potage (page 80). Similarly, Nahid Joon's take on Beef Soup with Beans, Chickpeas & Potatoes (page 86) transformed a simple national staple to an exquisite culinary experience.

Rice dishes are also typical of this region. Local legend has it that a cooked Cornish hen could reside in the center of a *kufteh tabrizi*, a large globe of rice mixed with herbs, nuts, dried fruits, and ground (minced) beef. Barberry Rice with Chicken (page 192) is a dish with complex flavors, courtesy of the Persian spice blend *advieh*. Nahid Joon took pride in preparing her own *advieh* (page 246), a prized gift she would so often share with friends.

✷

CASPIAN COAST

The lush land bordering the Caspian Sea is mountainous and forested with a coastal plain along the sea that is spotted with rice paddies. It has humid summers and cold winters. Caspian cuisine is influenced by incredible fish (sturgeon and sturgeon caviar are farmed in this region), the rice cultivated in the local rice paddies, fresh produce like its signature olives, and the abundance of fowl.

The staple food of the region is *kateh* rice (page 247) served with salted or smoked fish. It also includes tart and tangy stews, such as Sour Chicken Stew with Herbs (page 151) and Tomato & Celery Stew with Chicken (page 146). The Chicken Saffron Frittata (page 53), known locally as *chegh-ertmeh,* is infused with the aromas and flavors of saffron and citrus. Also distinctive to this region are delectable vegetarian dishes, such as Smoked Eggplant with Tomato (page 42) and fava (broad) beans with garlic and herbs (*baghala ghatogh*).

✷

CENTRAL PROVINCES OF ISFAHAN, KASHAN, AND YAZD

Central provinces include three notable cities in the central plains of Iran. Isfahan is situated in the foothills of the Zagros Mountains (and arguably among the most stunning and beautiful cities in the world). Kashan, a city of gardens, was a verdant oasis along the central deserts of Iran. The ancient Zoroastrian city of Yazd has a dry, sunny climate with rich soil. The Zayandeh Rud river, which flows through Isfahan, nourishes most of the rest of this region through a network of qanats. An ingenious engineering invention of ancient Persians, qanats consist of a network of underground aqueducts that transport water long distances through arid regions.

Grown in the desert climes of this region are the tastiest fruits: Persian quinces, mulberries, plums, pomegranates, and the prized and exquisitely juicy and native white cherries. The most fragrant roses are cultivated in this river basin as well. The villages of Qamsar and Neyasar are famous for their early spring rose festivals, where roses are harvested from the crack of dawn until mid-morning, when they're at their peak freshness and the petals are supple. (Rose petals lose their moisture under the strong sun.)

Rose water, dried rose petals, and rosebuds are staples of Persian cuisine. Rose water is used in desserts such as Cardamom & Rose Water Pudding (page 229). Dried rose petals are added to Cucumber-Herb Yogurt (page 38) and yogurt and sherbet drinks, while dried rosebuds are used to make tea. The most famous Isfahan dish is *beryouni*, a medley of ground (minced) lamb, beef, and spices served with traditional *sangak* bread. Meat & Yellow Split Pea Stew (page 160) and sweet, tangy veal and quince stew (page 158) are also staples within the region.

KERMAN

The province of Kerman is known for its exquisite carpets and spectacular star-studded desert sky. Notable produce includes dates, cumin, pistachios, and the most fragrant citruses.

Kerman cumin (*zireyeh Kerman*) is grown in the oasis town of Mahan. Cumin plants are drought tolerant and its seeds, grown in the hot desert climate, are incredibly aromatic. The Persian expression *zireh be Kerman bordan* (which means "taking cumin to Kerman") refers to a useless or redundant act—after all, who in their right mind would take cumin to Kerman, where the best can be found? Ground cumin is essential to the Persian Spice Blend (page 246). Nahid Joon always asked travelers to Iran to bring back cumin from Kerman, and she used it to create her signature advieh and to generously season rice dishes, stews, hearty soups, and pickles.

Pistachio orchards abound in Rafsanjan, in northern Kerman and border the southwestern edge of the great Lut Desert. There is arguably no pistachio as tasteful and plump as those from the orchards of Rafsanjan. Pistachio Soup (page 68) is a delectable dish.

The ancient city of Bam was once a strategic hub along the Silk Road, connecting it to India and China to the east and Egypt, Greece, and Rome to the west. It is home to one of the most delicious varieties of Iranian dates—with a thin, dark skin and sweet, soft, and succulent flesh. A simple Iranian meal may consist of a few dates, fresh bread, and Persian tea.

While date groves also abound in Jiroft, the region is best known for its citrus orchards, ranging from oranges and tangerines to the Persian sweet lemon and tart limes that are dried to add zest to many of our stews.

✳

KHUZESTAN AND SOUTHERN PERSIAN GULF PROVINCES

The provinces bordering the Persian Gulf, as well as the Iranian islands of Kish, Qeshm, and Hormuz, have a tropical climate with hot, humid summers and mild winters. It also has an ethnically diverse population of predominantly Persians, Arabs, and Baloch, but also Kurds, East Africans, Armenians, and Jews. Taking from all these influences, the cuisine of this region of Iran is diverse, centered on fresh seafood from the Persian Gulf (shrimp [prawns], oysters, calamari, lobster, crab) and native saltwater fish (pomfret, mackerel, grouper, flounder, tuna, and snapper). Spices and chilies are often added to give the fish and seafood dishes some heat.

Arab and Indian influences are also evident in the cuisine. For example, Spicy Tamarind Fish & Herb Stew (*ghelieh mahi*) combines the Arabic word *ghelieh* (stew) and the Farsi word *mahi* (fish). It is a popular dish made with a white fish in a sauce of tamarind paste, red pepper, and an array of spices and herbs. It is also interesting to note that the word "tamarind," often used in Iranian cuisine of the Gulf region, comes from the Arabic *tamr hindi*, meaning "the fruit of the Indian tamarind tree."

The region is also home to a variety of dates, which are eaten alone, added to desserts, or made into date molasses and powdered dates (often used as sweeteners in the cuisine). Other typical ingredients include dried Persian limes, sour oranges, and sumac, all of which impart a pleasant tartness to dishes.

CEREMONIES, HOLIDAYS, AND CELEBRATIONS

The First Persian Empire extended from the Balkans and Eastern Europe in the west to the Indus Valley in the east. This vast and diverse entity, the largest ever in its time, included multiple ethnic groups and nationalities. As a predominantly agrarian society, the culture of ancient Persia was closely guided by the natural elements and cycles.

Deeply influenced by ancient Persia, the celebrations in modern Iran often mark astronomical phenomena and change of seasons. Iranian folklore guide the mood and the rituals. An elaborate meal is an inherent part of a Persian celebration.

✻

NOWRUZ

Nowruz (meaning "New Day") is the most widely celebrated Iranian festivity. It marks the spring equinox and the beginning of the Persian New Year. Ancient Persians were followers of Zarathushtra, the first prophet with a monotheistic message. At the core of Zoroastrian belief is the concept of good and evil locked in an eternal struggle for domination. Nowruz is a celebration of the eventual triumph of good over evil, light over darkness, when winter is over and days become longer than nights. It is customary to visit friends and family, starting with older relatives.

The centerpiece of Nowruz celebrations is the *Haft Siin* (Seven Ss), an elaborate and festive display of seven items with names that start with an *S* (*siin*) in Persian. Although the exact components of the *Haft Siin* display may vary slightly from home to home, the following highlights the most customary ones:

- *Sabzeh* (sprouted seeds): rebirth and renewal
- *Siir* (garlic): good health
- *Sumac*: sunrise or spice of life
- *Seeb* (apples): health and beauty
- *Serkeh* (vinegar): patience
- *Samanu* (Persian sweet paste made from germinated wheat): fertility and sweetness of life
- *Senjed* (silver berries): love and affection

Other components that may be displayed alongside the *Haft Siin* include mirrors (self-reflection), goldfish in a bowl (movement and passage of time, also the zodiac sign Pisces, which coincides with the last month of the Persian calendar), colored eggs (fertility), wild rue (the smoke from its burning seeds is believed to ward off harm, or "keep the evil eye away"), and coins (prosperity). A colorful array of spring flowers including hyacinth, tulips, and pussy willows adorn the spread.

The traditions of Nowruz are also a feast for the senses. This might include the scent of hyacinth and rose water or the fragrances of almond and pistachio pastes and honey; the aroma of steamed rice with fresh herbs;

and the sizzle of battered white fish in olive oil. The Herb Frittata (page 50) is a popular dish on the lunch table during Nowruz.

Nowruz is observed for twelve days. On the thirteenth day of the year, it is customary to go to the countryside to avoid the bad omen of this day. The outing on the thirteenth (*sizdeh be dar*) marks the end of the Nowruz festivities.

The components of *Haft Siin* signify desires and hopes for health, joy, and prosperity throughout the year

TIRGAN

Tirgan is a midsummer celebration. *Tir* or *tishtar,* meaning “arrow” in modern Persian and Middle Persian, respectively, was believed to be the divine entity presiding over the brightest star in the sky and in control of thunder and rain. Tir or tishtar is invoked in midsummer to counter drought and enhance harvest.

Tirgan is also a celebration of courage, strength, and self-sacrifice, which are revered attributes among Persians. In Persian mythology, these qualities are personified in Arash the Archer (*Arash Kamangir*). Tirgan is celebrated on the day that Arash releases a fateful arrow from atop Mount Damavand to demarcate the border between Iran and Turaan (a historic region bordering Iran). The story is that Iran was defeated after sixty years of war with Turan. As the last act of humiliation, and to reduce the Iranian territory to a minimum, it was decided that an Iranian archer must shoot an arrow from Mount Damavand and the arrow’s landing place would mark the border between the two kingdoms. Arash volunteered for the task. He knew that he would have to put all his might into the arrow to ensure a vast territory for Iran and that he would have to give his life to this purpose. He climbed to the summit of Damavand and released his arrow. With Arash’s strength and commitment, the arrow traveled for days and a distance of over 1,400 miles (2,200 kilometers), landing on a walnut tree at the edge of Oxus River (*Amu Darya*) presently in Central Asia. (Afghanistan was then recognized as the border of ancient Iran and Turan.) According to legend, Arash perished as he released the arrow and his body was never found. Climbers of Mount Damavand believe they hear the echo of his voice guiding them through the demanding climb.

As summer advances, fruits and vegetables find their way onto the Persian table. Chicken & Peach Stew (page 142) and Meat & Yellow Split Pea Stew (page 160) are favorites.

✺

MEHRGAN

Mehrgan is a harvest festival celebrated on the autumn equinox. It is a tribute to Mithra, who is the divine entity in Zoroastrian belief and deemed to be the protector of love, friendship, and justice. Mithra was also believed to be the bestower of good fortune and abundant crops. Mehrgan, in origin, was a Thanksgiving celebration to reap the fruits of labor throughout the year. It was also a celebration of being blessed with ample food to survive the imminent winter. As the crops were harvested, so came the time for collecting taxes. It is said that Mehrgan was celebrated with pomp and pageantry in the Apadana Palace. Stone carvings from its remaining walls depict gift bearers with wine, food, and animals offerings on their way to pay their respect and dues to the king.

Many vegetables are harvested during fall. Veal & Quince Stew (page 158) is a delicious combination of dried summer fruit and autumnal vegetables.

Quince, a relative of apples and pears, is native to Iran and various parts of Asia. The fruit itself is not eaten raw. This aromatic fruit is used for Quince Jam (page 212), made in Iranian homes soon after the fall harvest. With its delightful rose color, sweet and tangy taste, and complex texture, the preserve is a must at many Persian breakfast tables.

✺

YALDA

The word *yalda*, meaning "birth," is believed to have its root in the Aramaic language. In Persian tradition, it refers to the first day of winter. The night of Shab e Yalda, customarily referred to as Yalda, is the longest of the year and marks the winter solstice. Yalda was considered the birthday of Mithra and the beginning of the arrival of light on the planet. The concept of Yalda is the most dualistic and romantic of all Persian celebrations.

Friends and family will gather on this evening, symbolically for solace, protection, and support. Together, they await the passing of the darkest night in the expectation of the birth of Mithra and the start of longer hours of daylight the next morning. Yalda celebrations are joyous and filled with laughter and storytelling. Persian poets have been inspired by the dark and long night of Yalda, some likening it to a lover's perpetual longing.

The dishes served at Yalda provide fortitude to endure the cold winter. Walnut, Chicken & Pomegranate Stew (page 148) is made with pomegranate juice and walnut paste. Herb & Noodle Potage (page 74) is a hearty noodle soup made with legumes, green leafy vegetables, dried yogurt (*kashk*), fried onions, and a garnish of fried mint.

HOW TO USE THIS BOOK

Persian cuisine is a symbol of national pride, reflecting centuries of culture and hospitality and a sophisticated sense for taste, aroma, and aesthetics. As such, each Iranian household holds itself to a high standard and has a strong view when it comes to Persian food. In reality, there is no one way or right way of making a Persian dish. A dish can be prepared differently, depending on the region and even households within that region. Personal preferences do impact Persian recipes. For instance, some prefer sweetness over tartness, buttery over dry, and many will adjust seasonings, spices, and herbs accordingly.

Saffron threads

In fact, Iranians taste their food as they make it. We suggest you do the same: taste as you go and feel free to improve. Use all five senses and your judgment to add that extra spoon of olive oil or lemon juice; reduce the amount of cinnamon (if you find it too strong); replace herbs or vegetables you dislike or cannot find them. If the sauce thickens too much, add some stock or water to thin it out. If it's too watery, simmer the dish longer until it reaches your desired consistency. Just remember, you are having a dialogue with the dish as you make it. It's meant to be a fun experience.

Most Persian dishes are made from ingredients you can find at regular supermarkets and gourmet food stores. For some of the more unusual items (such as saffron, sumac, dried barberries, dried Persian limes, Persian prunes, and *kashk*), look in Iranian, Middle Eastern, or Indian food stores and online. We always recommend using fresh produce and herbs over canned or dried options, unless specified otherwise in the recipe.

With Nahid Joon as our inspiration, we have included essential components she would have wanted in the book. "Staple Recipes" (page 246) showcases foundational recipes, seasonings, and such that are used throughout the book. A glossary (page 254) presents a collection of ingredients with their benefits. We suggest reading them before making recipes. "Menus" (page 250) offers ideas for creating memorable feasts in your own home.

When preparing a Persian meal for either your family or a larger gathering, please keep in mind that Iranians are always generous with the quantity and variety. A versatile, balanced, and generous meal is reflective of our hospitality. Therefore, a Persian table often has multiple dishes, balanced in ingredients and aesthetics, and is served family style. At every Persian lunch or dinner, you can expect: a few appetizers and mains; pita or Persian flatbread (*lavash*); Greek yogurt or yogurt-based dishes, fresh herbs with dried almonds or walnuts and feta (*sabzi khordan*); and Persian chutneys (*torshis*). Desserts are served separately, often comprising fresh or dried fruits or sweet treats. Don't be surprised—you may have leftovers. Please refrigerate or store them appropriately; Persian food tastes even better the next day.

Over time, as you cook the dishes presented in the following pages, you will develop your own opinion about how Persian food should taste, smell, and look. The one thing we all come to agree on is that Persian cooking exudes a joy of eating and a love for people. Making it, savoring it, and sharing it with family and friends is all part of this pleasurable experience. Enjoy!

APPETIZERS AND SIDE DISHES

Persian appetizers are generally presented as side dishes to accompany the main courses. Similar to the concept of a mezze spread, this bountiful arrangement makes for an enjoyable Persian meal and a delightful journey into the tastes and fragrances of our cuisine. (The word *mezze* derives from the Persian word *mazeh*, meaning "taste.")

At a dinner party, there will be at least one of the following: Herb Frittata (page 50), Chicken & Yellow Split Pea Patties (page 54), a yogurt dish, an array of salads, a few dips, a Persian Herb Platter (page 24), and a selection of breads to complete the feast.

Nahid Joon would present a selection of these appetizers daily, laid out on her beautiful tablecloth (*sofreh*).

HERB PLATTER

Sabzi Khordan + سبزی خوردن

Serves 6–8

Preparation time: 15 minutes, plus overnight soaking

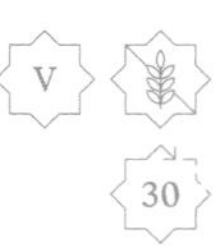

- 1–2 cups (4½–9 oz/120–250 g) walnuts, soaked in salted water overnight (see Note)
- Bunch of basil
- Bunch of cilantro (coriander)
- Bunch of tarragon
- Bunch of mint
- Bunch of radishes
- Bunch of scallions (spring onions)
- Bunch of chives (optional)
- 8 oz (225 g) feta
- Persian breads such as *barbari bread*, *sangak*, *taftoon*, or pita bread

This medley of fresh herbs, scallions (spring onions), walnuts, radishes, and feta accompanies every Persian meal. It can even be served as a starter or a replacement for salads. It is always served with at least one type of Persian bread.

My mother served this at every lunch and dinner when we lived in Iran. I would combine a piece of *naan lavash* with feta, walnuts, and a bunch of herbs to make into a sandwich. My mother would roll a thin lavash with all the ingredients for our school lunches. These days, I serve them as hors d'oeuvres at dinner parties: I simply wrap the ingredients in small squares of lavash, then tie them with chives.

Drain walnuts and pat dry with paper towels. Arrange all the ingredients on a large platter.

Note: Soaking walnuts in salted water aids digestibility and removes the tannins.

SHIRAZI SALAD

Salade Shirazi + سالاد شیرازی

Serves 6–8

Preparation time:
20 minutes

Cooking time:
5 minutes

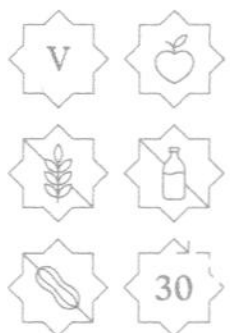

- 5 large tomatoes
- 8 radishes, coarsely chopped
- 5 Persian cucumbers, peeled and diced
- 4 shallots or 6 scallions (spring onions), finely chopped
- 1 cup (2 oz/55 g) finely chopped parsley or cilantro (coriander)
- 4 tablespoons finely chopped dill
- 4 tablespoons extra-virgin olive oil
- 3 tablespoons lemon juice
- 1 teaspoon pomegranate molasses (optional)
- 1 teaspoon salt
- ½ teaspoon black pepper
- 2 tablespoons pomegranate seeds, for garnish

If there ever was a national Iranian salad, it would be the Shirazi salad. Traditionally, it's dressed with olive oil and vinegar or lemon juice, but my mother loved the Turkish version with pomegranate molasses. She also scattered pomegranate seeds on top for the beautiful color.

Bring a medium saucepan of water to a boil. Cut an *X* in the bottom of the tomatoes, just deep enough to penetrate the skin. Carefully plunge them into the saucepan of boiling water, leaving them in for 10–15 seconds. Using a slotted spoon, remove the tomatoes from the water and place them in an ice water bath for 30 seconds to cool. Remove them from the water bath and peel the skin. Cut the tomatoes in half, then scoop out the seeds and discard. Chop the tomatoes.

In a bowl, combine all the ingredients and toss. Transfer to a serving bowl and garnish with the pomegranate seeds. Serve immediately.

SHRIMP SALAD

Salade Meygoo + سالاد میگو با انبه، آووکادو و سس شوید

Serves 6–8

Preparation time:
20–25 minutes

Cooking time:
5–10 minutes

30

- 4 teaspoons salt
- 2 lb (900 g) raw jumbo shrimp (tiger prawns), peeled, deveined, and thoroughly rinsed
- 1 cup (4½ oz/135 g) peas, thawed if frozen
- 3–4 semi-ripe avocados, coarsely chopped into ½-inch (1-cm) cubes
- 2–3 semi-ripe mangos, chopped into 1-inch (2.5-cm) cubes, plus extra for garnish
- ¾ cup (1½ oz/40 g) finely chopped dill, plus extra for garnish
- ¾ cup (4½ oz/135 g) pomegranate seeds, plus extra for garnish
- ¾ cup (6 fl oz/175 ml) extra-virgin olive oil
- ½ cup (4 oz/115 g) crème fraîche
- 4 tablespoons lemon juice
- 1 teaspoon sherry vinegar (optional)
- Black pepper, to taste

In 2008, I hosted a luncheon for forty guests at my gallery in honor of the exhibition *Selseleh Zelzeleh*. As there wasn't enough time to arrange for catering at this last-minute event, I called Nahid Joon in a panic and explained my dilemma. She prepared large salad platters and that was the start of my gallery luncheons.

One of the salads was her famous shrimp (prawn) salad. It has become the staple of many of my summer luncheons in New York, but it can be served any time of the year. You can also serve it as a light main course or on a soft brioche or baguette as a sandwich.

Bring 4 cups (32 fl oz/950 ml) of water to a boil in a medium saucepan. Add 1 tablespoon of salt. Add the jumbo shrimp (tiger prawns) and boil for 5–7 minutes, until the shrimp are opaque and cooked through. Using a slotted spoon, transfer the shrimp to a plate and pat dry with paper towels.

Bring 2 cups (16 fl oz/475 ml) of water to a boil in the same saucepan. Add the peas and cook for 1 minute. Drain, then transfer the peas to a bowl of ice water.

In a large bowl, combine the shrimp, peas, the remaining 1 teaspoon of salt, avocados, mangos, dill, pomegranate seeds, and pepper. Stir in the oil, crème fraîche, lemon juice, and vinegar, if using, and mix well. Season to taste with salt and pepper.

Serve in a shallow glass or silver bowl. Garnish with pomegranate seeds, dill, and mango.

LENTIL & QUINOA SALAD WITH HERBS

Serves 6–8

Preparation time:
45 minutes

Cooking time:
45 minutes

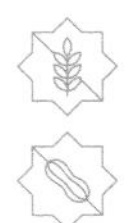

Salade adas va quinoa ba sabzi + سالاد عدس وکینوا با سبزی

- 2 tablespoons butter
- 2 cups (8 oz/225 g) dried barberries, rinsed
- 1 tablespoon sugar
- 2 cups (1 lb/450 g) dried Puy lentils
- 1 cup (8 fl oz/250 ml) and 2 tablespoons extra-virgin olive oil
- 1 cup (6½ oz/185 g) quinoa
- 1 cup (3½ oz/100 g) finely chopped scallions (spring onions)
- ½ cup (1 oz/30 g) finely chopped cilantro (coriander), plus extra for garnish
- ½ cup (2 oz/55 g) finely chopped chives
- ½ cup (1 oz/30 g) finely chopped parsley
- 4 tablespoons finely chopped dill
- ¾ cup (6 fl oz/175 ml) red wine vinegar or pomegranate molasses
- 2 tablespoons cumin seeds
- 1 tablespoon salt
- 2 teaspoons black pepper
- ½ teaspoon cayenne pepper
- 1½ cups (9¾ oz/275 g) pomegranate seeds, for garnish (optional)

Nahid Joon was fascinated that quinoa, as a grain, could act as a complete protein. She replaced the traditional bulgur in this recipe with quinoa and served this with her beet (beetroot) salad (page 41) for her vegetarian friends. The crunchy, nutty quinoa accompanied by fresh herbs and barberries makes for a very dynamic and refreshing dish.

Melt the butter in a large skillet over medium heat. Reduce the heat to low, then add the barberries and sugar. Mix for 2–3 minutes, until the sugar has melted.

Pick over the Puy lentils to remove any debris. Rinse the lentils under cold running water. In a medium saucepan, combine the lentils, 4 cups (32 fl oz/950 ml) of water, and 2 tablespoons of oil. Bring the water to a boil, then reduce the heat to a simmer and cook for 20–35 minutes, until the lentils are cooked through. Drain, then set aside.

Rinse the quinoa under cold running water, then drain. In a medium saucepan, combine the quinoa and 1½ cups (12 fl oz/350 ml) of water. Bring to a boil, then reduce the heat to medium-low. Cover and simmer for 15–20 minutes, until tender. Set aside to cool.

In a large bowl, combine the quinoa, lentils, scallions (spring onions), herbs, and barberries.

In a medium bowl, whisk 1 cup (8 fl oz/250 ml) of oil, vinegar, cumin, salt, pepper, and cayenne pepper. Pour over the salad and toss well. Season to taste, then garnish with pomegranate seeds, if using.

BRUSSELS SPROUT SALAD

Serves 6

Preparation time:
20 minutes

Salade Kalam Bruxelles ✢ سالاد کلم بروکسل

- 2 lb (900 g) Brussels sprouts, trimmed
- 3 green apples, finely chopped
- 3 cups (5½ oz/150 g) finely chopped dill
- 1⅓ cups (8 oz/225 g) crumbled feta, plus 2 tablespoons for garnish
- ½ cup (3¼ oz/90 g) pomegranate seeds, plus 2 tablespoons for garnish
- 1 cup (8 fl oz/250 ml) extra-virgin olive oil
- ¾ cup (6 fl oz/180 ml) lemon juice
- 2 tablespoons salt
- 1½ teaspoons black pepper

Contrary to what their name suggests, Brussels sprouts originated in Iran and Afghanistan. Nahid Joon loved the taste and antioxidant benefits of Brussels sprouts.

For Thanksgiving dinners, she roasted them with chestnuts and drizzled them with pomegranate molasses. When she served game meats such as pheasants, quails, or partridge, she'd make a Brussels sprout gratin with feta cheese and honey. It was only when she started making this salad that Brussels sprouts finally caught the family's attention. We love the crunchy, lemony, and refreshing combination of the pomegranate seeds, lemon, dill, and feta.

Using a knife, thinly slice the Brussels sprouts. (Alternatively, use a food processor with a slicing attachment.)

Combine all the ingredients in a large bowl. Mix until combined. Season to taste with extra salt and pepper.

Transfer to a serving bowl, then garnish with feta and pomegranate seeds.

PERSIAN CHICKEN SALAD

Serves 3–4

Preparation time:
45 minutes

Cooking time:
1 hour 20 minutes

Salade Olivier + سالاد اليويه

- 1 lb 4 oz (550 g) chicken breasts
- 1 large onion, quartered
- 2 bay leaves
- 1½ teaspoons salt
- 2 cups (16 fl oz/475 ml) chicken stock
- 2 russet (baking) potatoes, unpeeled
- 2 carrots, diced into ½-inch (1-cm) cubes
- 1½ cups (8 oz/225 g) peas, plus extra for garnish
- 7 eggs
- 2½ cups (20 fl oz/600 ml) mayonnaise
- 5 tablespoons lemon juice
- 2 tablespoons extra-virgin olive oil
- 2 teaspoons black pepper
- 1 cup (1¼ oz/35 g) finely chopped dill
- 1 cup (5½ oz/150 g) coarsely chopped cornichons, plus extra for garnish

Olivier Salad (also known as Stolichny Salad or Russian Salad) dates back to the 1860s at the famous Hermitage Restaurant in Moscow.

The Persian version is made with chicken breast, carrots, pickles, dill, and peas. It can be served as a main course, side dish, or in a baguette or *lavash* as a sandwich. Nahid Joon made her own mayonnaise for this dish. As a treat after school, she would take my brother and me to the André Delicatessen in Tehran, where we would eat the most delicious Olivier Salad in a crispy baguette.

In a large saucepan, combine the chicken breasts, onion, bay leaves, ½ teaspoon of salt, and the stock. Bring to a boil, then reduce the heat to medium. Cover and simmer for 45 minutes, or until the chicken is fully cooked.

Place the potatoes a large saucepan and add enough cold water to cover them by 1 inch (2.5 cm). Salt the water generously and bring to a boil. Reduce the heat to medium and simmer for 25 minutes, or until the potatoes can be easily pierced with a fork. Drain, then set aside to cool.

Peel the potatoes, then cut them into ½-inch (1-cm) cubes. Place in a large bowl.

Steam the carrots and peas for 2–3 minutes, until tender. Set aside to cool. Add to the bowl of potatoes.

Using a slotted spoon, transfer the chicken to a plate and set aside to cool. Dice into ½-inch (1-cm) cubes and add them to the bowl of vegetables.

Bring a saucepan of water to a boil. Add the eggs and boil for 8 minutes. Using a slotted spoon, gentle transfer the eggs to a colander and rinse under cold running water. Set aside to cool, then peel and dice into ¼-inch (5-mm) cubes. Add to the bowl of chicken and vegetables.

In a medium bowl, whisk together the mayonnaise, lemon juice, olive oil, the remaining 1 teaspoon of salt, and pepper. Pour the dressing into the bowl. Reserve 1 tablespoon of dill for garnish, then add the rest, along with the pickles, to the bowl. Toss well. Season to taste with salt and pepper.

Serve on a large platter. Garnish with the remaining dill, pickles, and peas.

EGGPLANT DIP

Kashke Bademjan + کشک بادمجان

Serves 6–8

Preparation time: 30 minutes

Cooking time: 45 minutes

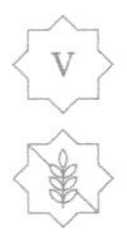

- 5 medium-large eggplants (aubergines), peeled, seeded, and quartered lengthwise
- 6 tablespoons salt
- ½ cup (2¼ oz/60 g) walnuts, plus 4 tablespoons chopped walnuts for garnish
- ¾ cup (6 fl oz/175 ml) virgin olive oil or butter
- 3 yellow onions, coarsely chopped
- 2 cloves garlic, coarsely chopped
- 5 tablespoons dried mint
- 1 tablespoon ground turmeric
- ¾ teaspoon black pepper
- ⅛ teaspoon cayenne pepper
- 10 oz (280 g) goat cheese or *kashk*
- 10 mint leaves, for garnish
- *Kashk*, for garnish (optional)

Eggplant (aubergine) was Nahid Joon's favorite vegetable, in every shape and form. She mostly used large black eggplants, but she also loved the purple miniature ones. As a child, I loved peeling the skin off her charred eggplants.

This delicious dip combines roasted eggplant with sautéed mint, crispy onions, and *kashk*, the liquid that remains after making sour milk or yogurt. Sour and tangy, kashk is available in specialty shops either in dried balls or as a liquid in a jar.

Nahid Joon prepared this dish almost weekly, and it was a special treat for her guests. When she moved to the United States, she had to use herb chèvre logs instead of kashk. She received so many compliments on this version that she continued using the chèvre, even when kashk became more readily available.

In a large bowl, combine the eggplants (aubergines), 5 tablespoons of salt, and enough water to keep the eggplants submerged. Set aside for 15 minutes, or until the water turns muddy green. Drain the eggplants, then squeeze out the water and pat dry with paper towels.

Meanwhile, place the walnuts in a food processor and blend for 1 minute, until it is coarsely ground and has the consistency of wet sand. Set aside.

Heat 4 tablespoons of oil in a medium skillet over medium-high heat. Add the onions and garlic and sauté for 7 minutes, until golden brown. Stir in the mint and turmeric. Turn off the heat and reserve 3 tablespoons of the onion mixture for garnish.

Heat the remaining ½ cup (4 fl oz/120 ml) of oil in a large saucepan over medium-high heat. Add the eggplant in a single layer, working in batches, if necessary, to avoid overcrowding. Fry the eggplants for 5–6 minutes on each side, until brown. Transfer to a paper towel–lined plate.

If you worked in batches, add the eggplants to the saucepan. Add the tablespoon of salt, the pepper, cayenne pepper, and 2 cups (16 fl oz/475 ml) of water. Simmer over low heat for 30 minutes, until the eggplants are soft. Drain, then transfer the eggplant to a large bowl. Using a fork or potato masher, mash the eggplants until chunky. Add the ground walnuts, onion mixture, and goat cheese and mix well.

Serve hot or cold in a deep platter. Garnish with the remaining chopped walnuts, reserved onion mixture, mint, and *kashk*, if using.

CUCUMBER-HERB YOGURT

Mast-o Khiar + ماست و خیار

Serves 6–8
as a side dish

Preparation time:
10 minutes, plus
10 minutes soaking

Cooking time:
5–10 minutes

- ½ cup (2½ oz/70 g) golden raisins (sultanas)
- 1⅓ cups (5½ oz/160 g) toasted walnuts
- 8 cups (3 lb/1.3 kg) Greek yogurt
- 12 Persian cucumbers, peeled and diced into ⅛-inch (3-mm) cubes
- 5 cups (9 oz/250 g) finely chopped dill, plus extra for garnish
- ½ cup (1 oz/30 g) finely chopped mint, plus extra for garnish
- ½ tablespoon salt
- ½ tablespoon black pepper
- 2 tablespoons dried rose petals, crushed, for garnish

Mast-o khiar is Farsi for "yogurt and cucumber." Similar to Indian raita, Greek tzatziki, or Turkish *cacik*, this dish accompanies almost every Persian meal of rice and stew. In Iran, we made our own yogurt from fresh cow's milk. We would put the yogurt in a cheesecloth (muslin) and hang it with a clothespin on a clothing rack in the garden, allowing the excess liquid to drain overnight. We'd use the yogurt in this recipe.

Cucumber-herb yogurt can be served with Persian breads. It can be served as a cold soup, by adding 1 cup (8 fl oz/250 ml) of water and a pinch of salt. When I'm in a rush, I have it for breakfast.

In a small bowl, soak the golden raisins (sultanas) in hot water for 10 minutes.

Meanwhile, put the walnuts in a saucepan and stir over medium heat for 5–8 minutes, until fragrant and brown. Keep them moving to prevent them from burning. Set aside to cool, then coarsely chop.

Drain the golden raisins. In a large bowl, combine the yogurt, cucumbers, raisins, 1 cup (4¼ oz/120 g) of walnuts, dill, mint, salt, and pepper. Mix well.

Transfer to a serving bowl and garnish with the remaining ⅓ cup (1 oz/30 g) of walnuts, dried rose petals, dill, and mint leaves.

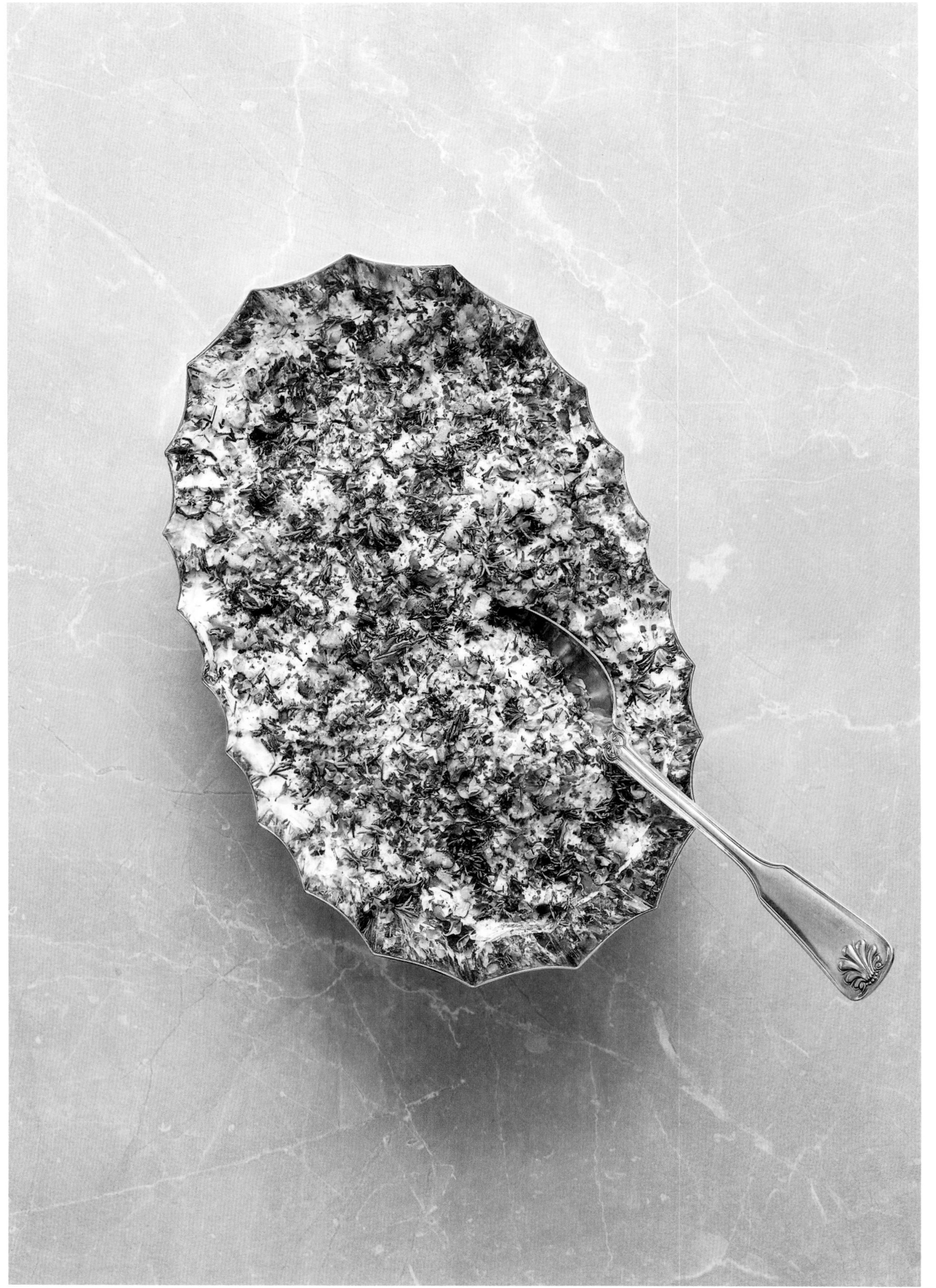

YOGURT & BEETS

Borani Laboo + بورانی لبو

Serves 4–6

Preparation time:
10 minutes

Cooking time:
1 hour

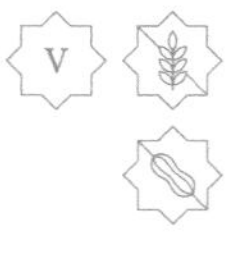

- 5 beets (beetroots), unpeeled
- 1½ cups (9 oz/250 g) Greek yogurt
- ½ cup (1 oz/30 g) coarsely chopped mint, plus extra for garnish
- 1½ teaspoons cumin seeds, lightly toasted
- ¾ teaspoon salt
- ½ teaspoon black pepper
- ⅛ teaspoon cayenne pepper
- 2 tablespoons extra-virgin olive oil
- Tarragon leaves, for garnish (optional)
- Persian flatbread (*lavash*), to serve

Borani laboo is beautiful—the combination of red beets (beetroots) with yogurt makes the most stunning pink color. My husband, Henry, loves this dish, so I always make it for him on Valentine's Day. I put a heart-shaped mold on the beet slices to turn the beet cubes into beet hearts. And the chopped mint adds a fresh contrast.

This vegetarian dish also has all the benefits and probiotics of yogurt and nutrients of beets, both of which are great for the gut. Serve it as a dip, side, or mixed with cooked lentils for a satisfying meal.

Preheat the oven to 350°F (180°C/Gas Mark 4).

Place the beets (beetroots) and 3 cups (25 fl oz/750 ml) of water in a deep ovenproof dish. Bake for 1 hour, or until the beets can be easily pierced with a fork. Remove and let cool.

Peel the skin off the beets. Chop the beets into ½-inch (1-cm) cubes. In a large bowl, combine all the ingredients together, except for the olive oil, and mix well.

Transfer to a serving bowl, drizzle the oil on top, and garnish with mint or tarragon leaves. Serve with Persian flatbread (*lavash*).

SMOKED EGGPLANT WITH TOMATO

Serves 4–6

Preparation time:
20 minutes

Cooking time:
1 hour 10 minutes

Mirza Ghasemi + میرزا قاسمی

- 5 eggplants (aubergines) (see Note)
- 4 large tomatoes
- 4 tablespoons virgin olive oil or butter
- 1 onion, finely chopped
- 15 cloves garlic, finely chopped
- 2 teaspoons salt
- 1 teaspoon black pepper
- 1 teaspoon ground turmeric
- 2–3 eggs (optional)
- 4 tablespoons walnuts, coarsely chopped, for garnish
- Chopped dill, for garnish
- Greek yogurt, for garnish (optional)
- Persian flatbread (*lavash*), to serve

This dish, which originates from the Caspian Sea region, is believed to be invented by and named after Mirza Ghasem Khan, the governor of the Mazandaran province during the reign of Nasseredin Shah of the Qajar dynasty. Charring the eggplant (aubergine) is key to the smokiness of the dish. It can be served as a hot or cold accompaniment to any meal or as a cold dip with Persian breads, such as *lavash*, *barbari*, or *sangak*.

Preheat the oven to 400°F (200°C/Gas Mark 6).

Using a knife, make a few incisions all around the eggplant (aubergine). Roast for 40–45 minutes. Set aside to cool slightly. Carefully peel off the skin. Chop the eggplant into small pieces.

Bring a medium saucepan of water to a boil. Cut an *X* in the bottom of the tomatoes, just deep enough to penetrate the skin. Carefully plunge them into the saucepan of boiling water, leaving them in for 10–15 seconds. Using a slotted spoon, remove the tomatoes from the water and place them in an ice water bath for 30 seconds to cool. Remove them from the water bath and peel the skin. Cut the tomatoes in half and, using a spoon, scoop out the seeds and discard. Cut the tomatoes into 1-inch (2.5-cm) cubes.

Heat the oil in a large saucepan over medium heat. Add the onion and sauté for 10–15 minutes, until softened and golden. Add the garlic and cook for another 2–3 minutes, until fragrant. Add the tomatoes, salt, pepper, and turmeric and mix well. Cook for 6–8 minutes, until the tomatoes are fully cooked and broken down. Stir in the eggplant, mix well, and cook for another 5 minutes. Move the mixture to the sides of the pan to create a space in the center. Add the eggs, if using, and cook for 2 minutes, or until halfway cooked. Mix them in.

Transfer to a serving plate. Add dollops of yogurt, if using, and garnish with walnuts and dill. Serve with Persian flatbread.

Note: Roasting the eggplants over an open flame is the most authentic way of preparing this dish. Place the eggplants on the grill and turn them continuously for 30–60 minutes, until completely black and softened.

CELERY ROOT, LEEK, & FENNEL PURÉE

Serves 6–8

Preparation time: 20 minutes

Cooking time: 40 minutes

Puree Risheh Karafs, Tareh Farangi va Razianeh + پوره ریشه کرفس، تره فرنگی و رازیانه

- ½ cup (4 fl oz/120 ml) and 3 tablespoons extra-virgin olive oil or melted butter
- 2 yellow onions, finely chopped
- 2 large leeks, white and light green parts only, coarsely chopped
- 4 celery roots (celeriac), cut into 1-inch (2.5-cm) cubes
- 3 fennel bulbs, cut into 1-inch (2.5-cm) cubes
- 6 cups (47 fl oz/1.4 L) vegetable stock
- 2½ tablespoons chopped thyme leaves, plus extra for garnish
- 1½ teaspoons salt
- 1 teaspoon black pepper
- 1 teaspoon ground nutmeg
- Pumpkin seeds, for garnish

Nahid Joon used fennel and celery root (celeriac) abundantly in soups and *aashes* or in accompaniments for meat dishes. For Thanksgiving, she would add leeks to the purée because it went so well with turkey. She would then top the dish with thyme for a boost of flavor. Although Nahid Joon made this dish with butter for richness, I prefer the lightness of olive oil.

Heat 3 tablespoons of oil in a large saucepan over medium-high heat. Add the onions and leeks and sauté for 5 minutes, until softened. Add the celery roots (celeriac), fennel, and stock. Cover, reduce the heat to medium, and simmer for 35 minutes, or until the vegetables are softened and mixture is dry. Set aside to cool.

Transfer the mixture to a food processor or blender. Add the thyme, salt, pepper, nutmeg, and the remaining ½ cup (4 fl oz/120 ml) of olive oil. Blend until creamy and smooth.

Ladle into a serving bowl. Garnish with thyme leaves and pumpkin seeds.

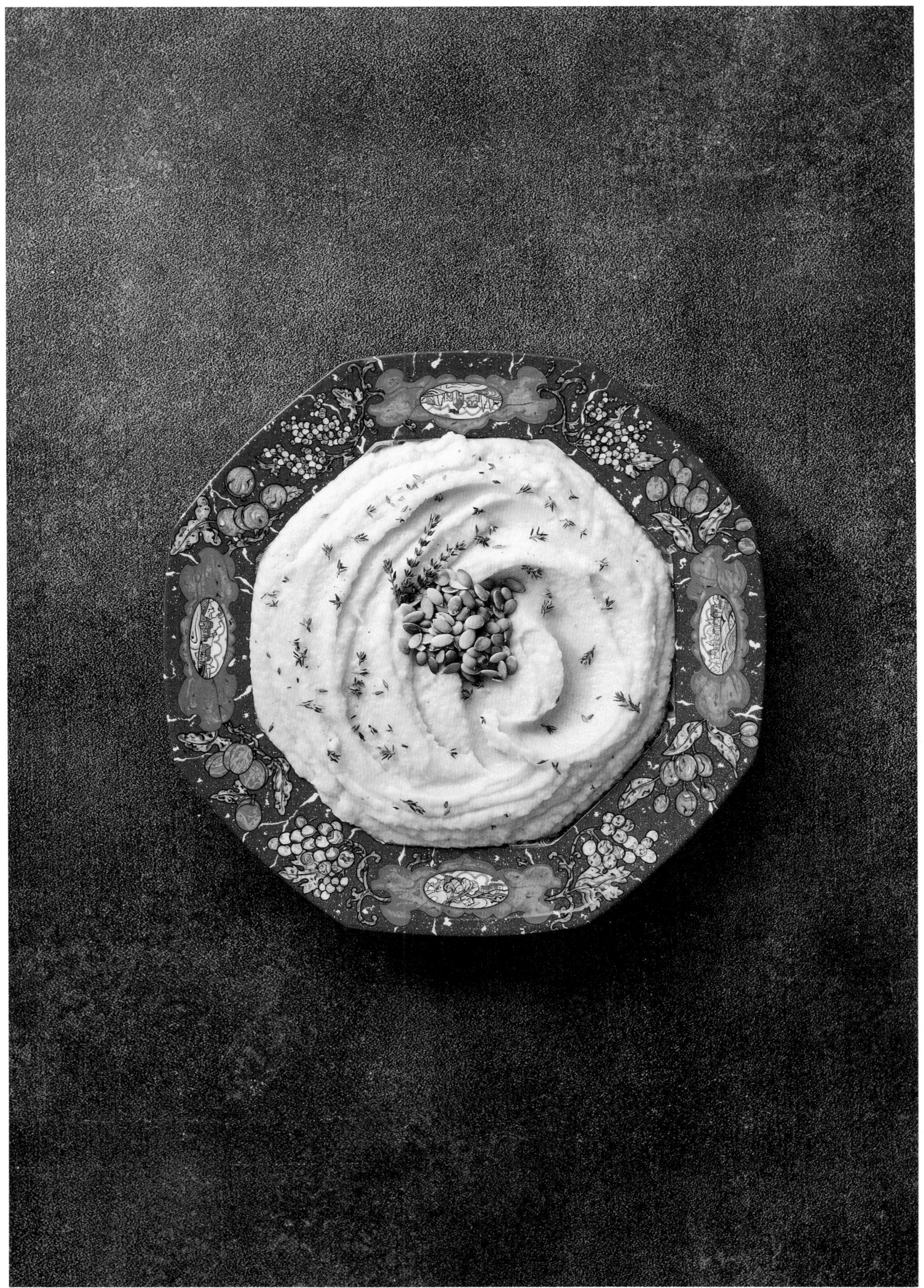

STUFFED GRAPE LEAVES

Dolmeh Barg-e Mo + دلمه برگ مو

Makes 40 dolmeh

Preparation time: 30 minutes, plus 1 hour soaking

Cooking time: 2 hours

- 1 × (16-oz/450-g) jar sour grape leaves (about 75 grape leaves) (see Note)
- ½ cup (4 fl oz/120 ml) virgin olive oil or butter
- 3 onions, grated
- 1½ lb (675 g) ground (minced) beef, with 15% fat
- 2 teaspoons salt
- 2 teaspoons Persian Spice Blend (page 246)
- 1 teaspoon black pepper
- ½ teaspoon ground turmeric
- ½ cup (3½ oz/100 g) basmati rice, well rinsed
- 8 scallions (spring onions), finely sliced
- Large bunch of dill, finely chopped
- Bunch of parsley, finely chopped
- ½ cup (4 fl oz/120 ml) lemon juice (about 4 lemons)
- 1 cup (6 oz/180 g) Greek yogurt
- 1 teaspoon baking soda (bicarbonate of soda)
- 2 tablespoons chopped parsley or cilantro (coriander), for garnish
- ⅓ cup (2¼ oz/60 g) sour grapes in brine (*ghooreh*), for garnish

When I was young, we had grape vines at our home. We would pick fresh leaves to wrap the dolmeh. I loved helping my mother prepare the leaves with the different fillings.

Grape leaves in brine can be found in most supermarkets. The leaves must be wrapped perfectly, so they remain closed during cooking.

Place the grape leaves in a medium saucepan. Add enough warm water to just cover the leaves. Bring the water to a quick boil over high heat. Drain, then transfer the leaves to a bowl of cold water. Set aside to soak for 1 hour, then drain.

Heat 3 tablespoons of oil in a medium saucepan over medium-high heat. Add the onions and sauté for 7–10 minutes, until softened and golden. Add the ground (minced) beef and stir frequently to break up the clumps. Season with 1 teaspoon of salt, the Persian spice blend, pepper, and turmeric. Cover and reduce the heat to low. Cook for 3–5 minutes, until the beef is cooked through and fat has rendered.

Increase the heat to medium-low. Pour in 2 cups (16 fl oz/475 ml) of water and cook for 10–15 minutes. Stir in the rice, cover, and boil again for 8–10 minutes, until the rice is partially cooked and the water has nearly evaporated. If needed, add more water until the rice is partially cooked.

Add the scallions (spring onions), dill, parsley, and lemon juice and mix well. Cook over medium-low heat for 20–30 minutes, or until the water has completely evaporated. Turn off the heat and set aside to cool. Stir in the yogurt.

Lay a grape leaf flat on a cutting board, rough side up. (If the grape leaf is torn or has deep edges, place another grape leaf on top to create a larger surface.)

Using a tablespoon, place the cooled filling in the center of each leaf, taking care not to overstuff the leaves. You should be able to fold the four corners and overlap in a snug fold. Carefully fold the edges from the sides of the leaf first, overlap to cover the filling, and wrap the dolmeh into a bundle. Repeat with the remaining grape leaves and filling.

Add 1 tablespoon of oil to a medium skillet. Arrange a snug single layer of stuffed grape leaves in the pan with the seam side down. This helps them remain closed while cooking. Sprinkle 1 teaspoon salt and baking soda (bicarbonate of soda) over the stuffed leaves. Add the remaining 4 tablespoons of oil and 1 cup (8 fl oz/250 ml) of water. Lay a few leaves over the stuffed grape leaves and place a heatproof plate or lid on top to keep the stuffed grape leave pressed down.

Cook them over medium heat for 1 hour, until most of the liquid has evaporated. Using a fork and spoon, gently transfer the stuffed grape leaves to a platter. Garnish with the parsley or cilantro and sour grapes. Serve hot or cold.

Note: Have extra vine leaves on hand, as some will tear while rolling the dolmeh.

STUFFED EGGPLANTS

Shekam Pareh + شکم پاره

Serves 6

Preparation time: 30 minutes

Cooking time: 1 hour 10 minutes

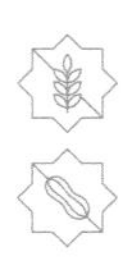

- 6 Italian or Japanese eggplants (aubergines) or 10 baby eggplants
- 5 teaspoons salt
- ¾ cup (6 fl oz/175 ml) and 5 tablespoons virgin olive oil
- 4 large onions, thinly sliced
- 15 cloves garlic, finely chopped
- 1 teaspoon ground turmeric
- 1½ lb (675 g) ground (minced) sirloin beef
- ½ teaspoon black pepper
- 3 tablespoons tomato paste (purée)
- ¾ cup (6 fl oz/175 ml) vegetable stock
- 1 jalapeño pepper, finely chopped
- 1 cup (2 oz/55 g) finely chopped parsley, plus extra for garnish
- 1 lb (450 g) cherry tomatoes, cut in half
- ½ teaspoon saffron threads
- 4 tablespoons butter
- 1 cup (8 oz/225 g) tomato purée (passata)
- Persian flatbread (*lavash*) or a side of salad, to serve

We grew long, purplish-black eggplants (aubergines) in our vegetable garden. During eggplant season, they'd be harvested frequently and we enjoyed them in various forms several times a week.

Nahid Joon adored *shekam pareh*. Since my husband is allergic to eggplant, she prepared a zucchini (courgette) version for him. We always thought the zucchini was a good substitute, but she said it was never the same. She would always say, "How can someone be allergic to eggplant and marry a Persian girl?"

Preheat the oven to 350°F (180°C/Gas Mark 4).

Make an incision lengthwise in each eggplant (aubergine), about 1¼-inches (3-cm) deep. Using a spoon, scoop out some of the eggplant to form a pocket (which you will later fill). Soak the eggplant in cold water, add 1 tablespoon of salt, and set aside for 10–15 minutes. Drain, then pat dry with paper towels. (This process helps to remove excess liquid and some of the bitterness.)

Heat ¾ cup (6 fl oz/175 ml) of oil in a large skillet over medium-high heat. Add the eggplants and cook for 4 minutes on each side, or until colored and slightly softened. Transfer the eggplants to a paper towel–lined plate to drain.

Heat the remaining 5 tablespoons of oil in another large skillet over medium heat. Add the onions and sauté for 10 minutes, until softened and golden. Add the garlic and turmeric and sauté for another 3–5 minutes, until fragrant.

Add the ground (minced) beef, 1 teaspoon of salt, the pepper, and tomato paste (purée) and sauté for 5 minutes, or until the beef is slightly cooked. Pour in half the stock and cook until slightly thickened. Remove from the heat, then stir in the jalapeño and parsley.

Transfer the eggplants to a baking dish. Gently pull in the sides of each eggplant to create a pocket for the filling. Using a teaspoon, fill the eggplants with the beef mixture. Place the tomatoes on top of the filled eggplants.

In a small bowl, bloom the saffron in 4 tablespoons of hot water. Melt the butter in a saucepan over medium heat. Add the tomato purée (passata), bloomed saffron water, the remaining stock, and the remaining 1 teaspoon of salt. Bring to a boil. Season with salt and pepper.

Drizzle half of the tomato sauce over and around the eggplants. Cover the dish with aluminum foil and bake for 35 minutes, or until the eggplants are thoroughly cooked. Uncover and bake for another 5–8 minutes, until the eggplants are fully softened. If needed, bake for another 5–10 minutes.

Using 2 large spatulas, carefully transfer the eggplants to 1–2 serving dishes. Ladle the remaining sauce over and around the eggplants. Garnish with the parsley.

Serve warm with Persian flatbread (*lavash*) or a side of salad.

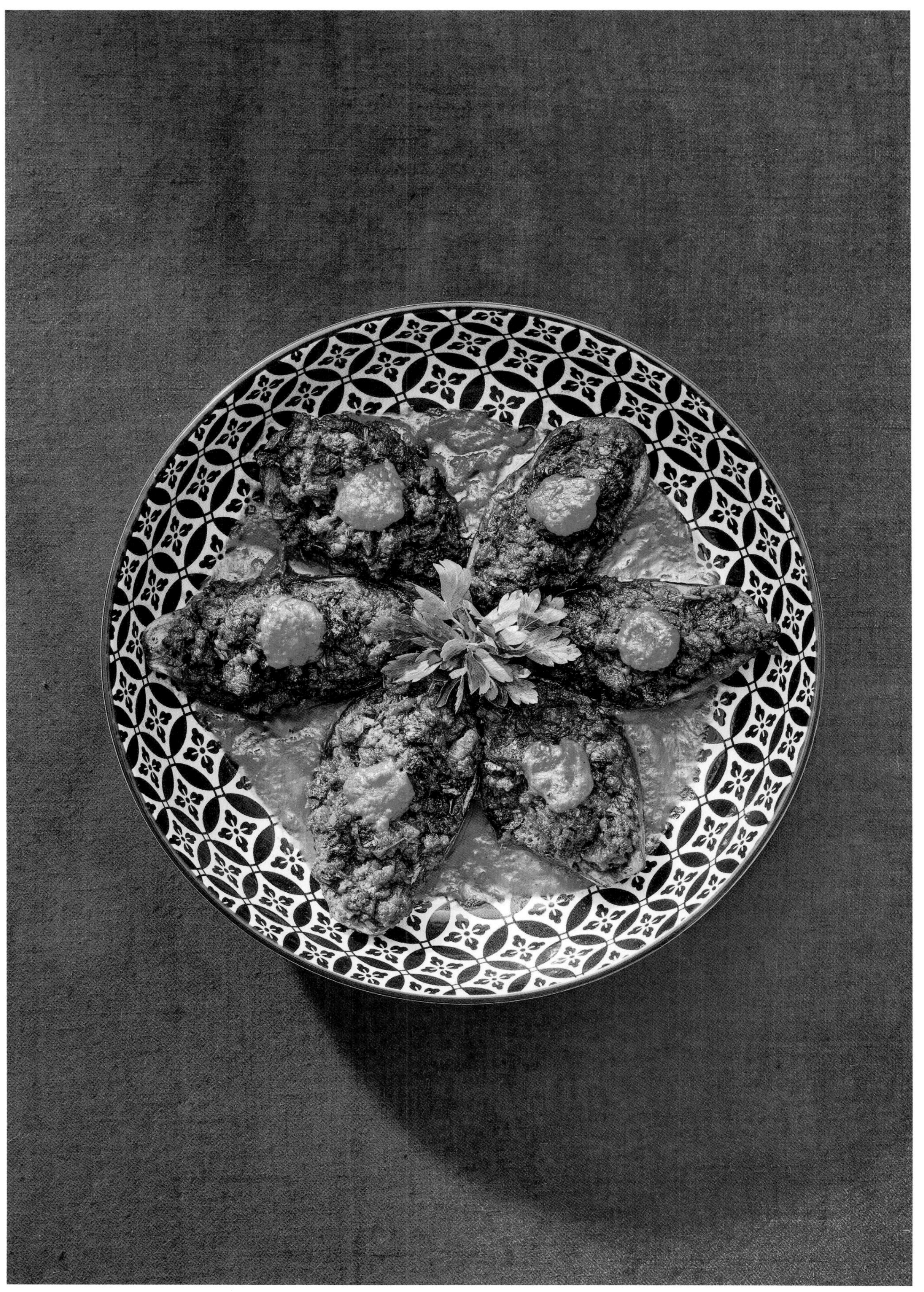

HERB FRITTATA

Kookoo Sabzi + کوکو سبزی

Serves 8–10

Preparation time:
30 minutes, plus
20 minutes soaking

Cooking time:
55–60 minutes

For the frittata:
- 6 cups (12 oz/350 g) finely chopped cilantro (coriander)
- 6 cups (12 oz/350 g) finely chopped parsley
- 3 cups (12 oz/350 g) finely chopped chives or scallions (spring onions)
- ⅔ cup (5 fl oz/150 ml) virgin olive oil
- 2 onions, finely chopped
- 2 cloves garlic, finely chopped
- 8 eggs
- 2 teaspoons salt
- 1 teaspoon black pepper
- 1 teaspoon baking powder
- 1 teaspoon ground turmeric
- 1 teaspoon Persian Spice Blend (page 246)
- 1 tablespoon all-purpose (plain) flour
- 2 cups (9 oz/250 g) walnuts, coarsely chopped

For the garnish:
- 1 tablespoon butter
- 4 tablespoons dried barberries, soaked in cold water for 20 minutes
- 1 tablespoon sugar
- 1 teaspoon rose water

The Persian frittata is similar to an Italian frittata or crustless French quiche and a blank canvas made for herb, spice, and flavor embellishments. It can be made with mostly herbs (as in this recipe); eggplant (aubergine) and zucchini (courgette); green beans and meat; or chicken and saffron (page 53). While it can be prepared on a stovetop, it is more commonly baked in an oven and then cut into small squares or pie slices. It can be served hot or cold as an appetizer, side dish, or main course.

Make the frittata. Preheat the oven to 500°F (260°C/Gas Mark 10).

In a large bowl, combine the herbs and mix well.

Heat 6 tablespoons of oil in a large skillet over medium-high heat. Add the herb mixture and sauté for 4–6 minutes, until shiny.

Heat 1 tablespoon of oil in a medium skillet over medium heat. Add the onions and garlic and sauté for 7–10 minutes, until softened and lightly golden. Set aside to cool.

In a large bowl, combine the eggs, salt, pepper, baking powder, turmeric, and Persian spice blend. Add the cooled herbs, onion mixture, flour, and walnuts. Using a silicone spatula, gently fold the mixture and take care not to overmix.

Add the remaining 3 tablespoons of oil to a nonstick ovenproof dish, about 10 × 16 inches (25 × 40 cm). Tilt the dish to coat the base in oil. Add the herb mixture and gently smooth the top using a silicone spatula. Bake for 10 minutes.

Reduce the oven temperature to 350°F (180°C/Gas Mark 4) and cook for another 30 minutes, until golden. If you would like it to be crispier, reduce the heat to 300°F (150°C/Gas Mark 2) and cook for another 10 minutes.

Make the garnish. Combine all the ingredients in a medium skillet. Sauté over medium heat for 4 minutes, until the barberries are soft. Barberries burn very easily, so stir frequently.

Garnish with the caramelized barberries. Slice, then serve.

CHICKEN SAFFRON FRITTATA

Serves 8–10

Preparation time:
30 minutes

Cooking time:
3 hours

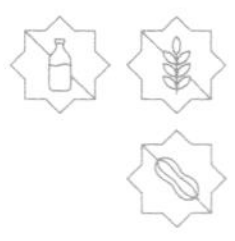

Kookoo Morgh + کوکو مرغ

For the frittata:

- 4–6 boneless, skinless chicken breasts (2 lb/900 g)
- 5 cups (40 fl oz/1.2 L) chicken stock or water
- 1 teaspoon saffron threads
- 1 quantity Golden Fried Onions (page 246)
- 4 tablespoons tomato paste (purée)
- Juice of 2 lemons
- 2 teaspoons salt
- 1 teaspoon black pepper
- 8 eggs
- 2 tablespoons extra-virgin olive oil

For the garnish:

- ½ bunch cilantro (coriander), coarsely chopped
- ½ bunch chives, coarsely chopped
- ½ onion, thinly sliced

This dish, known locally as *cheghertmeh*, hails from the lush province of Gilan in northern Iran, bordering the Caspian Sea. The recipe is by Nayer Modjtabai, a childhood friend of Nahid Joon. Nahid and Nayer were among ten girls who sat together in class and became very close friends. This enduring friendship continued long after high school, marriage, children, and grandchildren, and even after Nahid moved to New York.

The next generation became classmates and remain the closest of friends today. Even after the 1979 revolution, when Nayer Joon and Nahid Joon were separated and settled in opposite corners of the world, they made every effort to travel long distances to see each other. They shared each other's happiness and sorrow throughout the years. Nayer Joon's daughters—Leila, Vida, Avid, and Neda—are all my best friends, and we have been exchanging recipes since college.

Make the frittata. Preheat the oven to 350°F (180°C/Gas Mark 4).

Rinse the chicken under cold running water. In a large saucepan, combine the chicken and stock, cover, and cook over medium heat for 45 minutes, until the chicken is cooked and the stock as reduced by half. Set aside to cool.

In a small bowl, bloom the saffron in 4 tablespoons of hot water. Set aside.

Transfer the chicken to a cutting board. Shred it with your hands or a sharp knife, then return it to the saucepan of stock. Add the golden fried onions, tomato paste (purée), lemon juice, bloomed saffron water, salt, and pepper. Cook over low heat for 1 hour. Check often to make sure it doesn't get dry. If it does, add a splash of chicken stock or water. Set aside to cool.

Crack the eggs into a bowl and whisk until frothy. Fold the cooled chicken mixture into the egg batter. (If the chicken is too hot, it will cook the eggs.) Mix well.

Add the oil to a 8 × 12-inch (20 × 30-cm) nonstick ovenproof dish and tilt to coat the entire pan evenly. Pour the chicken mixture into the dish and smooth the surface. Bake for 1¼ hours, until the mixture is set and golden brown.

Garnish with herbs and onion. Using a sharp knife, cut into 2-inch (5-cm) squares and serve immediately.

CHICKEN & YELLOW SPLIT PEA PATTIES

Makes 18–20 patties

Preparation time:
30 minutes

Cooking time:
1 hour 10 minutes

Shami e Morgh + شامی مرغ

- 4 boneless, skinless chicken breasts, chopped into 2-inch (5-cm) cubes
- 2 teaspoons salt
- 1 teaspoon black pepper
- 1 teaspoon baking soda (bicarbonate of soda)
- ½ teaspoon ground turmeric
- 2 cups (16 fl oz/475 ml) and 2 tablespoons virgin olive oil or butter, plus extra if needed
- 2 onions, coarsely chopped
- 1⅔ cups (1 lb 13 oz/825 g) dried yellow split peas, rinsed
- 1½ cups (12 fl oz/350 ml) chicken stock
- 1 teaspoon ground saffron
- 2 teaspoons Persian Spice Blend (page 246)
- 3 eggs
- 1–2 tablespoons rice flour, if needed
- 1 cup (5½ oz/160 g) all-purpose (plain) flour

Shami is one of Iran's most prevalent dishes. It can be served as hors d'oeuvres or as a main, accompanied with bread, fresh herbs, salad, rice, and relishes. It is also great for lunch in a baguette with cucumbers and pickles.

In a large bowl, combine the chicken, 1 teaspoon of salt, ½ teaspoon of pepper, the baking soda (bicarbonate of soda), and turmeric. Mix until the chicken is fully coated.

Heat 2 tablespoons of oil in a medium saucepan over medium-high heat. Add the chicken and cook for 5 minutes, until lightly browned. Add the onions, then cover and reduce the heat to medium. Simmer for 20 minutes, until onions are tender and the chicken juices are absorbed. Set aside to cool.

In a medium saucepan, combine the yellow split peas, the remaining 1 teaspoon of salt and ½ teaspoon of pepper, and stock. The stock should cover the split peas by 1 inch (2.5 cm). If needed, top it up with water or more stock. Bring to a boil over high heat, then reduce the heat to medium. Simmer for 35–40 minutes, uncovered, and stir occasionally, until the split peas are fully cooked. Set aside to cool.

In a small bowl, bloom the saffron in 1 tablespoon of hot water.

Transfer the split peas to a food processor. Add the chicken mixture, Persian spice blend, and bloomed saffron water and blend until smooth and homogeneous. The texture should be dry and powdery.

Transfer the mixture to a large bowl. Add the egg one at a time, mixing well after each addition. The mixture should be sticky and hold its form. If needed, add the rice flour. Cook a teaspoon of the mixture in a skillet over medium heat. Taste, and then adjust the seasoning of the remaining mixture as needed.

Put the flour on a plate. Wet your hands and roll a small handful of the mixture into a ball. In the palm of your hands, flatten it into a round patty, about ½ inch (1 cm) thick. Coat the patty lightly on all sides with flour and set aside. Repeat with the remaining mixture.

Heat the remaining 2 cups (16 fl oz/475 ml) of oil in a deep skillet over high heat until hot. There should be enough oil to deep-fry the patties and ensure they are evenly golden. Working in batches to avoid overcrowding, carefully lower a few patties into the oil. Deep-fry for 2 minutes on each side, until crisp and golden brown. Transfer the patties to a paper towel–lined plate. Repeat with the remaining patties. Discard the oil halfway through frying and add fresh oil to the skillet.

Serve hot or cold.

CHICKEN PATTIES

Kotlet e Morgh + کتلت مرغ

Makes 28–30 patties

Preparation time:
45 minutes

Cooking time:
35–40 minutes

- 1½ lb (625 g) russet (baking) potatoes, peeled
- 2 lb (900 g) ground (minced) chicken
- 4 onions, grated and drained (see Note)
- 1 egg
- 1 egg yolk
- 6 scallions (spring onions), finely chopped
- 2 teaspoons ground turmeric
- 1 teaspoon salt
- 1 teaspoon black pepper
- 1½ cups (3 oz/85 g) bread crumbs
- 2 cups (16 fl oz/475 ml) virgin olive oil or ghee (clarified butter)

For the garnish (optional):
- 2 tablespoons finely chopped dill
- 2 tablespoons finely chopped cilantro (coriander)
- Sliced radishes, basil leaves, tarragon, cherry tomatoes, and/or pickles

Persian *kotlets* are typically made with ground (minced) veal or beef, but Nahid Joon also made them with chicken. She would serve them hot as a main course with vegetables, fresh herbs, salad, bread, and yogurt. When we were lucky, she would prepare sandwiches with the leftovers—with cucumbers, pickles, and fresh dill—for our school lunches. It was one of our favorite lunchbox meals.

Place the potatoes in a large saucepan and add enough salted water to cover them by 2 inches (5 cm). Bring to a boil over high heat, then reduce the heat to medium and simmer for 15–20 minutes, until the potatoes can be easily pierced with a knife. Drain, then set aside to cool slightly.

Mash the potatoes. Add the ground (minced) chicken, onions, egg, egg yolk, scallions (spring onions), turmeric, salt, and pepper. Using your hands, mix well for 4–5 minutes, until a smooth, homogeneous paste is formed. Dip your hands in warm water occasionally to help with the stickiness of the mixture.

Spread the bread crumbs on a large plate or cutting board. Wet your hands and shape a golf ball–sized portion of the mixture into a ball. In the palm of your hands, flatten it into an oval shape, about ¼ inch (5 mm) thick. Coat both sides in bread crumbs and transfer to a large plate. Repeat with the remaining mixture. At this point, you can freeze the patties for later use.

Heat the oil in a large skillet over medium-high heat until hot. Working in batches to avoid overcrowding, add the patties to the skillet. Fry on each side for 10 minutes, until golden brown and cooked through. Transfer to a paper towel–lined plate to drain the excess oil. Repeat with the remaining patties.

Add garnishes, if using, and serve hot or cold.

Note: You may use a food processor to grate the onions.

BEEF PATTIES

Kotlet-e Goosht + کتلت گوشت

Makes 28–30 patties

Preparation time:
30 minutes

Cooking time:
25–30 minutes

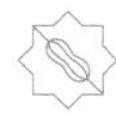

- 1½ lb (625 g) russet (baking) potatoes, quartered
- 1 tablespoon salt
- 2 lb (900 g) lean twice-ground (minced) sirloin beef (see Note)
- 4 onions, grated and drained (see Note)
- 1 tablespoon dried parsley
- 2 teaspoons ground turmeric
- 2 teaspoons Persian Spice Blend (page 246)
- 1 teaspoon black pepper
- ½ teaspoon baking soda (bicarbonate of soda)
- 1 tablespoon soy sauce
- 3 eggs
- 1½ cups (3 oz/85 g) bread crumbs
- 2 cups (16 fl oz/475 ml) grapeseed oil or ghee (clarified butter)
- Chopped parsley, for garnish
- Chopped cilantro (coriander), for garnish

Nahid Joon's oval-shaped beef patties (larger than most) were so crispy on the outside and juicy on the inside. Traditionally, the patties are served as a room-temperature appetizer or a side dish at dinner parties, but she always prepared them as a main course accompanied by vegetables, fresh herbs, salad, bread, and yogurt.

When we were children, Nahid Joon would put leftover patties in *lavash* or baguettes along with sliced pickles and tarragon for our school lunch. The patties can be made in large quantities and kept in the refrigerator or frozen for future use.

The size of the patties is a matter of taste. These patties are on the small side, but you can make them larger if desired. Simply scoop a ball of meat, about 2½ inches (6 cm) in diameter, and flatten into an oval shape. Cook for 6–8 minutes on each side, until golden brown and cooked through.

Place the potatoes in a large saucepan and add enough water to cover them by 2 inches (5 cm). Add 1 teaspoon of salt. Bring the water to a boil over high heat, then reduce the heat to medium and simmer for 15–20 minutes, until the potatoes can be easily pierced with a knife. Drain, then set aside to cool.

Process the potatoes through a potato ricer or grate them on a box grater. Put the grated potatoes in a large bowl. Add the beef, onions, parsley, turmeric, Persian spice blend, the remaining 2 teaspoons of salt, pepper, baking soda (bicarbonate of soda), soy sauce, and eggs. Using your hands, mix for 4–5 minutes, until the mixture forms a smooth, homogeneous paste. Dip your hands in warm water occasionally to help with the stickiness of the mixture.

Spread the bread crumbs on a large plate or cutting board. Wet your hands and shape a golf ball–sized portion of the mixture into a ball. In the palm of your hands, flatten it into an oval shape, about ¼ inch (5 mm) thick. Coat both sides of the patty in bread crumbs and transfer to a large plate. Repeat with the remaining mixture. At this point, you can freeze the patties for later use.

Heat the oil in a large skillet over high heat. Working in batches to avoid overcrowding, carefully lower the patties into the skillet. Deep-fry them for 4–5 minutes. Turn, then fry for another 4–5 minutes, until golden brown on both sides. Transfer to a paper towel–lined plate to drain. Repeat with the remaining patties.

Transfer to a serving platter, sprinkle with parsley and cilantro (coriander), and serve immediately. Alternatively, keep the patties warm in a covered ovenproof dish. When ready to serve, warm them in the oven at 400°F (200°C/Gas Mark 6) for 5–10 minutes.

Notes: Instead of beef, you can use ground (minced) lamb or a combination of both.

You can use a food processor to grate the onions.

BEEF PATTIES WITH TOMATO SAUCE

Makes 14–16 patties

Preparation time:
30 minutes

Cooking time:
40 minutes

Shami ba Gojeh Farangi + شامی با گوجه فرنگی

- 1 cup (8 fl oz/250 ml) and 2 tablespoons virgin olive oil or butter
- 4 tablespoons unbleached all-purpose (plain) flour
- 2 lb (900 g) ground (minced) sirloin beef
- 2 onions, grated and drained (see Note)
- 1 teaspoon salt
- 1 teaspoon black pepper
- 1 teaspoon ground turmeric
- 2 eggs
- 4 tablespoons tomato paste (purée)
- 3 tablespoons lemon juice
- ½ cup (2 oz/55 g) finely chopped scallions (spring onions) or chives, for garnish

This succulent and juicy *shami* was Nahid Joon's specialty. Add fresh herbs if you wish—mint, basil, and tarragon make delicious additions. The dish also pairs well with Nahid Joon's Cilantro Chutney (page 209).

Heat 2 tablespoons of oil in a medium skillet over medium heat. Add the flour and fry for 4–6 minutes, until lightly golden. Set aside to cool.

In a large bowl, combine the ground (minced) beef, onions, salt, pepper, turmeric, fried flour, and eggs. Using your hands, mix for 4–5 minutes, until the mixture forms a smooth, homogeneous paste. Wet your hands and shape a golf ball-sized portion of the mixture into a ball. In the palm of your hands, flatten it into a patty, about ¾ inch (2 cm) thick. Repeat with the remaining mixture. At this point, you can freeze the patties for later use.

Heat the remaining oil in a deep skillet over high heat. Working in batches to avoid overcrowding, carefully add the patties to the pan. Fry for 2 minutes on each side, until golden brown. Transfer to a paper towel–lined plate to drain. Repeat with the remaining patties.

Place the fried patties in a medium saucepan.

In a bowl, whisk the tomato paste (purée), lemon juice, and 1 cup (8 fl oz/250 ml) warm water. Pour the mixture over the patties. Cover and cook over low heat for 30 minutes.

Using a slotted spoon, carefully transfer the patties to a serving platter and spoon the tomato sauce on top. Garnish with scallions (spring onions).

Note: You can use a food processor to grate the onions.

AUNTIE EVELYN'S VEAL CUTLETS

Serves 4–6

Preparation time: 20 minutes

Cooking time: 20 minutes

Kotlet-e Goosaleh ✢ کتلت گوساله

- 2 small Idaho potatoes, quartered
- 3 slices white bread
- ½ cup (4 fl oz/120 ml) whole (full-fat) milk
- 1 lb (450 g) ground (minced) veal
- 1 small onion, grated and drained (see Note)
- 2 eggs
- 1 teaspoon salt
- ½ teaspoon black pepper
- ½ teaspoon ground turmeric
- 1½ cups (3 oz/85 g) bread crumbs
- ¾ cup (6 fl oz/175 ml) virgin olive oil or ghee (clarified butter)
- 5–6 basil leaves, for garnish
- 5–6 cherry tomatoes, for garnish

Auntie Evelyn was our nursery school teacher at Miss Hekmat Nursery School in Tehran. She would bake us delicious treats. We all loved her dearly and begged to be in her class.

In New York, Auntie Evelyn continues to send us her warm, delicious lemon cake and succulent cutlets.

Place the potatoes in a saucepan and add enough cold water to cover them. Bring to a boil and cook for 10–15 minutes, until tender. Drain, then set aside to cool. Peel, then purée until smooth.

Soak the bread in milk until softened.

In a large bowl, combine the veal, onion, eggs, and potatoes. Add the soaked bread, salt, pepper, turmeric, and ½ cup (1 oz/30 g) of bread crumbs. Using your hands, mix for 4–5 minutes, until the mixture forms a smooth, homogeneous paste. Dip your hands in warm water occasionally to help with the stickiness of the mixture.

Pour the remaining 1 cup (2 oz/55 g) of bread crumbs on a large plate. Wet your hands and shape a golf ball–sized portion of the mixture into a ball. In the palm of your hands, flatten it into an oval shape, about ½ inch (1 cm) thick.

Coat both sides of the cutlet in bread crumbs and transfer to a large plate. Repeat with the remaining mixture. At this point, you can freeze the cutlets for later use.

Heat the oil in a large skillet over medium-high heat. Working in batches to avoid overcrowding, carefully lower the cutlets into the skillet. Deep-fry the cutlets for 4–5 minutes. Turn, then fry for another 4–5 minutes, until golden brown on both sides. Transfer to a paper towel–lined plate to drain. Repeat with the remaining cutlets.

Arrange the cutlets on a serving platter. Garnish with basil leaves and cherry tomatoes.

Note: You may use a food processor to grate the onions.

SOUPS AND POTAGES

Persian meat broth (*abgoosht*) is the every man's dish in Iran. Along with Kebabs with Rice (page 131), it is the dish prepared most often by Iranians. When growing up, I would see a wood-burning fire next to every construction site, with a steaming pot of abgoosht being prepared for the workers' lunch. This is a dish that can be made either with expensive cuts of meat or a modest slab of mutton fat, beef or lamb, chickpeas, tomatoes, potatoes, and onions.

Nahid Joon served her abgoosht in two ways. One version has the broth and meat separated, then the meat mashed with a mortar and pestle into a chunky paste and served atop of Persian bread (*lavash*) alongside the broth. The other version is a tasty, slow-cooked stew with tender morsels of meat. A touch of turmeric and tomato paste (purée) gives the broth its beautiful orange hue.

Nahid Joon would always put a tablespoon of the mashed meat on top of small squares of lavash bread and tie it with a chive. It is a delicious hors d'oeuvre that can be served at room temperature. She would also prepare delicious abgoosht sandwiches for our lunchboxes.

Aash, a thick, hearty herb potage, comes in an array of flavors. The base ingredients are herbs or vegetables, but legumes, grains, chicken, beef, lamb, and spices are added. For my family, *aash* was the first course of every lunch and dinner during the cold months, or it was a main course accompanied by a salad and Persian bread, such as *barbari*, *sangak*, *taftoon*, or pita.

RED BORSCHT

Borscht + بورشت

Serves 5–6

Preparation time: 30 minutes

Cooking time: 1–1 hour 35 minutes

- 2 tablespoons virgin olive oil
- 1 onion, finely chopped
- 1 clove garlic, finely chopped
- 2 veal shanks, cut into 3-inch (7.5-cm) pieces, or 1 lb (450 g) stewing lamb or beef (see Note)
- 1½ tablespoons salt
- 1 tablespoon black pepper
- 4 cups (32 fl oz/950 ml) beef stock (see Note)
- 4 bay leaves
- 5 carrots, diced
- ½ head celery, diced
- 4 beets (beetroots), peeled and diced into ½-inch (1-cm) cubes (see Note)
- 2 large russet (baking) potatoes, diced into ½-inch (1-cm) cubes
- ½ large celery root (celeriac), diced into ½-inch (1-cm) cubes
- 1 × (28-oz/800-g) can crushed tomatoes
- ⅓ cup (2½ oz/70 g) tomato paste (purée)
- ½ large white cabbage, shredded
- 1 cup (8 fl oz/250 ml) red wine vinegar
- 1 cup (1¾ oz/50 g) finely chopped dill
- ½ cup (3½ oz/100 g) crème fraîche, for garnish
- Persian bread (*lavash*), to serve

My father and his siblings were born in Samarkand, Russia, before the Bolshevik Revolution. At the end of the revolution, his family immigrated to Iran and settled in Tehran. When my mother married my father in 1951, she was proficient in Persian cooking, especially Azerbaijani cuisine, which she learned from her mother. Nahid Joon's sisters-in-law told my mom that she had to learn to cook Russian and Uzbeki cuisine to be a good cook. They taught her how to make one of my father's favorite meals, Russian borscht.

When we were young, my brother and I always looked forward to the winter months when hearty bowls of borscht would be waiting for us when we came home from school.

Use gloves when handling beets (beetroots) to prevent your fingertips from staining.

Heat 1 tablespoon of oil in a large, heavy saucepan over medium heat. Add the onion and cook for 5–7 minutes, until softened. Add the garlic and cook for 1–2 minutes, until fragrant.

Season the veal generously with salt and pepper and add to the saucepan. Sear for 4 minutes on each side, until browned. Add the stock and bay leaves. Reduce the heat to medium-low and simmer for 20–25 minutes.

Meanwhile, heat the remaining tablespoon of oil in a large skillet over medium heat. Add the carrots and celery and sauté for 5 minutes, or until softened. Add the beets (beetroots) and cook for another 5 minutes.

Transfer the sautéed vegetables to the saucepan with the meat. Add the potatoes, celery root (celeriac), crushed tomatoes, and tomato paste (purée). Cover and simmer for 20–25 minutes, until the vegetables are softened. Add the cabbage and vinegar. Season to taste with salt and pepper. Reduce the heat to low and cook for another 30 minutes.

Transfer the shanks to a cutting board and remove the meat from the bones. Shred the meat and add it to the saucepan. (If using stewing meat, skip this step.) Season to taste with salt and/or vinegar.

To serve, stir in half of the dill. Ladle the borscht into shallow bowls. Top with crème fraîche and the remaining dill. Serve immediately with Persian bread (*lavash*).

Note: For a vegetarian borscht, use vegetable stock and replace the meat with canned white beans, drained and rinsed.

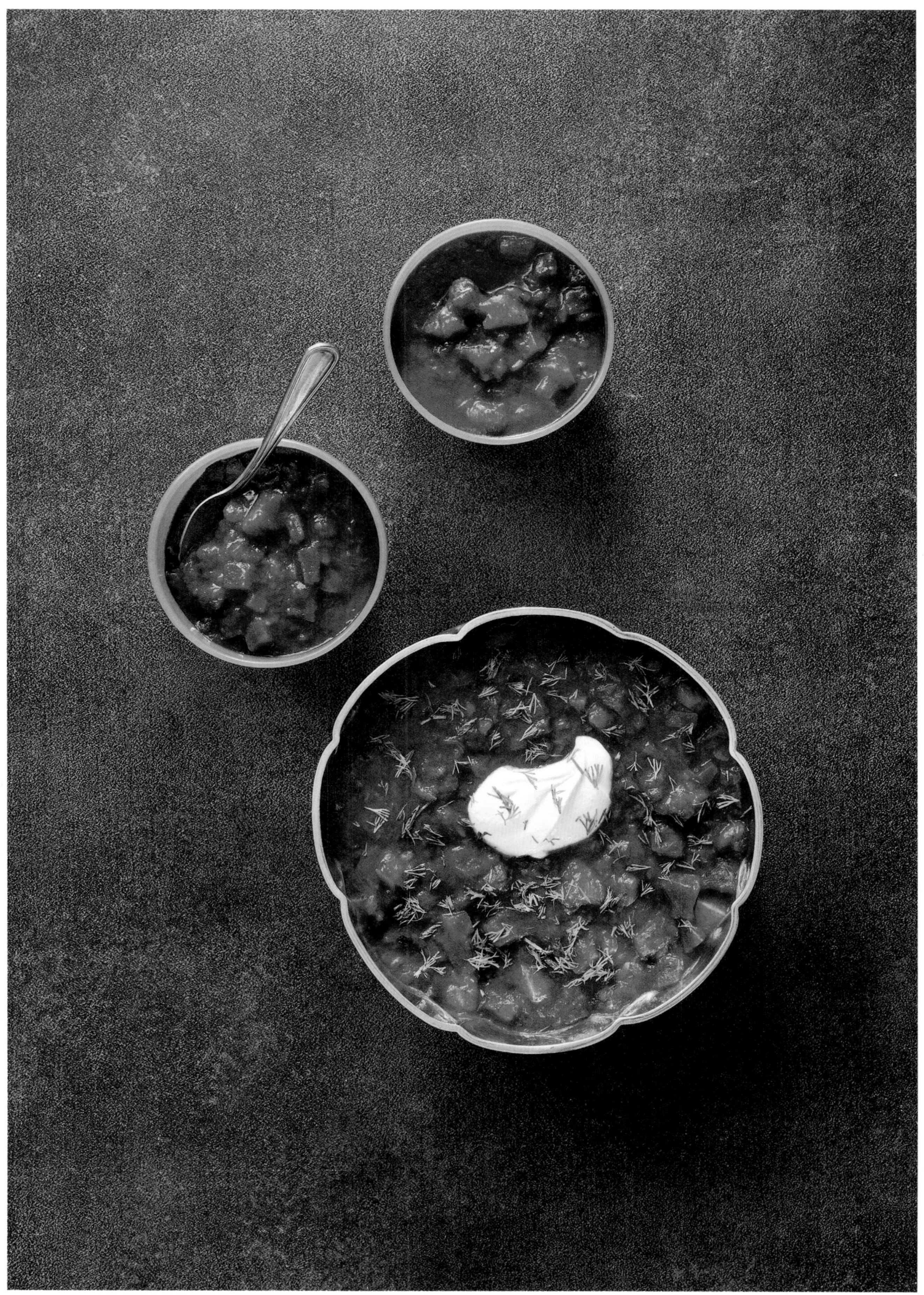

PISTACHIO SOUP

Soup-e Pesteh + سوپ پسته

Serves 6–8

Preparation time:
25 minutes

Cooking time:
1–1 hour 30 minutes

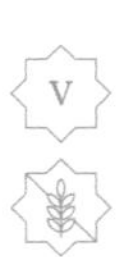

- 3 cups (12 oz/350 g) unsalted, shelled raw pistachios
- ½ teaspoon ground saffron
- ⅓ cup (2¾ fl oz/80 ml) virgin olive oil
- 1½ tablespoons grated ginger
- 1 teaspoon ground coriander
- ½ teaspoon chili powder
- ½ teaspoon ground turmeric
- 2 leeks, white and light greens parts only, finely chopped
- 2 teaspoons salt
- ½ teaspoon black pepper
- ½ cup (2¼ oz/60 g) finely chopped cilantro (coriander)
- ½ cup (1 oz/30 g) finely chopped parsley
- 1 cup (8 fl oz/250 ml) orange juice
- ½ cup (4 fl oz/120 ml) lemon juice
- ½ cup (3 oz/85 g) Greek yogurt

For the garnish:

- 4 tablespoons dried rose petals
- 4 tablespoons slivered pistachios
- ½ cup (3¼ oz/90 g) pomegranate seeds

In March 2017, our dear family friend and fashion designer Nazzy Beglari was looking forward to hosting Nahid Joon for a Nowruz (Persian New Year) dinner at her home in Abu Dhabi, but she was anxious. Two years prior, Nazzy's husband Peter called her from New York to report that the food he had just enjoyed at Nahid Joon's was the most delicious Thanksgiving dinner. Being a vegan, Nazzy prepared the tastiest vegan Persian New Year feast.

This pistachio soup is one of Nazzy's favorite recipes passed on from her Azeri grandmother. After tasting it, Nahid Joon immediately asked for the recipe.

Put the raw pistachios in a food processor and pulse for 1–2 minutes, until finely ground. Slowly add 1 cup (8 fl oz/250 ml) of water and pulse until a fine paste forms. Set aside.

In a medium bowl, bloom the saffron in 4 tablespoons of hot water.

Heat the oil in a stockpot over medium heat. Add the ginger, ground coriander, chili powder, and turmeric and sauté for 1 minute, or until fragrant. Add the leeks, salt, and pepper and sauté for another 8 minutes, until the leeks are slightly golden. Add the pistachio paste and 6 cups (47 fl oz/1.4 L) of water. Stir, then bring to a boil over high heat. Cover, then reduce the heat to medium and simmer for 1 hour.

Stir in the cilantro (coriander) and parsley. Pour in the orange and lemon juice.

Working in batches if necessary, transfer the soup to a blender and purée for 3 minutes, until smooth and silky. Return the soup to the stockpot. If necessary, add water to thin it out. Season to taste with salt and pepper.

Add the yogurt to the bloomed saffron water and whisk until combined. To serve, ladle the soup into individual bowls and add 1–2 teaspoons of the saffron yogurt in a swirl. Garnish each bowl with rose petals, pistachios, and pomegranate seeds.

KNUCKLE POWER SOUP

Soup-e Pacheh + سوپ پاچه

Serves 10

Preparation time:
10 minutes

Cooking time:
10–15 hours

- 6 lb (2.7 kg) veal knuckle bones, thoroughly washed
- 4 bay leaves
- 2 stalks celery, chopped
- 1 onion, chopped
- 1 large bell pepper, chopped
- ½ head garlic, chopped
- 2 tablespoons black peppercorns
- 1 tablespoon salt
- 1 tablespoon white wine vinegar
- Lemon slices or ground cinnamon, to serve (optional)
- Your favorite chutneys (page 204–9), to serve (optional)

This bone marrow soup is from Faranak Amirsaleh, my dear friend who called Nahid Joon her New York mom. Her mother, Fati Ghassemieh, was one of Nahid Joon's best friends and a true auntie to me. Nahid and Faranak were always exchanging recipes, as Faranak is an amazing chef in her own right. The eye of the knuckle is rich in flavor and full of collagen. For these reasons, Faranak calls this recipe "Knuckle Power Soup," because it strengthens bones, nails, and hair and energizes you for the whole day.

This hearty and fortifying soup requires a full day to cook, but your patience will be rewarded. Thickened by the gelatin of the knuckles, it is often served in the winter or after a night out of partying and drinking to settle the stomach. Having it daily is said to benefit the gut.

Put the veal bones into a large saucepan of water and bring to a quick boil. Drain.

Return the drained bones to the saucepan. Add the remaining ingredients and 2½ quarts (2.3 L) of water. If the ingredients are not completely submerged, top up the water. Simmer for 10–15 hours, occasionally skimming the foam from the surface, until the soup is gelatinous and any meat has detached from the bone. The longer the simmer, the better the soup.

Strain the soup, then transfer it to small containers and refrigerate overnight. To serve, remove and discard the congealed fat from the surface and reheat. Ladle the soup into bowls and serve with lemon, cinnamon, and chutney, if using.

The soup can be stored in the freezer for up to 3 months.

HERB POTAGE

Aash-e Sabzi + آش سبزی

Serves 8–10

Preparation time:
40 minutes, plus
3–12 hours of soaking

Cooking time:
1 hour 45 minutes

For the potage:

- ½ cup (4 oz/115 g) dried yellow split peas, rinsed
- ½ cup (4 oz/115 g) dried green lentils, rinsed
- 1 cup (7 oz/200 g) basmati rice, well rinsed
- 2 tablespoons virgin olive oil or butter
- 1 small onion, grated
- ½ teaspoon ground turmeric
- 2 cups (6 oz/180 g) coarsely chopped spinach
- 1 cup (3½ oz/100 g) thinly sliced scallions (spring onions)
- 1 cup (2 oz/55 g) coarsely chopped basil
- 1 cup (2 oz/55 g) coarsely chopped parsley
- 2 teaspoons salt
- 1 teaspoon black pepper
- 2 cups (12 oz/350 g) Greek yogurt, plus extra for garnish (optional)

For the meatballs:

- 1 lb (450 g) ground (minced) beef (15% fat), lamb, or turkey
- 1 small onion, grated
- 1 clove garlic, finely chopped
- 1 egg
- ½ cup (3 oz/85 g) cooked basmati rice
- 4 tablespoons finely chopped parsley
- 4 tablespoons finely chopped mint
- ½ teaspoon salt
- ¼ teaspoon black pepper
- 3 tablespoons virgin olive oil or butter

My grandparents lived in an old house with coal stoves. During very cold winters in Tehran, they would build a *korsi* in their sunroom, a low table with a built-in coal-burning grill, covered in blankets and surrounded by cushions. My grandmother's korsi was adorned with antique Persian and Indian textiles called *termehs*. They were embroidered with metallic paisley and floral patterns. My brother and I would count the days until winter so we could visit our grandparents and stretch out our legs to feel the korsi's warmth.

Our meals during this time of the year would start with a traditional herb potage, followed by Azerbaijani food—often rice and a deliciously fragrant *khoresh*—prepared by my grandmother, whom I lovingly called *nanou*.

Make the potage. In a large bowl, combine the split peas and lentils. Soak in hot water for at least 3 hours or overnight. Drain.

Place the rice in a separate bowl, cover with salted lukewarm water, and soak for 30 minutes or overnight. Drain.

Heat the oil in a large saucepan over medium heat. Add three-quarters of the grated onion and sauté for 7–10 minutes, until golden brown. Stir in the turmeric and pour in 6 cups (47 fl oz/1.4 L) of water. Add the rice, split peas, and lentils and stir to combine. The water should measure slightly more than half of the saucepan. Top up with more if needed.

Bring to a boil. Add the spinach, scallions (spring onions), basil, and parsley. Add the salt and pepper. Boil for 30 minutes, stirring frequently to prevent the bottom of the soup from burning. Reduce the heat to medium-low and simmer for 30 minutes, stirring frequently, until the ingredients are suspended in the water and do not sink when stirred.

Make the meatballs. Meanwhile, in a large bowl, combine all the ingredients except for the oil. Mix well, kneading by hand, until the mixture is homogeneous. Using a spoon, push the meat to one side of the bowl until the juices come out. Drain the liquid.

Add 2 tablespoons of the oil and knead until soft and smooth. Wet your hands, then shape a generous tablespoon of the meat mixture into a ball. Repeat with the remaining mixture.

Heat the remaining 1 tablespoon of oil in a large skillet over medium-high heat. Fry the meatballs for 2 minutes, until brown. Flip and sear for another 2 minutes, until brown. Transfer to a paper towel–lined plate. (They will be fully cooked in the soup.)

Bring the potage to a boil. Carefully add the meatballs, then reduce the heat to medium-low. Partially cover and simmer for 30 minutes. If needed, thin out the soup with more water. Turn off the heat, then season to taste. Stir in the yogurt, if using. (The addition of the yogurt transforms this dish into *aash-e-maast*.)

Ladle the soup into shallow serving bowls. Add a dollop of yogurt on top, if using.

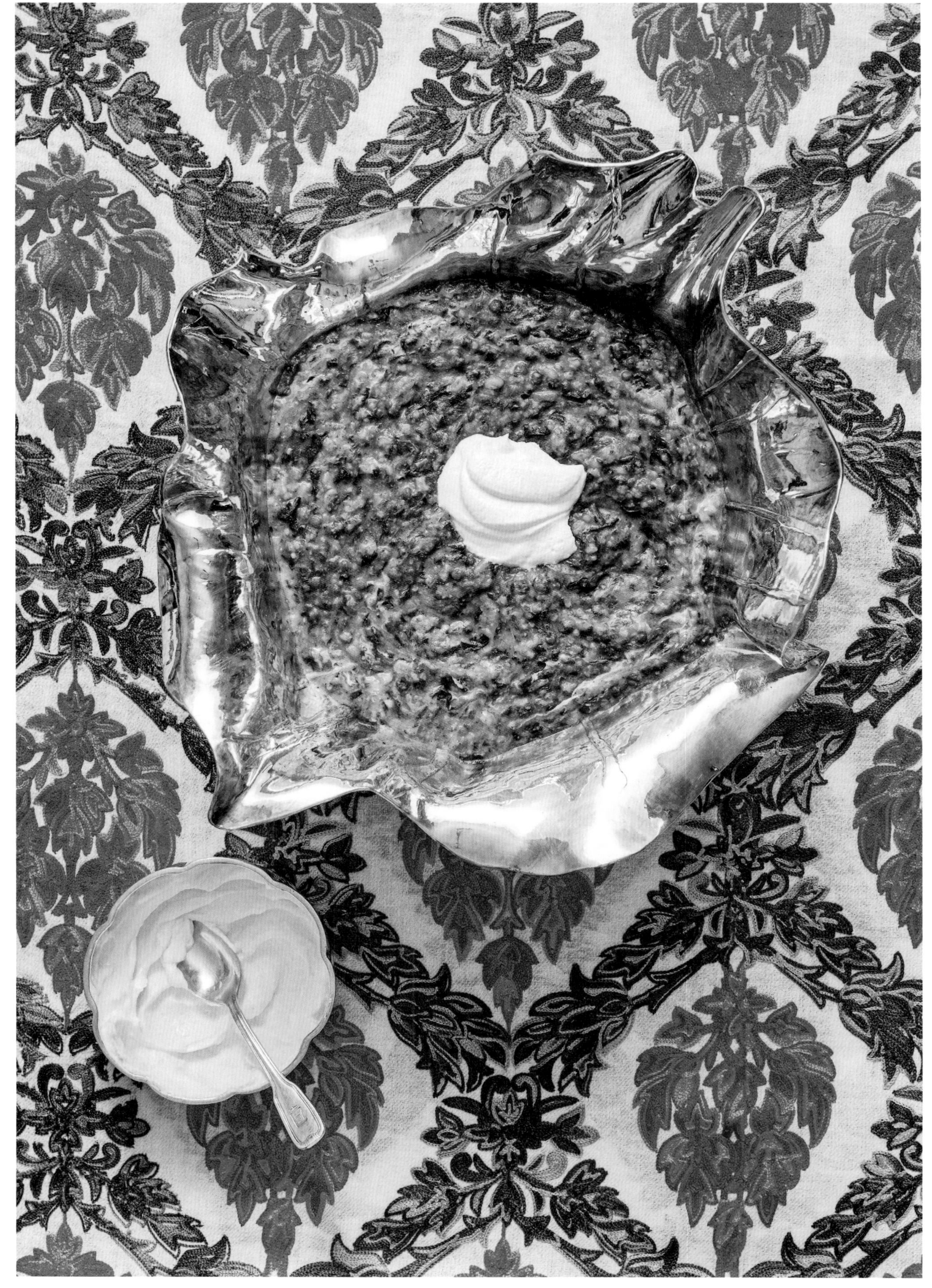

HERB & NOODLE POTAGE

Serves 8–10

Preparation time: 25 minutes, plus overnight soaking

Cooking time: 2 hours 40 minutes

Aash-e Reshteh + آش رشته

For the potage:

- ½ cup (3 oz/85 g) dried chickpeas, soaked overnight
- 2 tablespoons virgin olive oil or butter
- 2 onions, thinly sliced
- 8 cloves garlic, finely chopped
- 1 cup (2 oz/55 g) coarsely chopped mint or 4 tablespoons dried mint
- 1 teaspoon salt
- 1 teaspoon black pepper
- 1 teaspoon ground turmeric
- ½ cup (3 oz/85 g) dried red kidney beans, soaked overnight
- ½ cup (3 oz/85 g) dried pinto beans, soaked overnight
- 4½ × (32-fl oz/950-ml) cartons vegetable stock
- 1 cup (8 oz/225 g) dried green lentils, soaked overnight
- 5 cups (15 oz/425 g) coarsely chopped spinach
- 2 cups (4 oz/115 g) coarsely chopped parsley
- 2 cups (7 oz/200 g) thinly sliced scallions (spring onions)
- 1 cup (1¾ oz/50 g) coarsely chopped dill
- 2 beets (beetroots), peeled and cut into ½-inch (1-cm) cubes
- 9 oz/250 g Persian noodles (*reshteh*)
- 1½ cups (12 fl oz/350 ml) *kashk*, whey, or buttermilk

For the garnish:

- 2 tablespoons virgin olive oil or butter
- 1 onion, thinly sliced
- 4 cloves garlic, finely chopped
- 1 tablespoon dried mint
- 3–4 tablespoons *kashk* or Greek yogurt

Aash-e reshteh is the most popular of Persian potages. Served as a starter or a hearty main, it is most satisfying with beans, herbs, and a starchy, enriched wheat noodle known as *reshteh*. My grandmother would make the best herb and noodle potage—I was always keen to visit her home, sit around her *korsi*, and enjoy this delicacy. Anytime I go to Nasim Alikhani's Persian restaurant Sofreh in Brooklyn, I revel in their delicious *aash-e reshteh*, which brings back memories of my grandmother Nanou's cuisine.

If you're short on time, replace the dried beans with 1½ cups (9 oz/250 g) canned beans, drained and rinsed. Add them with the noodles and skip the first 45 minutes of cooking.

Make the potage. Drain the chickpeas and remove the skins. Set aside.

Heat the oil or butter in a heavy saucepan over medium heat. Add the onions and sauté for 7–10 minutes, until softened and golden. Add the garlic and cook for 2–4 minutes, until fragrant. Season with mint, salt, pepper, and turmeric. Add the chickpeas and drained kidney and pinto beans and sauté for another 2 minutes.

Pour in the stock and bring to a boil. Reduce the heat to medium-low, cover, and simmer for 45 minutes. Add the drained lentils and cook for another 45 minutes.

Add the spinach, parsley, scallions (spring onions), dill, and beets (beetroots) and bring to a boil. Reduce the heat to medium-low and cook for another 30 minutes, or until the vegetables are soft. Add the noodles and cook over medium heat for another 20 minutes, stirring frequently to prevent the noodles from sticking together. Reduce the heat and stir in the *kashk*. Add more stock or water if the soup is too thick. Season to taste and keep warm.

Make the garnish. Heat the oil in a medium skillet over medium heat. Add the onion and garlic and sauté for 7–10 minutes, until the onion is translucent and golden. Add the dried mint and mix.

Ladle the potage into individual bowls or a deep serving bowl. Garnish with the onion-mint mixture and kashk.

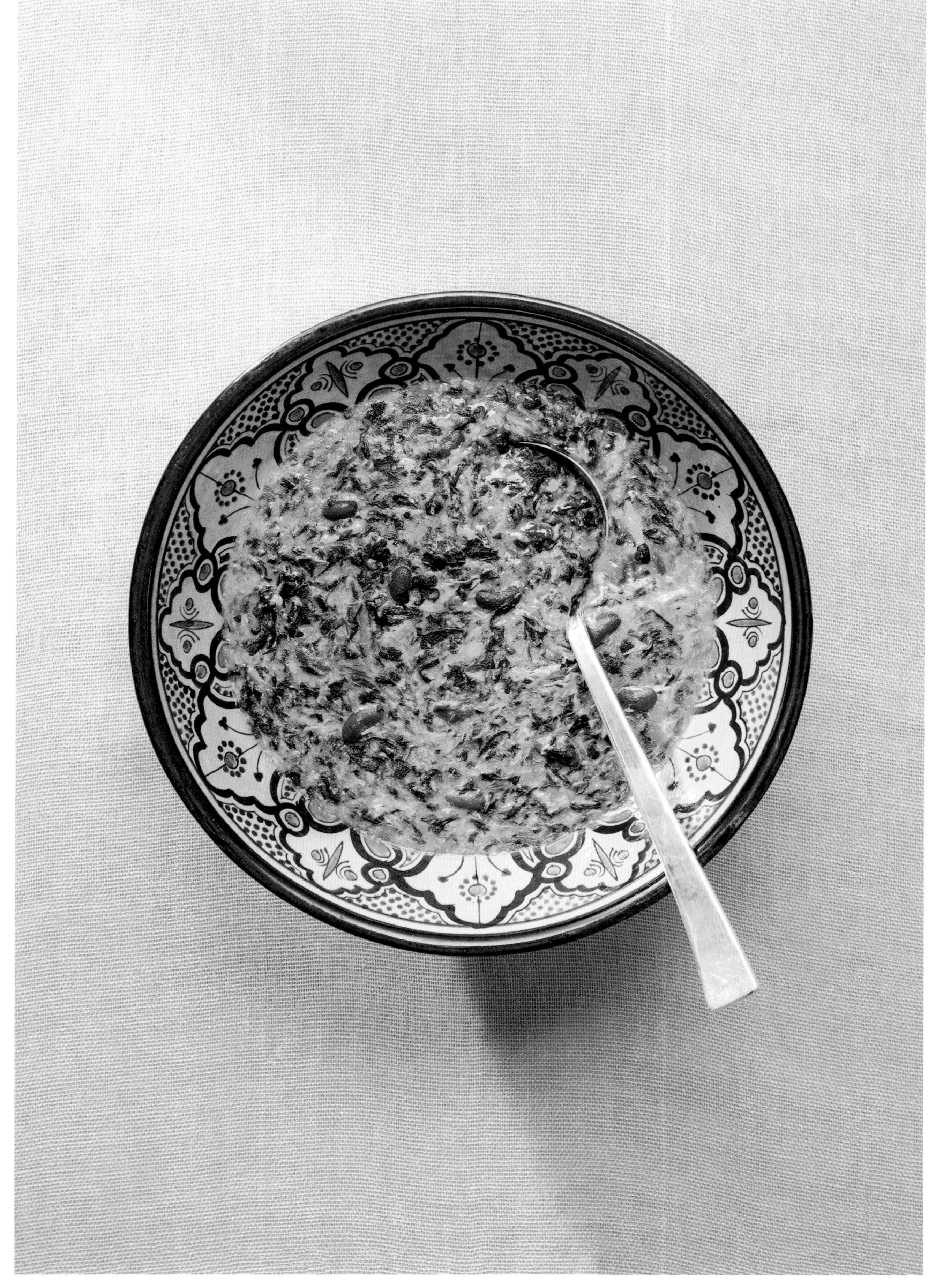

SPINACH EGG DROP HERB POTAGE WITH MEATBALLS

Serves 6-8

Preparation time:
30-45 minutes, plus overnight soaking

Cooking time:
1-1 hour 30 minutes

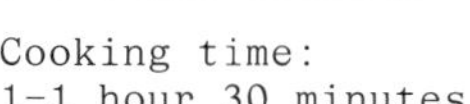

Aash-e Saak + آش ساک

- 1 cup (6½ oz/185 g) dried red kidney beans, soaked overnight, or 3 cups (1 lb 2 oz/500 g) canned red kidney beans, drained and rinsed
- 4 cups (32 fl oz/950 ml) vegetable stock
- 1 quantity uncooked Meatballs (see page 72)
- 3 cloves garlic, finely chopped
- 1 small onion, finely chopped
- 6 cups (1 lb 6 oz/625 g) coarsely chopped spinach
- 2 teaspoons ground turmeric
- 4 tablespoons rice flour
- 1 cup (8 fl oz/250 ml) verjus (see Note)
- 3 eggs, beaten
- 2 teaspoons salt
- 1 teaspoon black pepper
- ½ cup (1 oz/30 g) finely chopped parsley or cilantro (coriander), for garnish (optional)

My grandmother and mother both loved cooking hearty *aash-e-saak* in the winter. I just love the citrusy and sour flavors.

When I make *aash* in New York, I think of those cold Tehran winter nights, sitting around the *korsi* and listening to my grandparents share stories of our family and the battles my grandfather Salar fought in his lifetime to protect his birthplace Azerbaijan against the Russians and the Ottoman Empire.

Combined the drained kidney beans and 4 cups (32 fl oz/950 ml) of water in a medium saucepan. Bring to a boil, then reduce the heat to medium. Cover and simmer for 35 minutes, or until soft. Drain and set aside. (If using canned kidney beans, skip this step.)

In a large saucepan, combine the stock and 4 cups (32 fl oz/950 ml) of water and bring to a boil. Carefully lower the meatballs into the pan. Reduce the heat to medium. Add the garlic, onion, spinach, and turmeric and stir to combine.

In a small bowl, whisk the rice flour and verjus until smooth. Add the mixture to the saucepan and stir until the soup starts to thicken. Cook over medium heat for 20–25 minutes, until the meatballs are fully cooked.

Add the eggs and kidney beans and stir to combine. Season with salt and pepper. Cook for another 10–15 minutes, stirring frequently. Season to taste.

Ladle warm soup into serving bowls and garnish with the parsley, if using.

Note: If you can't find verjus, substitute it with ¾ cup (6 fl oz/175 ml) of lemon juice, depending on the desired sourness. Lemon juice is slightly more sour than verjus.

POMEGRANATE & HERB POTAGE

Aash-e Anar + آش انار

Serves 10–12

Preparation time:
30 minutes, plus
30 minutes soaking

Cooking time:
2 hours

- 1 cup (7 oz/200 g) basmati rice
- 2 tablespoons virgin olive oil or butter
- 1 large onion, grated
- ½ teaspoon ground turmeric
- ½ cup (4 oz/115 g) dried yellow split peas, rinsed
- ½ cup (4 oz/115 g) dried green lentils
- 8 cups (1 lb 8 oz/675 g) coarsely chopped spinach
- 2 cups (2¾ oz/80 g) coarsely chopped beet greens
- 2 cups (7 oz/200 g) thinly sliced scallions (spring onions)
- 2 cups (4 oz/115 g) coarsely chopped basil
- 2 cups (4 oz/115 g) coarsely chopped parsley
- 1 quantity uncooked Meatballs (see page 72)
- 5 cups (40 fl oz/1.2 L) pomegranate juice
- ½ cup (4 fl oz/120 ml) verjus (see Note)
- 2 tablespoons tomato paste (purée)
- 2 teaspoons salt
- 1 tablespoon black pepper
- 2–3 tablespoons sugar (optional)
- Pomegranate seeds, for garnish

This tangy and sweet *aash* is my favorite, by far. When pomegranates are in season in Iran, during the fall and winter, we would enjoy this dish every week with fresh pomegranate juice. Every other time of the year, my mother used pomegranate molasses, which gives the *aash* a deep, fruity taste. Nahid Joon would serve the potage in ceramic bowls shaped like pomegranates.

If you prefer it sweeter in taste, you can add sugar. Nahid Joon did not.

Rinse the rice under cold running water until the water runs clear. Transfer the rice to a bowl, cover with salted lukewarm water, and soak for 30 minutes. (You can also soak it overnight.) Drain.

Heat the oil or butter over medium heat in a large saucepan. Add the onion and sauté for 7–10 minutes, until softened. Stir in the turmeric and pour in 2 quarts (2 L) of water. Add the rice, split peas, and lentils and stir to combine. The water should measure slightly more than half of the saucepan. Bring to a boil.

Add the spinach, beet greens, scallions (spring onions), basil, and parsley. Boil for 15 minutes, stirring frequently to prevent the bottom of the soup from burning. Reduce the heat to medium and cook for 1 hour, stirring frequently, until the ingredients are suspended in the water and do not sink to the bottom of the saucepan when stirred.

Bring the potage to a boil and carefully add the meatballs. Add the pomegranate juice, verjus, tomato paste (purée), salt, and pepper. Boil for 3 minutes. Season to taste. If you prefer a more sour potage, add more lemon and pomegranate juice. For a sweet-sour taste, add the sugar.

Reduce the heat to low and partially cover. Simmer for 30 minutes. If the *aash* seems too thick, thin it out with more water. Stir occasionally to prevent the ingredients from sticking to the bottom of the saucepan and burning. Season to taste.

Ladle the warm potage into shallow serving bowls. Garnish with pomegranate seeds.

Note: If you can't find verjus, substitute it with ½ cup (4 fl oz/120 ml) of lemon juice, depending on the desired sourness. Lemon juice is slightly more sour than verjus.

BARLEY & HERB POTAGE

Serves 8

Preparation time:
1 hour 30 minutes

Cooking time:
3 hours

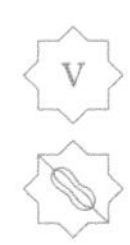

Aash-e Jo + آش جو

For the potage:

- 1½ cups (10½ oz/300 g) pearl barley
- 2 teaspoons salt
- 3 tablespoons virgin olive oil or butter
- 2 onions, finely chopped
- 3 tablespoons dried mint
- ½ teaspoon ground turmeric
- 2 cups (6 oz/180 g) coarsely chopped spinach
- 2 cups (4 oz/115 g) coarsely chopped parsley
- 1½ cups (5½ oz/150 g) thinly sliced scallions (spring onions)
- 1 cup (8 oz/225 g) dried green lentils
- ½ cup (6½ oz/185 g) dried red kidney beans (see Note)
- ½ cup (6½ oz/185 g) dried pinto beans (see Note)
- 1 teaspoon black pepper
- 1 cup (8 fl oz/250 ml) *kashk*, whey, or buttermilk

For the garnish:

- 4 tablespoons virgin olive oil or butter
- 1 large yellow onion, thinly sliced
- 4 cloves garlic, finely chopped
- 3 tablespoons dried mint

With the addition of beans and barley, this hearty and nutritious *aash* is a meal in itself. It is vegetarian, though you could always add beef or veal. Sometimes, my mother would add a log of chèvre in place of the *kashk* for richness.

The barley needs to be prepared in advance.

Make the potage. Combine the barley, 1 teaspoon of salt, and 3½ cups (27 fl oz/800 ml) of water in a medium saucepan. Leave uncovered and bring to a boil. Boil for 3–4 minutes, then reduce the heat to medium-low. Simmer for 20–30 minutes, until the barley is tender. Place the barley and remaining water in a food processor and purée.

Heat the oil in a large saucepan over medium heat. Add the onions and sauté for 7–10 minutes, until softened. Stir in the mint and turmeric and cook for 2–3 minutes. Add 2 quarts (2 L) of water, the barley purée, and the remaining ingredients. Season with the remaining teaspoon of salt. Bring to a boil and stir frequently to prevent the bottom from burning. Reduce the heat to medium-low and partially cover. Simmer for 2 hours, stirring frequently until the ingredients are suspended in the liquid when stirred. Add ¾ cup (6 fl oz/175 ml) of the *kashk* and stir for 3 minutes. Season to taste. (Kashk is quite salty.)

Make the garnish. Heat the oil in a small skillet over medium heat. Add the onion and sauté for 12–15 minutes, until golden brown. Add the garlic and mint and sauté for another 2–3 minutes. Transfer to a paper towel–lined plate.

Ladle the soup into a shallow serving bowl. Drizzle the rest of the kashk on top and garnish with crispy onions and mint.

Notes: If you're short on time, you can replace the dried beans with 1½ cups (9 oz/250 g) canned beans, drained and rinsed. Reduce the simmering time of the soup to 1 hour.

You can add ½ cup (3 oz/85 g) of cooked and skinned chickpeas for a heartier potage.

For a sharper taste, stir in ½ cup (4 fl oz/120 ml) of verjus.

GILANI BEAN & HERB POTAGE

Aash-e Gilani + آش گیلانی

Serves 10

Preparation time: 45 minutes, plus overnight soaking

Cooking time: 2 hours

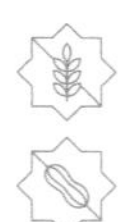

- ½ cup (3 oz/85 g) dried chickpeas (see Note)
- ½ cup (3 oz/85 g) dried pinto beans (see Note)
- ½ cup (3 oz/85 g) dried red kidney beans (see Note)
- 2 tablespoons virgin olive oil or butter
- 3 onions, grated
- 1 tablespoon ground turmeric
- 5 cups (40 fl oz/1.2 L) vegetable stock
- 2 beet greens, coarsely chopped into ½-inch (1-cm) pieces
- 4 cups (8 oz/225 g) coarsely chopped parsley
- 4 cups (8 oz/225 g) coarsely chopped cilantro (coriander)
- 2 cups (7 oz/200 g) thinly sliced scallions (spring onions)
- 1 tablespoon salt
- 1 teaspoon black pepper
- 1 quantity uncooked Meatballs (see page 72)
- 2 tablespoons rice flour
- 1 cup (8 fl oz/250 ml) verjus, plus extra if desired
- 2 eggs, beaten

A medley of legumes, herbs, and eggs come together to make this satisfying dish from the province of Gilan on the Caspian Sea. The verjus adds a pleasant tang.

In the winter, Nahid Joon served this hot *aash* with meatballs. In the summer, she added another cup of stock, and served it as a light, chilled soup. Both versions can be topped with a dollop of yogurt.

This soup can be made with another Persian dried herb called *khalwash*. You can rub it between your palms and put it into the verjus. Add it to the soup at the final cooking stage, just before serving.

In a large bowl, combine the chickpeas and beans and add enough water to cover. Soak overnight. Drain.

Heat the oil in a stockpot over medium heat. Add the onions and sauté for 7–10 minutes, until they begin to turn golden brown. Stir in the turmeric. Pour in the stock and 6 cups (47 fl oz/1.4 L) of water. Add the drained chickpeas, both beans, and beet greens. The water should fill the pot halfway, otherwise the soup will be mushy. Add more water if needed.

Bring to a boil. Add the parsley, cilantro (coriander), scallions (spring onions), salt, and pepper. Boil for 30 minutes, stirring frequently to prevent the bottom of the soup from burning. Reduce the heat to medium and simmer for 30 minutes, stirring frequently until the ingredients are suspended in the water when stirred and do not sink to the bottom.

Bring to a boil and carefully add the meatballs. Reduce the heat to medium-low, partially cover, and simmer for 30 minutes. If the soup seems too thick, add more water.

Dissolve the rice flour in 5 tablespoons of water and whisk to form a paste. Add it to the saucepan and boil for 10 minutes. If it is too watery, dissolve some more rice flour in water and add it in. Add the verjus and boil for another 10 minutes. Season to taste and turn off the heat Add the eggs to the pan and mix well.

Ladle the soup into shallow serving bowls.

Note: If you're short on time, replace each of the dried beans with 1 cup (6 oz/180 g) canned beans, drained and rinsed.

TOMATO & HERB POTAGE

Serves 10

Preparation time: 25 minutes

Cooking time: 4 hours 20 minutes

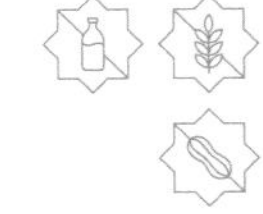

Aash-e Gojeh Farangi + آش گوجه فرنگی

- 2 tablespoons virgin olive oil
- 1 yellow onion, finely chopped
- 2 cloves garlic, finely chopped
- 1 lb (450 g) ground (minced) beef
- 1 tablespoon ground cumin
- 2 teaspoons ground turmeric
- 2 teaspoons salt
- 1 teaspoon black pepper
- 20 scallions (spring onions), finely sliced
- 2 × (12-oz/250-g) packages frozen spinach
- 4 cups (1 lb/450 g) finely chopped cilantro (coriander)
- 2 cups (4 oz/115 g) finely chopped parsley, plus extra for garnish
- 4 tablespoons finely chopped mint
- 1 cup (7 oz/200 g) basmati rice, well rinsed
- 2 × (28-oz/800-g) cans crushed tomatoes
- 1 tomato, for garnish (optional)

Nahid Joon loved this simple Azerbaijani dish that her cousin Maryam Panahy Ansary always served at her lavish lunches and dinner parties. This recipe was passed down from generation to generation in the Panahy family. Maryam Joon learned it from her aunt, Razieh Khanom, who was the family's matriarch and a venerated chef.

Heat the oil in a large saucepan over medium-high heat. Add the onion and garlic and sauté for 7–10 minutes, until the onion is softened and golden. Add the beef and cook for 7–10 minutes, until lightly brown, breaking it up with a wooden spoon. Reduce the heat to medium. Add the cumin, turmeric, salt, and pepper and stir to combine.

Add the scallions (spring onions), spinach, cilantro (coriander), parsley, and mint. Pour in 3¾ quarts (3.6 L) of water. Reduce the heat to medium-low and cover. Simmer for 3 hours, stirring occasionally, until the greens are soft.

Add the rice and crushed tomatoes. Simmer for 1 hour, or until the rice is fully cooked.

Peel the skin off the tomato in one long strip, if using. Roll it into a rose shape. Garnish the rice with the decorative rose and parsley. Serve.

BEEF SOUP WITH BEANS, CHICKPEAS & POTATOES

Serves 6–8

Preparation time:
30 minutes, plus overnight soaking

Cooking time:
3 hours 30 minutes

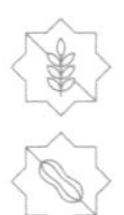

Abgoosht + آبگوشت

- 4 tablespoons virgin olive oil or butter
- 2 large onions, diced
- 2 lb (900 g) bone-in beef short ribs or bone-in lamb shanks (see Note)
- ½ cup (3 oz/85 g) dried white beans, soaked overnight (see Note)
- ½ cup (3 oz/85 g) dried chickpeas, soaked overnight (see Note)
- 2 teaspoons ground turmeric
- 2 teaspoons salt
- ½ teaspoon black pepper
- ¼ teaspoon ground saffron
- 4 white potatoes
- 4 dried Persian limes, pierced
- 2 Roma tomatoes, cut in half
- ½ cup (4 oz/115 g) dried yellow split peas, soaked overnight
- 4 tablespoons tomato paste (purée)
- 4 tablespoons coarsely chopped parsley, for garnish

With its tantalizing turmeric and saffron aroma, this versatile soup is Iran's most popular dish. The meat and ingredients are mashed and served as an accompaniment to the soup. However, you can leave all the ingredients intact in the soup. This makes for a hearty stew that can be served with Persian bread (*lavash*).

Heat the oil in a large saucepan over medium heat. Add the onions and sauté for 7–10 minutes, until golden brown. Set aside.

Rinse the meat under cold running water, then add it to the pan. Pour in 7 cups (1¾ quarts/1.7 L) of water. Bring to a boil, occasionally skimming the froth from the surface. Add the drained white beans and chickpeas, turmeric, salt, and pepper. Cover, then reduce the heat to low and simmer for 1½ hours. The meat should be submerged in the liquid. Add more water if needed.

In a small bowl, bloom the saffron in 4 tablespoons of hot water. Set aside.

Add a potato to the pan. Add the dried Persian limes, tomatoes, drained yellow split peas, tomato paste (purée), and bloomed saffron water. Cover and simmer for another 30 minutes. Transfer the cooked potato to a bowl and set aside to cool. Mash the potato, then add it back to the saucepan. This helps to thicken the mixture.

Quarter the rest of the potatoes and add them to the pan. Cover and simmer for 90 minutes, until the stock has thickened and the potatoes can be easily pierced with a fork.

Carefully squeeze the Persian limes to release the juices into the saucepan, then discard the rinds. Using a slotted spoon, remove the meat, cooked beans, vegetables, and potatoes and allow to cool. Debone the meat, then mash it until lumpy. Using a mortar and pestle or food processor, mash the meat and beans until smooth. Season to taste with salt and pepper.

Plate the meat on a separate side dish, sprinkle with parsley, and serve with a bowl of the hot stock.

Notes: You can replace the short ribs with 1¾ lb (800 g) cubed beef or lamb.

To save on time, replaced dried beans with 1½ cups (9 oz/250 g) canned beans, drained and rinsed.

PERSIAN CHICKEN SOUP WITH POTATOES

Serves 6–8

Preparation time: 20 minutes

Cooking time: 2 hours

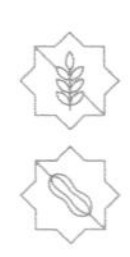

Abgoosht Morgh + آبگوشت مرغ

- ¼ teaspoon ground saffron
- 4 tablespoons virgin olive oil or butter
- 2 onions, grated
- 8 boneless, skinless chicken thighs, cut into 2-inch (5-cm) cubes
- ¾ cup (6 oz/180 g) dried yellow split peas, rinsed
- 2½ teaspoons salt
- 1½ teaspoons black pepper
- ½ teaspoon ground turmeric
- 2 potatoes
- 1 tablespoon dried Persian lime powder (see Note)
- 3 dried Persian limes
- 4 tablespoons tomato paste (purée)
- 4 tablespoons coarsely chopped parsley, for garnish

To serve:

- Persian bread, such as *barbari*, *sangak*, *taftoon*, or pita bread
- 1 small onion, coarsely chopped
- 1 small scallion (spring onion), coarsely chopped
- ½ cup (2 oz/55 g) coarsely chopped chives

When Nahid Joon moved to the United States in the early 1980s—long before Australian and New Zealand lamb were being imported into the country—she struggled to find good-quality lamb. Persian lamb is extremely lean, as the herds of sheep in Iran are reared across mountainous terrain.

She improvised by using chicken, which was leaner, in her *abgoosht*—my father's favorite winter stew. This light, healthy rendition pairs well with Persian bread, pickles, and salad.

In a small bowl, bloom the saffron in 4 tablespoons of hot water. Set aside.

Heat the oil in a large saucepan over medium heat. Add the onions and sauté for 7–10 minutes, until golden brown. Add the chicken and sauté for 10 minutes to slightly brown on all sides. Add the split peas, salt, pepper, turmeric, and bloomed saffron water.

Pour in 2 quarts (2 L) of water and bring to a boil. Reduce the heat to low and add a whole potato. Cook for 30 minutes, or until the potato can be easily pierced with a fork. Transfer the potato to a bowl and mash it with a fork. Add it back to the pan. Stir in the dried Persian lime powder.

Using a sharp knife, make a few small holes in the Persian limes. Add them to the saucepan. Cut the remaining potato into 1-inch (2.5-cm) cubes and add it to the pan. Add the tomato paste (purée). Simmer for 1 hour, or until the potatoes are fully cooked. Season to taste. To serve, squeeze in the juice of the Persian limes. You can leave them in the soup or remove them, but they are not to be eaten.

Transfer the meat and potatoes to the bowls, then ladle the broth and legumes on top. Garnish with parsley. Serve warm with a selection of bread, chopped onions, scallions (spring onions), and chives on the side.

Note: If you can't find dried Persian lime powder, substitute with an additional 6 Persian limes.

FEASTING WITH THE GREAT KING

Jake Stavis

Toward the end of the sixth century BCE, the Persians of southwestern Iran came to control the largest empire the world had yet seen. At its peak, the Achaemenid Empire, named for the ruling dynasty, stretched from Thrace in the west to northern India in the east, encompassing Iran, Mesopotamia, Anatolia, Egypt, and parts of Central Asia. Even more impressive perhaps, this empire remained mostly intact for about 200 years, successfully bringing together different languages, cultures, economies, and sociopolitical organizations. Despite the enormity of their achievements, the Achaemenids remain largely misunderstood, in no small part due to Classical Greek texts written to foster a Hellenic sense of identity in contrast to a barbaric East. Generations of scholars have uncritically relied on Classical authors, especially Herodotus, to describe the Persian court as one of excessive wealth, despotic power, and indulgent luxury. However, if we instead look to material culture from the Persians themselves, we might better understand their grand banqueting practices and convivial drinking as foundational to an innovative royal ideology, integrating carefully orchestrated acts of generosity and decorum.

A relatively minor population of nomadic origin, the Persians took charge of an enormous conglomeration of states and peoples, and unlike previous imperial powers in the region such as the Assyrians, they could not extend their system of governance over the newly acquired territories. Instead, they adopted a rather pragmatic solution, inserting themselves into existing political structures and playing into the heterogeneity of their empire. Local governors called *satraps* served at the behest of the great "King of Kings," the binding force incarnate who unified the state. A relief from the Hall of a Hundred Columns at Persepolis illustrates the foundational throne of Achaemenid kingship: the Persian monarch sits atop a tiered platform, supported by the satraps, each one distinguished by culturally specific dress and coiffure. They carry the royal dais on their fingertips with ease, conveying a trademark sense of order and harmony bestowed by the king. This new visual language of power is manifested throughout royal building projects, stages for major religious celebrations and elaborate feasts, demonstrating both the diversity of the empire and the role of the king in holding it together. That same image of imperial harmony was brought to life in the banquets themselves, sites for the manifestation of power relations through the exchange of food and drink.

Prior to the conquest of Babylon in 539 BCE, the Persians did not have major cities or their own tradition of monumental architecture. In lieu of one capital they ultimately built several, drawing on material resources, specialized craft traditions, and labor from throughout the empire. The great king split his time between residences at Persepolis, Susa, Ecbatana, and Babylon in accordance with the seasons, but it was at Persepolis where he and his court observed the new year's festival in the spring, possibly a predecessor to the holiday we now call Nowruz. Delegations from across the empire entered through a monumental portal, fittingly called the Gate of All Nations, then processed along different routes depending on their role, ultimately delivering tribute to the great king, including a range of craftwork, as well as raw materials and livestock. Many of the buildings at Persepolis were faced with limestone reliefs, and those adorning the Apadana Palace likely represent aspects of this annual new year's festival. The delegates are once again distinguished by culturally specific clothing and grooming and the gifts they offered the king.

Broadly, this vision stands in stark contrast to earlier reliefs from the Assyrians, an explicitly militaristic authority scaring its subjects into submission. Instead of violent force, casualties, prisoners, and looted goods, we see a harmonious vision of an empire and its subjects uniting in celebration, their annual tax payments pointedly recast as gifts for the just and benevolent king. Early scholarship of Achaemenid art especially derided such compositions as dull and repetitive, often making such value judgments through comparison with Western aesthetic norms; instead, we might better understand the rhythmic composition as capturing an eternal motion of the empire, propelled by the vision of the great king at its center. To gather in homage to the King of Kings was to recommit to this vision.

Besides these representatives from the provinces, we encounter numerous palace guards and courtiers and servants bearing food and drink for an abundant feast. Some carry bowls and what appear to be wineskins, while others hold live animals. Greek writers emphasize both the quantity and range of ingredients procured for the royal table, including horses, camels, cows, donkeys, deer, and birds of all sizes, plus flours, spices, herbs, and oils aplenty. They also note variation according to region—the king enjoyed dishes scented with saffron when he was in the northern regions of Iran, and further south in Babylon, the heart of date country, he sipped a combination of palm wine mixed with grape. Administrative texts from Persepolis hint at the massive quantities, if not the wide variety, of the products destined for the royal court. Like the monumental building projects, we might understand such banquets as a sort of microcosm of empire, drawing on the vast resources and labor at the king's disposal, while also clearly communicating power dynamics.

The feast itself provided a setting for participants to vie for power and cement their ties to the great king, especially through the exchange of drink and luxury tableware. Animal-shaped vessels feature prominently among the tributary reliefs and are among the finest examples of Achaemenid craftsmanship found in museums around the world (often, most frustratingly, without sound provenience). One particularly noteworthy type is the rhyton, composed of the forepart of an animal or composite beast and a tall beaker, sometimes curved like a horn. A small outlet in the chest or mouth allowed liquid to flow through the vessel, which could then be caught with a conventional cup or directly in the mouth of the drinker (while we call these *rhyta* after the Greek word meaning "to flow," the Persian designation for these vessels remains unknown). It is believed these vessels are a sleeker version of earlier Iron Age terracotta beakers found in Iran and elsewhere in the Near East, also with animal heads and foreparts but lacking the second outlet. Such vessels were clearly not utilitarian designs, but rather symbolically charged cups, combining the iconography of royalty alongside precious materials, only to be used by those with specialty knowledge.

An example from the Metropolitan Museum of Art (The Met) features a reclining ram, perhaps a wild mouflon, its forelegs folded under its body and its hind legs extended up the beaker. Images of combat between the royal hero and wild beasts such as this one were integral to the formation of a mythological cosmos, frequently occurring on monumental reliefs and cylinder seals alike in the Near East for millennia. To drink from such a vessel places the drinker in that same agonistic position, subduing the beast by draining it of its life force and reiterating an act of control. Moreover, to drink from such a vessel in the king's presence was at once a demonstration of skill and a declaration of status among the true elite.

Fluted, shallow bowls are another characteristic Achaemenid form associated with the royal table. The size, weight, and inscriptions of some lead scholars to believe they were particularly suited for gifting. Perhaps an even greater honor than dining with the great king was to be gifted royal tableware—such vessels were prized not only for their craftsmanship, often hammered and chased from a single sheet of metal, but also for their material weight. This one in The Met's collection is part of a set of four nearly identical vessels said to have come from Hamedan, varying only slightly in size and all bearing the same inscription: "Artaxerxes, the great king, king of kings, king of lands, son of Xerxes the king, Xerxes son of Darius the king, the Achaemenid: in his house, this silver bowl was made."

Scholars often call this type of bowl by its Greek name, *phiale mesomphalos*, meaning "with a central navel." In Greece, these were primarily used to serve libations, inserting a finger into the central cavity to hold the bowl while tilting it to pour. Smaller bowls of a similar shape were used in the Near East not only for liquid offerings but also as drinking cups, balanced on the fingertips in an elegant fashion. The size, and therefore the volume, of this phiale inscribed with the name and titles of Artaxerxes is truly majestic. Nearly a foot in diameter, it is difficult to imagine comfortably drinking from such a bowl, though it's clear that vessels such as these were not crafted for practical purposes.

Much has changed since the time of the Achaemenid kings, but an appreciation for the art of feasting has persisted in Iran across the millennia. One might suggest that ancient traditions of eating, drinking, and hospitality, intricately interwoven with dynamics of power and conveying social relations, may have laid the groundwork for the development of *taarof*. While the dishes and details have of course varied with the introduction of new ingredients, cooking and preservation techniques, and political arrangements, that characteristically Iranian form of etiquette may have first found its expression around the royal table long ago.

—Jake Stavis, PhD, Hagop Kevorkian Curatorial Fellow (2019–2021), The Metropolitan Museum of Art, New York

MEAT, POULTRY, AND FISH

In ancient Iran, the people consumed lamb, beef, poultry, pork, and fish. These days, pork is not consumed in Iran for religious reasons, similar to many other countries in this region. Persians usually prepare meats in a stew, or *khoresht* (page 133), which is served with rice and bread. Meat tends not to be prepared on its own, except for marinated and grilled meats on skewers (*kebabs*), which are regarded as one of Iran's national foods.

Lamb is the protein of choice in Iran. By the mid-twentieth century, beef became prevalent and spread across the country. Chicken, once a delicacy, was consumed more regularly after the influx of Western culture and poultry farming. *Jujeh kebab* (grilled marinated chicken on skewers) is now a popular dish both in Iran and among the Persian diaspora in the West. Fish, once a rarity consumed only in coastal areas of Iran, is now a popular treat.

Nahid Joon prepared her kebabs with beef and her stews with veal, beef, and the occasional lamb. As for poultry, she favored the delicate Cornish hen, but she also used poussin and other game. Once she immigrated to the United States, she continued to experiment with fish and added spices, nuts, and seeds to create tasty, Persian-inspired recipes.

CHICKEN WITH MORELS

Morgh ba Gharch-e Morel ✣
مرغ با سس قارچ

Serves 4

Preparation time:
15 minutes, plus
20 minutes soaking

Cooking time:
1 hour

- 12 oz (350 g) fresh morel mushrooms or 1¾ oz (50 g) dried
- 5 tablespoons white wine vinegar
- 3 tablespoons butter
- 2 shallots, diced
- 1¼ teaspoons salt
- ¾ teaspoon black pepper
- ½ cup (4 fl oz/120 ml) sherry
- 2 cups (16 fl oz/475 ml) chicken stock
- 2 tablespoons heavy (double) cream
- 3 tablespoons virgin olive oil or butter
- 4 boneless chicken breasts, skin-on
- 2 cloves garlic, finely chopped
- ½ bunch thyme

Morels are seasonal and grow in the wild. Nahid Joon loved this luxurious delicacy more than any other mushroom. In the United States, she had a difficult time finding morels but managed to finally find them at D'Artagnan, a specialty food purveyor in New Jersey.

When Nahid Joon wanted to make a lighter dish, she would use crème fraîche instead of heavy (double) cream.

In a large bowl, combine the morels, vinegar, and enough hot water to cover them. Soak for 20 minutes. (This step is crucial for cleaning the morels and getting rid of all the dirt.) Drain, then rinse thoroughly under cold running water until the water runs clear. Place the morels on a large paper towel–lined plate and set aside to dry.

Heat the butter in a large skillet over medium heat until melted. Add the shallots and sauté for 6–8 minutes, until translucent. Add the morels, 1 teaspoon of salt, and the pepper and mix well.

Add the sherry and stir for 8 minutes, or until the sauce thickens. Pour in the stock, reduce the heat to low, and cover. Simmer for 20 minutes, stirring occasionally, until the sauce has thickened. Turn off the heat, then stir in the heavy (double) cream. Transfer the mixture to a blender and purée until smooth.

Heat the oil in a large skillet over medium heat. Add the chicken and sear, skin side down, for 3 minutes. Turn and cook for another 3 minutes, until golden. Reduce the heat to medium-low, then add the garlic and thyme. Cover and gently simmer for 20–25 minutes, until cooked through. Season to taste with salt and pepper.

Transfer to a serving platter, pour the morel sauce on top, and serve.

BRAISED TURMERIC CHICKEN

Serves 8

Preparation: 10 minutes

Cooking Time: 45–50 minutes

Morgh ba Zardchoobeh + مرغ با زرد چوبه

- 1 teaspoon ground saffron
- 4 tablespoons virgin olive oil or butter
- 3 onions, finely chopped
- 16 boneless, skinless chicken thighs or 8 boneless, skinless chicken breasts, cut in half
- 1 teaspoon ground turmeric
- 1 teaspoon salt
- ½ teaspoon black pepper
- 2 tablespoons lemon juice
- Dried barberries, rinsed, for garnish (optional)
- 4 tablespoons coarsely chopped cilantro (coriander) or parsley, for garnish
- Your favorite rice dish (page 170), to serve

Nahid Joon made this dish at least four times a week. The chicken is juicy, moist, and subtly spiced and designed to be enjoyed with rice dishes. Its aroma permeates the hallways of my apartment whenever I prepare it. I love cooking with turmeric; it is such a powerful antioxidant.

In a small bowl, bloom the saffron in ⅓ cup (2½ fl oz/75 ml) of hot water.

Heat the oil or butter in a large saucepan over medium-high heat. Add the onions and sauté for 7–10 minutes, until golden. Add the chicken and brown for 4 minutes on each side. If necessary, work in batches to avoid overcrowding.

Add the turmeric, salt, pepper, lemon juice, and 4 cups (32 fl oz/950 ml) of water. Cook over medium heat for 30–35 minutes, until the liquid has thickened and the chicken is cooked through. There should be enough liquid to cover a quarter of the chicken. If not, add more water.

Garnish with barberries or herbs. Serve with your favorite rice dish.

POUSSIN WITH POMEGRANATE SAUCE

Serves 8

Preparation time:
10 minutes, plus
1 hour chilling

Cooking time:
1½–2 hours

Jujeh ba Sauce Anar + جوجه با سس انار

- 4 poussins or Cornish hens, or 8 quails, cavity cleaned
- 6 tablespoons extra-virgin olive oil
- 6 cloves garlic, finely chopped
- ½ cup (1½ oz/40 g) finely chopped thyme leaves, plus extra for garnish
- ½ cup (1½ oz/40 g) finely chopped rosemary, plus extra for garnish
- 1½ teaspoons salt
- 2 teaspoons black pepper
- 6 tablespoons pomegranate molasses
- 1 peach, quartered and pitted
- 1 nectarine, quartered and pitted
- 1 red apple, peeled, cored, and quartered
- 1 D'Anjou pear, peeled, cored, and quartered
- 1 × (24-oz/675-g) jar pitted cherries in syrup (optional)
- 2 tablespoons pomegranate seeds, for garnish

When we lived in Iran, Nahid Joon would often skewer whole quail, grouse, and pigeon and broil them on an open coal-fire brazier (*manghal*). They would emanate the most delicious aroma of pomegranate molasses, rosemary, and thyme.

As she didn't have a terrace when we moved to New York, Nahid Joon would roast the game birds in her oven, making them very crispy. Poussin or Cornish hen were added to the menu if she couldn't find grouse or quail.

Roasted game can accompany many Persian rice dishes, or they can be had on their own with roasted pears, apples, pears, and quince.

Preheat the oven to 375°F (190°C/Gas Mark 5).

Wash the poussins under cold running water, then thoroughly pat dry the inside and outside with paper towels.

In a medium bowl, combine 4 tablespoons of olive oil, garlic, thyme, rosemary, 1 teaspoon of salt, the pepper, and pomegranate molasses. Rub the marinate over the poussins and inside the cavity, making sure to get into all the nooks. Leave uncovered and refrigerate for 1 hour.

In a medium bowl, combine the peach, nectarine, apple, and pear. Add the remaining 2 tablespoons of oil and ½ teaspoon of salt and toss to combine. Transfer the poussins to a large ovenproof dish or roasting pan and arrange the fruit around them. Do not overcrowd the dish. If necessary, use two pans.

Roast for 1½–2 hours and baste every 15 minutes in the juices, until the skin is roasted and the poussins are cooked through. (If roasting quail, reduce the time by 15 minutes.)

Meanwhile, if using, heat the cherries and syrup in a small saucepan over low heat for 45 minutes, until the syrup has reduced and thickened.

Transfer the chicken to a platter and arrange the fruit around them. Pour the remaining juice into a medium saucepan and cook over medium-high heat for 3 minutes, or until the juice thickens to a sauce. Stir the sauce frequently to prevent it from burning.

Pour the fruit sauce over the poussins, then add a dollop of the cherry sauce on top. Sprinkle with pomegranate seeds, then garnish with sprigs of thyme and rosemary. Serve.

CORNISH HEN WITH ROSEMARY & THYME

Serves 4

Preparation time:
20–30 minutes

Cooking time:
45–50 minutes

Jujeh ba Rosemarie va Avishan + جوجه کورنیش با رزماری و آویشن

- 1 teaspoon ground saffron
- 4 small Cornish hens, washed and quartered
- 2 teaspoons salt
- 1 teaspoon black pepper
- ½ teaspoon ground turmeric
- ½ cup (4 fl oz/120 ml) extra-virgin olive oil
- ½ cup (4 oz/115 g) melted butter
- 4 large onions, thinly sliced
- 12 sprigs rosemary, plus extra for garnish
- 12 sprigs thyme, leaves only
- Juice of 3 lemons
- Lemon wedges, for garnish

Nahid Joon would baste the Cornish hens with butter, rosemary, thyme, and turmeric, making them so succulent and flavorful. My mother would slice them in half and arrange them around rice dishes. This recipe can also be prepared with poussin, quail, or partridge, but the cooking time will need to be adjusted.

Preheat the oven to 400°F (200°C/Gas Mark 6).

In a small bowl, bloom the saffron in 4 tablespoons of hot water.

Season the Cornish hens with salt, pepper, and turmeric.

In a large ovenproof dish, combine the oil and half of the butter. Spread the onions evenly along the bottom of the dish. Place the Cornish hens on top, insert the rosemary into the cavity, and sprinkle with thyme leaves. Pour over the remaining half of the butter. Roast for 30 minutes, until golden, turning the Cornish hen often so that they cook evenly and basting occasionally.

In a small bowl, combine the lemon juice and bloomed saffron water. Pour this mixture over the Cornish hens and cook for another 15–20 minutes.

Serve on a platter and garnish with lemon wedges and rosemary.

HAMBURGERS

Hamburger + همبرگر

Serves 8

Preparation time:
15 minutes

Cooking time:
10–15 minutes

- 2 lb (900 g) ground (minced) sirloin beef
- 2 large onions, grated and drained (see Note)
- 1 cup (2 oz/55 g) coarsely chopped cilantro (coriander)
- 4 tablespoons soy sauce
- 2 tablespoons ground cumin
- 2 teaspoons garlic powder
- 1½ teaspoons salt
- 1½ teaspoons black pepper
- 2 eggs
- 8 slices white cheddar cheese (optional)
- 4 tablespoons virgin olive oil or butter
- 8 hamburger buns
- Assorted lettuce, sliced tomatoes, and Persian pickles (optional)
- Herb Platter (page 24), to serve (optional)

My son Philip once told Nahid Joon about the burger he enjoyed at a favorite burger spot in New York. She replied without skipping a beat, "You think that was a good burger, I can make you one that is ten times better!"

The next evening, the smell of hamburgers filled the air as he approached Nahid Joon's front door. As he sat down at the dinner table, she emerged with a platter of twelve giant cheeseburgers! He said, "Nana, you and I are the only ones eating tonight, why did you make twelve cheeseburgers?" With a big smile, she replied, "I do not know how to cook for two people, I know how to cook for twelve."

Philip was transfixed by the flavors: the traditional tastes of an American burger with the spices of Persian kebab and notes of East Asian flavors. "Anytime you want the best burger, you can come here." And he did just that.

In a large bowl, combine the sirloin, onions, cilantro (coriander), soy sauce, cumin, garlic powder, salt, pepper, and eggs. Using your hands, mix until the mixture is smooth and homogeneous. (Dip your hands in warm water occasionally to help with its stickiness.)

Preheat the grill to 375°F (190°C). (See Note.)

Wet your hands. Shape a portion of the mixture, slightly larger than the size of a tennis ball, into a ball. Flatten it into a ¾-inch (2-cm)-thick patty. Place the formed patty on a baking sheet and make an indention in the center to prevent it from puffing up while cooking. Repeat with the remaining mixture.

Place the patties on the grill and cook for 4–5 minutes on each side, until they have reached the desired doneness. If needed, cook for another 2–3 minutes on each side. If you are adding cheese, place the slices on top of the patties 1 minute before they're cooked through.

Serve on buns with lettuce, tomatoes, Persian pickles, and the herb platter, if desired.

Notes: To fry the patties on the stovetop, heat 4 tablespoons of oil in a large cast-iron skillet. Carefully place the patties in the pan, taking care not to overcrowd the patties. Fry on each side for 4–5 minutes. Cook for another 2–3 minutes on each side, until the patties have reached the desired doneness. Add the cheese at the final minute and cook until melted.

You may use a food processor to grate the onions.

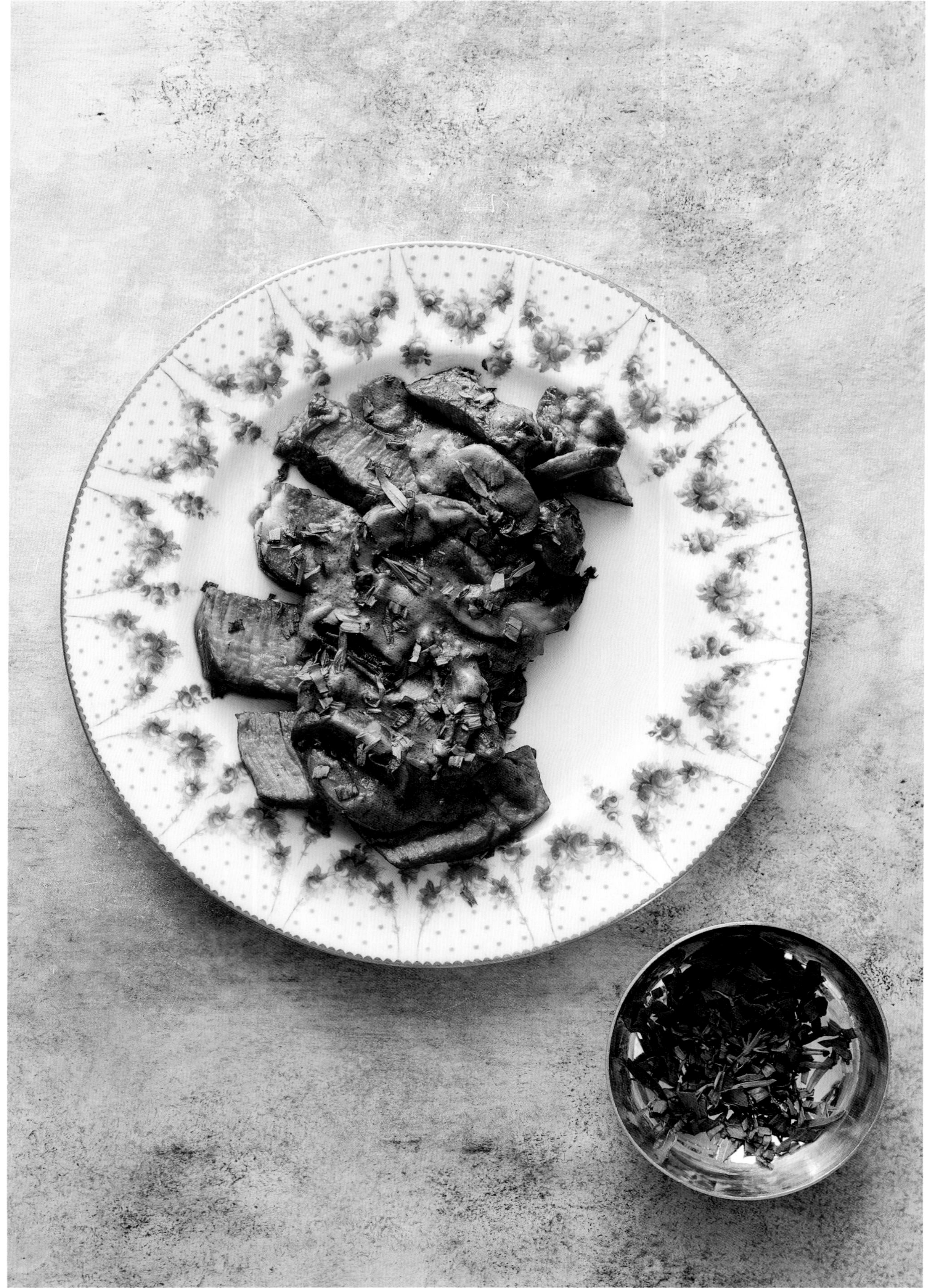

FILET MIGNON WITH TARRAGON & MUSHROOM SAUCE

Filet Mignon ba Sauce Gharch + فیله مینیون با سس قارچ

Serves 4

Preparation time: 30 minutes

Cooking time: 55–65 minutes

- 4 tablespoons butter
- 2 shallots, finely sliced
- 2½ cups (5 oz/140 g) tarragon leaves, plus extra for garnish
- 4 tablespoons extra-virgin olive oil
- 1 lb 2 oz (500 g) assorted mushrooms, finely sliced
- ½ cup (3½ oz/100 g) crème fraîche
- ¾ teaspoon salt
- ¾ teaspoon black pepper
- 4 filet mignon steaks

Tarragon was Nahid Joon's favorite herb, and it's also the feature herb in her Herb Platter (page 24). Persians love it and use it abundantly, as do the French, who use it in so many dishes and sauces.

My mom's filet mignon was delicious, and everyone loved this sauce. (The extremely fragrant tarragon fills a room with its aroma.) It's made with shiitake, cremini, and oyster mushrooms, though other mushrooms can also be used.

Preheat the oven to 350°F (180°C/ Gas Mark 4).

Heat 2 tablespoons of butter in a medium saucepan over medium heat. Add the shallots and sauté for 10–12 minutes, until soft and golden. Set aside.

In a food processor, combine the tarragon and oil. Blend for 3 minutes, or until smooth.

Heat the remaining 2 tablespoons of butter in a large skillet over medium heat. Add the mushrooms and sauté for 12 minutes, until cooked through. Stir in the tarragon oil and fried shallots. Reduce the heat to low, then stir in the crème fraîche. Cook for another 10 minutes, stirring occasionally to prevent the sauce from burning. Add ¼ teaspoon of salt and pinch of pepper and stir. Adjust seasoning to taste.

Place the steaks in a large ovenproof dish. Rub the remaining ½ teaspoon of salt and the pepper over the meat. Cook for 20 minutes for medium (25 minutes for medium-well or 30 minutes for well done.) The cooking time will vary, depending on the size of your steaks. Set aside to rest for 10 minutes.

Transfer the steaks to a large cutting board. Cut into 1-inch (2.5-cm)-thick slices. If the steak is still raw once sliced, place the meat back into the dish and reheat in the oven for 2–3 minutes.

To serve, heat up the tarragon and mushroom sauce until warmed through. Arrange the sliced steak on a serving platter, then pour the sauce on top. Garnish with tarragon. Serve immediately.

Note: This sauce works well with other cuts of beef, veal, and lamb.

CURRY MEATBALLS

Koofteh Curry + کوفته کاری

Makes 12–14 meatballs

Preparation time:
30 minutes, plus
1–2 hours chilling

Cooking time:
1 hour

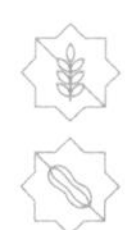

- ½ teaspoon ground saffron
- 1½ cups (10½ oz/300 g) basmati rice, well rinsed
- 2 teaspoons salt
- 3 lb (1.3 kg) ground (minced) sirloin beef, bison, or turkey
- 6 eggs
- 3 cups (12 oz/350 g) finely chopped chives or scallions (spring onions), plus extra for garnish (see Note)
- 1½ cups (1 oz/30 g) finely chopped oregano
- 1½ cups (4¼ oz/120 g) finely chopped thyme leaves
- 1 tablespoon Persian Spice Blend (page 246)
- 1 teaspoon black pepper
- ½ cup (4 fl oz/120 ml) virgin olive oil or butter
- 6 large onions, finely chopped
- 4 cups (32 fl oz/950 ml) crushed tomatoes
- 4 cups (32 fl oz/950 ml) chicken or beef stock
- 2 tablespoons curry powder
- Dried barberries, rinsed, for garnish (optional)
- Chelow (page 248), to serve

Nahid Joon used curry blends abundantly: in her famous Rice with Curry (page 186), Curry Stew with Fruits (page 152), and here in this original recipe. Every time I'd travel to the Middle East, she'd ask me to bring her different spices, curry blends, and masalas.

In a small bowl, bloom the saffron in ½ cup (4 fl oz/120 ml) of hot water. Set aside.

Combine the rice, ½ teaspoon of salt, and 2 cups (16 fl oz/475 ml) of water in a medium saucepan. Parboil, uncovered, over medium heat for 8 minutes, or until most of the liquid is absorbed and the rice is al dente. Using a colander, rinse the rice under running cold water. Drain, then set aside.

In a large bowl, combine the sirloin, eggs, chives, oregano, thyme, parboiled rice, Persian spice blend, and pepper. Add the remaining 1½ teaspoons of salt and the bloomed saffron water. Mix well to combine.

Wet your hands. Shape a portion of the mixture into a large meatball, about 3½ inches (9 cm) in diameter. Place on a tray and repeat with the remaining mixture. Makes 12–14 meatballs. Refrigerate for 1–2 hours until firm.

Heat the oil in a large saucepan over medium heat. Add the onions and sauté for 7–10 minutes, until lightly golden. Add the crushed tomatoes, stock, and curry powder and cook for 10–15 minutes, until the sauce has slightly thickened. Gently lower the meatballs into the saucepan, reduce the heat to low, and simmer for 30 minutes, until cooked. Occasionally, very gently turn the meatballs.

Carefully transfer the meatballs to 1–2 serving platters. Pour the sauce on top, then garnish with chives or barberries. Serve with rice.

Note: You may use a food processor to finely chop the oregano and thyme, but I recommend chopping the chives by hand to prevent them from bruising. Fresh oregano and thyme can be replaced with 3 tablespoons dried.

TABRIZI MEATBALLS

Koofteh Tabrizi + کوفته تبریزی

Makes 4 large meatballs

Preparation time:
1 hour, plus 3 hours soaking

Cooking time:
1 hour 30 minutes

For the meatballs:
- 2 cups (1 lb/450 g) dried yellow split peas, rinsed and soaked in hot water for at least 3 hours or overnight
- 2½ teaspoons salt
- 1 cup (7 oz/200 g) basmati rice, well rinsed
- ½ teaspoon ground turmeric
- 1 cup (8 fl oz/250 ml) chicken stock
- 1 tablespoon virgin olive oil
- 2 large onions, finely chopped
- 1½ cups (4½ oz/130 g) Blanched Orange Peels (page 246)
- 2 tablespoons Persian Spice Blend (page 246)
- 2 teaspoons black pepper
- ½ teaspoon curry powder
- ½ teaspoon ground saffron
- 2 lb (900 g) ground (minced) beef, 85% lean
- 2 cups (8 oz/225 g) finely chopped chives
- 1 cup (¾ oz/20 g) oregano leaves
- ½ cup (1 oz/30 g) finely chopped parsley
- 4 tablespoons dried thyme
- 3 eggs, beaten
- 4 hard-boiled eggs, cut in half
- 4 teaspoons slivered almonds
- 4 teaspoons slivered pistachios
- 8 prunes, pitted and quartered
- 8 walnuts, quartered
- 4 tablespoons dried barberries, rinsed

For the sauce:
- 6 tablespoons virgin olive oil
- 1 large onion, diced
- 2 cloves garlic, finely chopped
- 2 cups (16 fl oz/475 ml) chicken stock
- 2 cups (16 fl oz/475 ml) tomato juice
- 2 cups (16 fl oz/475 ml) tomato sauce
- 4 tablespoons tomato paste (purée)
- 1 tablespoon ground turmeric
- 1 teaspoon salt
- 1 teaspoon black pepper

For the garnish:
- 4 tablespoons virgin olive oil
- 1 large onion, thinly sliced
- 4 tablespoons dried barberries, rinsed
- 1 teaspoon sugar
- 6 tablespoons coarsely chopped cilantro (coriander)

This meatball originates from Tabriz, the capital of East Azerbaijan and the birthplace of my grandmother, Nosrat Khanom. Traditional yet complex, it consists of extra-large meatballs stuffed with hard-boiled eggs, nuts, dried fruits, and berries. The preparation is essential to the dish's success. My grandmother Nanou was an expert in making an extra-large meatball, wrapping it in cheesecloth (muslin) to hold it together.

Make the meatballs. Drain the yellow split peas, then rinse under cold running water. In a small saucepan, combine the split peas, ¼ teaspoon of salt, and enough water to cover the peas by 1 inch (2.5 cm). Cook, uncovered, over medium heat for 15–20 minutes, until softened. Drain, then set aside.

In a small saucepan, combine the rice, turmeric, ¼ teaspoon of salt, stock, oil, and 1 cup (8 fl oz/250 ml) of water. Simmer over medium heat for 20 minutes, until most of the liquid is absorbed and the rice is al dente. Drain, then rinse under running cold water. Set aside.

In a large bowl, combine the split peas, rice, onion, and orange peels. Transfer the mixture to a food processor, add the remaining 2 teaspoons of salt, the Persian spice blend, pepper, and curry powder and blend until smooth.

In a small bowl, bloom the saffron in 4 tablespoons of hot water.

In a large bowl, combine the split pea paste and beef and mix well. Stir in the herbs. Add the bloomed saffron water and eggs. Mix with your hands for 5 minutes, until well blended. The mixture should hold together when you pick it up. Refrigerate for 1 hour.

Meanwhile, make the sauce. Heat the oil in a medium saucepan over medium heat. Add the onion and garlic and sauté for 8–10 minutes, until golden. Add the stock, tomato juice, tomato sauce, tomato paste (purée), turmeric, salt, and pepper. Simmer on low heat for 3 minutes, until thickened. Set aside.

Divide the meat mixture into 4 equal portions. Sprinkle a few drops of water into a large bowl. Divide a meatball in half. Spread one-half along the side of the bowl, ensuring it is smooth. Add two egg halves to the center of the meat mixture. Add 1 teaspoon of almonds, 1 teaspoon of pistachios, 2 prunes, 4 walnut pieces, and 1 tablespoon of barberries. Cover the filling with the other half of the meatball. Wet your hands and press the two halves together and around the filling to form a smooth, seamless ball. Repeat with the remaining meatballs. To prevent the meatballs from falling apart, wrap them individually in cheesecloths (muslins) and tie a knot on top to close.

Slide the meatballs, one at a time, into the sauce. (The meatballs should sit snugly together to hold their shape.) Simmer on low heat, uncovered, for 30 minutes. Cover the saucepan, increase the heat to medium-low, and cook for another 1 hour. Baste the meatballs frequently with the sauce. Set aside for 15 minutes.

Make the garnish. Heat 3 tablespoons of oil in a large skillet over medium-high heat. Add the onion and sauté for 7–10 minutes, until golden brown. Transfer the onion to a paper towel–lined plate and set aside.

Soak the barberries in 4 tablespoons of hot water for 10 minutes. Drain. Combine the barberries, the remaining 1 tablespoon of oil, and sugar and sauté over medium heat for 4 minutes, until caramelized.

Transfer the meatballs to a platter and drizzle the remaining sauce on top. To serve, cut each meatball in half, then top each with the fried onions, cilantro (coriander), and caramelized barberries.

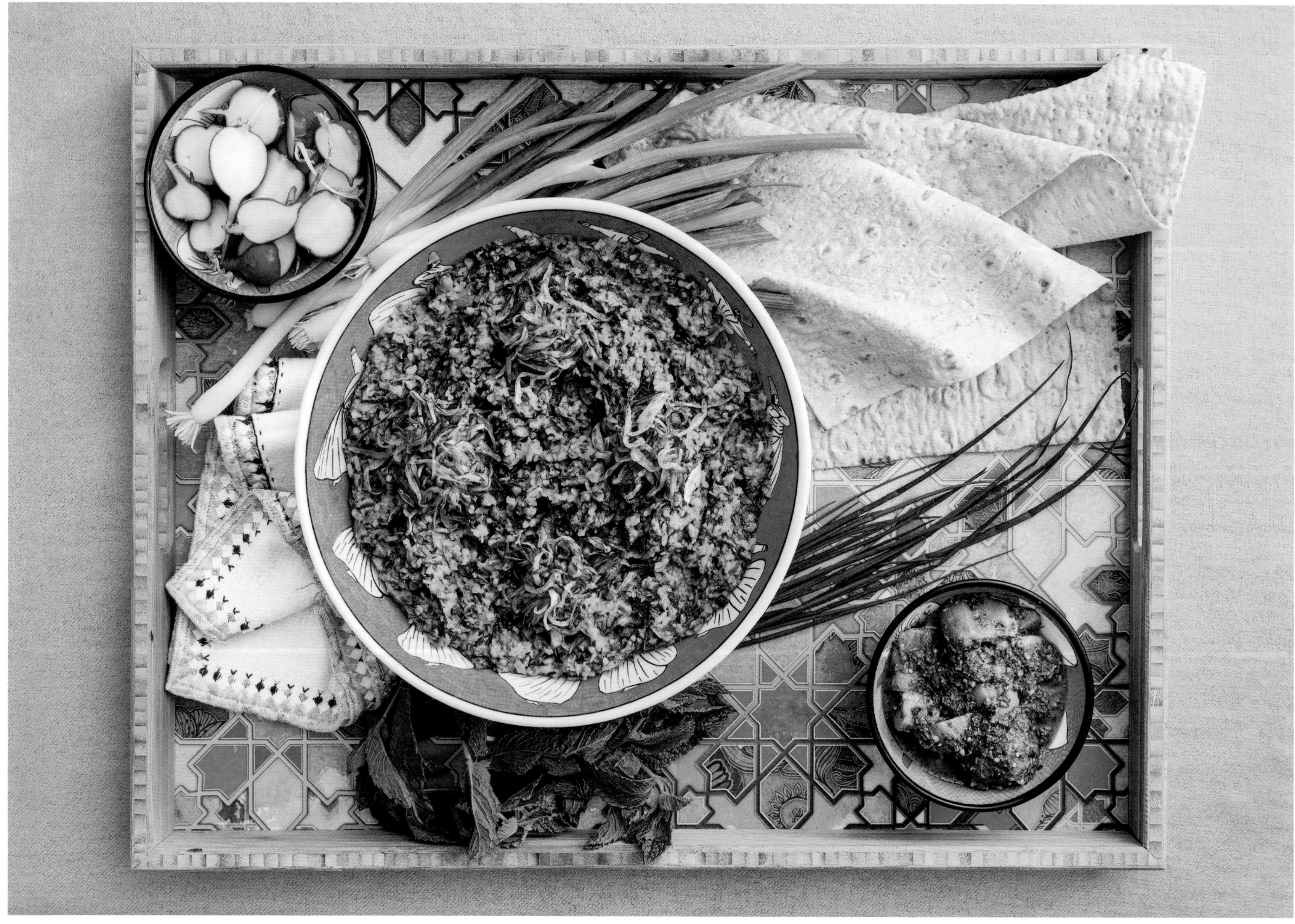

MASHED LAMB & MUNG BEANS

Maash-o Ghomri + ماش و قمری

Serves 4 as a main or
6–8 as an appetizer

Preparation time:
20 minutes

Cooking time:
1 hour 30 minutes

- 1 cup (7 oz/200 g) mung beans, soaked overnight and rinsed
- 2½ teaspoons salt
- ½ cup (3½ oz/100 g) basmati rice, well rinsed
- ¾ cup (6 fl oz/175 ml) virgin olive oil or butter
- 2 onions, diced
- 1 lb (450 g) ground (minced) lamb
- 1 teaspoon ground turmeric
- ½ teaspoon black pepper
- 2 kohlrabies or large turnips, grated
- 1 cup (2 oz/55 g) finely chopped parsley
- 1 cup (2 oz/55 g) finely chopped cilantro (coriander)
- 1 cup (2 oz/55 g) finely chopped tarragon
- 1 cup (1¾ oz/50 g) finely chopped dill
- 1 cup (4 oz/115 g) finely chopped chives
- 1 teaspoon fenugreek
- ½ teaspoon saffron threads

From the onset of the Iranian Revolution in 1979, Nahid Joon had lived in exile and missed Iran. Hostessing with homemade Persian dishes kept her country's traditions alive. Through sharing "bread and salt" (a Farsi expression meaning sharing your privileges as a pact of a friendship), Maryam Massoudi remembers Nahid Joon as a beautiful, strong, and intelligent matriarch—the doyenne of the Iranian community in New York and the "Irreplaceable One" who gathered everyone around her table with love and affection.

Masho ghomri is one of the greatest and least-known specialties of Isfahan, one of the most beautiful cities in Iran. Delicious, nutritious, and aromatic, it is made with lamb, kohlrabies, mung beans, rice, herbs, and onions. In great tradition, Maryam Joon would prepare this dish for Nahid Joon whenever they celebrated Nowruz together.

In a small saucepan, combine the mung beans, 1 teaspoon of salt, and 3 cups (25 fl oz/750 ml) of water. Bring to a boil, then reduce the heat to low. Cover and simmer for 30 minutes, until tender. Drain, then set aside.

Meanwhile, in another small saucepan, combine the rice, 1 teaspoon of salt, and 2 cups (16 fl oz/475 ml) of water. Bring to a boil, then reduce the heat to low. Cover and gently simmer for 20 minutes, until fully cooked. Drain, then set aside.

Heat 4 tablespoons of oil in a large saucepan over medium heat. Add three-quarters of the onions and sauté for 7–10 minutes, until golden. Add the lamb, turmeric, pepper, and the remaining ½ teaspoon salt. Cook for 10 minutes, stirring occasionally. Add the kohlrabies, parsley, cilantro (coriander), tarragon, dill, chives, fenugreek, cooked mung beans, and rice. Cook for another 30 minutes over low heat. With a potato masher, mash the mixture until smooth.

Heat the remaining ½ cup (4 fl oz/120 ml) of oil in a small pan over medium-high heat. Add the remaining onions and sauté for 7–10 minutes, until brown and crispy. Transfer to a paper towel–lined plate to drain.

In a small bowl, bloom the saffron in 4 tablespoons of hot water.

Transfer the lamb mixture to a serving platter. Top with the fried onions and bloomed saffron water and serve.

LEG OF LAMB

Raan-e Bareh + ران بره

Serves 6

Preparation time: 20 minutes

Cooking time: 2 hours 30 minutes

- ½ teaspoon ground saffron
- 1 bone-in leg of lamb, skin and fat trimmed, or veal shanks
- 4 tablespoons virgin olive oil or butter
- 2 onions, coarsely chopped
- 4 cloves garlic, crushed
- 1 teaspoon ground turmeric
- 1 teaspoon salt
- ½ teaspoon black pepper
- 1½ cups (12 fl oz/350 ml) hot chicken stock, plus extra if needed
- 4 tablespoons finely chopped chives, for garnish
- Celery Root, Leek & Fennel Purée (page 44), to serve (optional)

Nahid Joon's leg of lamb would cook low and slow (about two hours) until juicy, tender morsels of meat would fall off the bone. Depending on the mood of the dinner, Nahid Joon would add spices to the lamb or keep it simple, like in this recipe, with a turmeric and saffron blend to let the lamb flavor take center stage.

She always served this with her delicious Celery Root, Leek & Fennel Purée (page 44).

In a small bowl, bloom the saffron in 4 tablespoons of hot water. Set aside.

Wash the leg of lamb, then pat dry with paper towels.

Heat 3 tablespoons of oil in a large saucepan over high heat. Add the lamb and sear for 12 minutes, until all sides are browned. Set aside.

Heat the remaining 1 tablespoon of oil in the same saucepan over medium heat. Add the onions and sauté for 7–10 minutes, until slightly golden. Add the garlic and sauté for another 2–3 minutes, until fragrant. Place the lamb in the saucepan. Add the bloomed saffron water, turmeric, salt, and pepper.

Add the stock to the pan. Reduce the heat to very low, cover, and slowly cook for 2 hours, or until the meat falls off the bone and the sauce has thickened. The meat should always be covered halfway with liquid. Add more stock or water if needed.

To serve, transfer the lamb onto a platter and spoon the remaining sauce on top. Garnish with chives and serve with the celery root, leek, and fennel purée, if using.

RACK OF LAMB IN SAUCE

Serves 6

Preparation time:
15 minutes

Cooking time:
1 hour 30 minutes

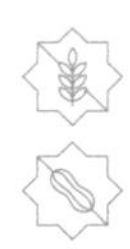

Dand-e Bareh ba Sauce + دنده بره با سس

- ½ teaspoon ground saffron
- 5½ tablespoons butter
- 1 cup (2 oz/55 g) finely chopped mint
- 3 bone-in racks of lamb, fat and skin trimmed
- ½ cup (4 fl oz/120 ml) virgin olive oil or butter
- 3 onions, coarsely chopped
- 4 cloves garlic, crushed
- ½ teaspoon salt
- ½ teaspoon black pepper
- 1 cup (8 fl oz/250 ml) chicken stock
- Bunch of chives or scallions (spring onions), finely chopped, for garnish
- 1 Persian flatbread (*lavash*), to serve

For Easter, Nahid Joon always made a rack of lamb with saffron. In the West, particularly in England and the United States, lamb dishes were accompanied by mint jelly. Nahid Joon didn't enjoy the sweetness, so she improvised by sprinkling fried mint (*naana dagh*) over the lamb before serving.

In a small bowl, bloom the saffron in ½ cup (4 fl oz/120 ml) of hot water. Set aside.

Melt 4 tablespoons of butter in a small saucepan over medium heat. Add the mint and fry for 3–5 minutes, until golden brown. Transfer to a paper towel–lined plate and set aside.

Wash the racks of lamb, then pat dry with paper towels.

Heat the oil in a large saucepan over high heat. Working in batches, add the lamb racks and sear on each side for 6 minutes, until browned. Transfer the lamb racks to a baking sheet.

Add the onions to the same saucepan and sauté over medium heat for 10–15 minutes, until slightly golden. Add the garlic and sauté for another 2–3 minutes, until fragrant. Add the lamb racks, salt, pepper, and bloomed saffron water. Mix well to ensure all sides of the lamb are covered with onions.

Place the stock and the remaining 1½ tablespoons butter in a separate saucepan and warm through, stirring to combine. Pour the mixture into the pan with the lamb. Cover, reduce the heat to very low, and cook for 1 hour, or until the meat is tender and the sauce has thickened.

To serve, place a Persian flatbread on a large serving platter and arrange the lamb on top. Drizzle the sauce over the lamb racks, then garnish with the fried mint and chives.

POACHED SALMON WITH GREEN SAUCE

Mahi Ghezel-ala ba Sauce Sabz ✢ ماهی قزل آلا با سس سبز

Serves 6–8

Preparation time:
20 minutes

Cooking time:
1 hour 45 minutes

- 1 × (4 lb/1.8 kg) whole skinless salmon fillet
- 2 cups (16 fl oz/475 ml) vegetable stock
- 6 carrots, coarsely chopped
- 6 stalks celery, coarsely chopped
- 1 shallot, quartered
- 2 teaspoons salt
- 2 teaspoons black pepper
- 1 cup (2 oz/55 g) coarsely chopped mint
- 1 cup (2 oz/55 g) coarsely chopped cilantro (coriander)
- 1 cup (2 oz/55 g) coarsely chopped parsley
- 1 cup (½ oz/15 g) basil leaves
- ½ cup (4 fl oz/120 ml) extra-virgin olive oil
- 4 tablespoons lemon juice
- Chopped chives and/or lemon wedges, for garnish

My mother's cooking was defined by her abundant use of fresh herbs, and this salmon dish is no exception. The fresh and vibrant green sauce makes the ideal accompaniment to the perfectly cooked, melt-in-your-mouth salmon. Delicious warm or cold, this is a dish often served for lunch.

Preheat the oven to 250°F (120°C/Gas Mark ½).

Wash the salmon fillets under cold running water, then pat dry with paper towels. Place the salmon in a large ovenproof dish.

In a large saucepan, combine the stock, carrots, celery, shallot, and 1 teaspoon each of salt and pepper. Pour in 4 cups (32 fl oz/950 ml) of water and bring to a boil. Reduce the heat to medium-low and simmer, uncovered, for 15 minutes. Pour the hot liquid over the salmon until completely submerged. If needed, top up with boiling water.

Bake the salmon for 1½ hours, or until salmon is firm and just cooked through. Set aside to cool slightly.

Meanwhile, in a blender, combine the mint, cilantro (coriander), parsley, basil, and the remaining 1 teaspoon each of salt and pepper. Gradually add the oil and lemon juice and blend until emulsified.

Carefully transfer the salmon fillets to a serving platter and pour the green sauce over top. Garnish with chives and/or lemon wedges and serve.

WHOLE ROASTED FISH WITH HERBS

Serves 4

Preparation time: 20 minutes, plus 1–2 hours chilling

Cooking time: 25–30 minutes

Mahi ba Geshniz va Pooneh Koohi

ماهی با گشنیز و پونه کوهی +

- 1 cup (2 oz/55 g) finely chopped cilantro (coriander) or (4 oz/115 g) chives, plus extra for garnish
- ½ cup (¼ oz/10 g) oregano or thyme, plus extra sprigs for garnish
- 2 tablespoons grated ginger
- 2 teaspoons salt
- 1 teaspoon black pepper
- Zest of 3 limes
- Zest of 2 lemons
- ½ cup (4 fl oz/120 ml) virgin olive oil or butter
- 2 tablespoons lemon juice
- 1 × (2-lb/900-g) fish such as salmon, sea bass, snapper, or halibut, cleaned
- Lemon or lime wedges, for garnish (optional)
- Dried barberries, rinsed, for garnish (optional)

One summer, my brother Mamady and I had caught forty blue fish off the coast of Montauk in Long Island, New York. We brought them all home and Nahid Joon immediately marinated them with what she had available in her kitchen. We barbecued them for lunch, and it became one of her best dishes.

She concocted this dish with ginger, cilantro (coriander), lemon, and thyme. The blend works well with meaty fish such as sea bass, snapper, halibut, or salmon.

In a blender, combine all the ingredients except for the fish. Blend until the sauce is semi-smooth.

Rinse the fish under cold running water, then pat dry with paper towels. Pour some of the sauce in a large roasting pan, add the fish, and pour the remaining sauce on top. Cover and refrigerate for 1–2 hours.

Preheat the oven to 325°F (160°C/Gas Mark 3). Remove the fish from the refrigerator. Bake, uncovered, for 25–30 minutes.

Transfer the fish to a large serving platter. Decorate with sprigs of fresh herbs and chopped cilantro (coriander). Serve immediately with lemon and barberries, if using.

STUFFED FISH WITH HERBS & NUTS

Serves 4

Preparation time:
20 minutes, plus
1–8 hours marinating

Cooking time:
30 minutes

Mahiye Shekam Por ÷ ماهی شکم پر

- 4 × (1-lb/450-g) sea bass or branzino, cleaned
- ½ cup (4 fl oz/120 ml) and 2 tablespoons extra-virgin olive oil, plus extra for greasing
- ½ cup (4 fl oz/120 ml) lemon juice
- 4 tablespoons orange juice
- ¾ cup (3 oz/85 g) dried barberries, plus extra for garnish, rinsed (optional)
- 1 teaspoon sugar
- 5 cloves garlic, finely chopped
- 1 cup (2 oz/55 g) coarsely chopped cilantro (coriander)
- 1 cup (4 oz/115 g) coarsely chopped chives
- 1 cup (2 oz/55 g) coarsely chopped tarragon
- ½ cup (1 oz/30 g) coarsely chopped mint
- ½ cup (2 oz/55 g) slivered pistachios
- 4 tablespoons slivered almonds
- 2 teaspoons salt
- 1 teaspoon black pepper
- 1 teaspoon ground turmeric
- 5 tablespoons pomegranate molasses
- ½ cup (3¼ oz/90 g) pomegranate seeds
- Lemon or lime slices, for garnish (optional)

My grandmother Nostrat Khanom (or *Nanou* to her grandchildren) would serve us this fish in the summers when we visited. She had an enchanting garden with many fruit trees, including cherry, apricot, peach, and mulberry.

We would stuff branzino with seasonal herbs and nuts. She would marinate the fish in citrus, then sprinkle pomegranate molasses over the top just before cooking. Once cooked, the fish would be garnished with herbs, slivered pistachios, and barberries. I make this recipe at least twice a month, and it tastes as amazing as it looks.

Rinse the fish under cold running water, then pat dry with paper towels.

In a large bowl, combine 4 tablespoons of oil, 4 tablespoons of lemon juice, and the orange juice. Add the fish, then cover and refrigerate to marinate for at least 1 hour or overnight.

Preheat the oven to 400°F (200°C/Gas Mark 6). Line a baking sheet with well-oiled parchment paper.

Heat 2 tablespoons of oil in a medium saucepan over medium-high heat. Add the barberries and sugar and cook for 2–3 minutes, stirring continuously, until caramelized.

Heat the remaining 4 tablespoons oil in a medium saucepan over medium-high heat. Add the cooked barberries, garlic, cilantro (coriander), chives, tarragon, mint, pistachios, almonds, salt, pepper, and turmeric. Sauté for 3 minutes, or until the herbs are wilted and the garlic is soft. Reserve 3 tablespoons for garnish.

In a small bowl, mix the pomegranate molasses and 3 tablespoons of water and set aside.

Place the fish on the prepared baking sheet. Brush the marinade over the fish and inside the cavity. Fill each fish with herb-nut mixture. Drizzle the diluted pomegranate molasses over the fish, reserving 1 tablespoon for garnish. Bake for 25 minutes, or until fully cooked.

To serve, sprinkle the remaining herb-nut mixture over the fish and top with pomegranate seeds and diluted pomegranate molasses. If desired, add the lemon slices. Serve immediately.

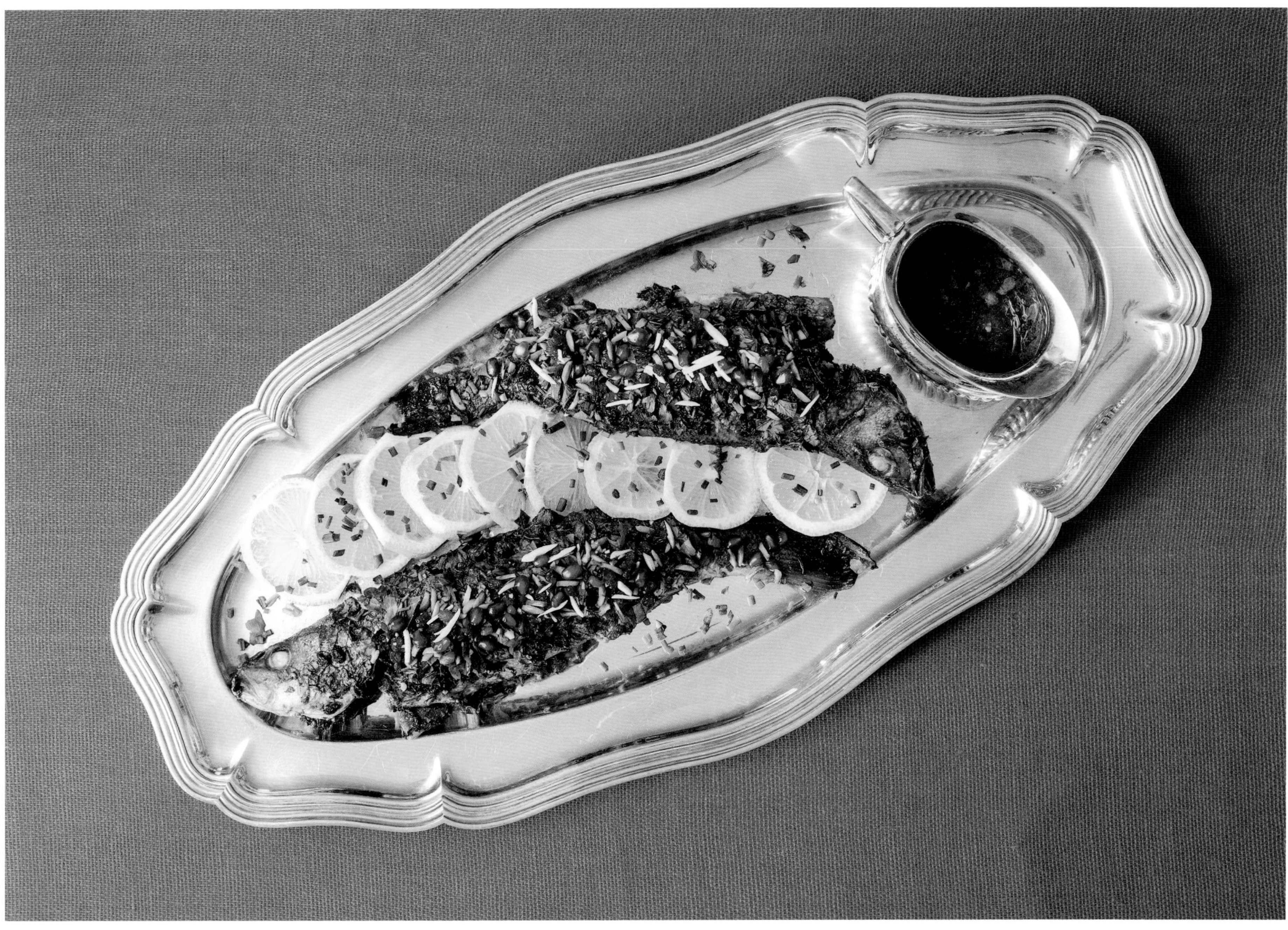

CHICKEN KEBABS

Jujeh Kebab + جوجه کباب

Serves 8–10

Preparation time:
35–45 minutes, plus
24 hours of marinating

Cooking time:
20–30 minutes

For the chicken skewers:
- ½ tablespoon ground saffron
- 4 lb (1.8 kg) boneless, skinless chicken breasts, cut into 2-inch (5-cm) cubes
- 1–2 red bell peppers, seeded, deveined, and cut into chunks (optional)
- 10 cloves garlic, coarsely chopped
- 2 large onions, coarsely chopped
- ½ jalapeño pepper, coarsely chopped
- 1 tablespoon salt
- 2 teaspoons ground turmeric
- 2 teaspoons black pepper
- 2 cups (12 oz/350 g) Greek yogurt
- 6 tablespoons extra-virgin olive oil
- Juice of 1 lemon or lime

For the basting sauce:
- ½ tablespoon ground saffron
- ½ cup (4 oz/115 g) melted butter
- Juice of 1 lemon or lime

To serve:
- Persian flatbread (*lavash*) or pita bread
- Grilled tomatoes
- Scallions (spring onions)
- Sprigs of parsley, tarragon, or basil
- Radishes
- Lemon wedges
- Sumac

Majid Tavakolian, who makes the best kebabs in the New York tri-state area, is the son of Nahid Joon's best childhood friend, Soraya. He is also the husband of one of the book's contributors, Bahar. Majid was my playmate growing up when we were children. His jokes always made us laugh.

When Majid moved to New York, Nahid Joon opened her home to him and he was truly a son to her. He eventually married Bahar, and Nahid Joon shared all of her recipes with the young couple. (Bahar translated sixty of them from Farsi to English.)

This is Majid's adaptation of Nahid Joon's original recipe.

Make the chicken skewers. In a small bowl, bloom the saffron in 4 tablespoons of hot water. Set aside for 2 minutes.

In a large bowl, combine the chicken, bloomed saffron water, and the remaining ingredients. Mix well, then marinate in the refrigerator for 24 hours (and no longer than this). Separate the chicken pieces from the marinade mixture.

Make the basting sauce. In a small bowl, bloom the saffron in 4 tablespoons of hot water. Set aside for 2 minutes. Combine all the ingredients a saucepan and heat over medium heat. Stir until homogeneous.

Preheat a grill over high heat until very hot. (If using charcoal, the hot charcoals should be smoldering.) Place pieces of chicken and peppers, if using, on a flat metal skewer about 1 inch (2.5 cm) wide. Repeat with the remaining chicken.

Place the skewers on the grill and lightly brush them with the basting sauce. Reduce the heat to medium-high. Turn them every few minutes and occasionally baste them to keep the meat moist. Season the chicken with salt and cook for 10–12 minutes, until the chicken is fully cooked through.

Transfer to a large serving platter. Garnish with the grilled tomatoes, scallions (spring onions), herbs, radishes, lemon wedges, and sumac. Serve with bread on the side.

BEEF KEBABS

Kebab Barg + کباب برگ

Serves 4–5

Preparation time:
35–45 minutes, plus
24 hours of marinating

Cooking time:
20–25 minutes

- 1 large onion, finely chopped
- 1½ tablespoons extra-virgin olive oil
- 1 tablespoon Greek yogurt
- 1 tablespoon Dijon mustard
- 1 teaspoon black pepper
- 1 lb (450 g) filet mignon, cleaned and fat trimmed, cut against the grain to ½ × ¾ × 2 inches (1 × 2 × 5 cm) (see Note)
- ½ tablespoon salt
- 2 tablespoons melted butter
- Sumac, for sprinkling
- Grilled peppers, tomatoes, and pearl onions, to serve
- White rice, to serve

Nahid Joon's beef kebabs were the juiciest and most succulent. The best-quality filet mignon would be marinated overnight, then brushed with butter on grill. As this is a costly dish to make, it can be scaled down if there are fewer diners.

In a large bowl, combine the onion, oil, yogurt, mustard, pepper, and filet mignon and mix well. Cover and refrigerate for 24 hours.

Preheat a grill or broiler over high heat.

Remove the marinated meat from the refrigerator. Discard the onions.

Place 6 pieces of kebabs on a flat 20-inch (50-cm) skewer about 1 inch (2.5 cm) wide. Once on the skewer, use the sharp edge of a knife to pound the meat several times. This breaks down the fibers and tenderizes the meat. Straighten the meat into a line. Season the kebabs with salt. (Don't be afraid to add just a bit more than what your instincts may tell you.)

Make sure the grill is hot. (If using charcoal, the hot charcoals should be smoldering.) Place the skewers on the grill and turn a few times for 8–12 minutes, depending on your desired doneness, until uniformly cooked. Do not overcook the meat, as it will become dry.

Sprinkle with the sumac. Serve immediately with the grilled peppers, tomatoes, pearl onions, and rice.

Note: You can broil the kebabs instead of grilling them. Presoak wooden skewers for 2 hours. Preheat the broiler over high heat. Use 2 wooden skewers, spaced 1 inch (2.5 cm) apart, to skewer the meat. Place them in a roasting pan and brush with 4 tablespoons of melted butter. Place the pan 3 inches (7.5 cm) below the broiler and broil for 10 minutes on one side. Turn the skewers over and broil the other side for 5–6 minutes. Do not overcook the meat, as it will become dry.

GROUND LAMB OR BEEF KEBABS

Kebab Koobideh + کباب کوبیده

Serves 6–8

Preparation time: 30 minutes

Cooking time: 15 minutes

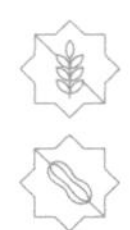

- ½ teaspoon ground saffron (optional)
- 2 lb (900 g) twice-ground (minced) lamb shoulder or sirloin beef
- 3 large onions, grated and drained (see Note)
- 3 cloves garlic, finely chopped
- 1 tablespoon baking soda (bicarbonate of soda)
- 2 teaspoons salt
- 1 teaspoon black pepper
- 1 egg yolk
- ½ cup (4 oz/115 g) butter, plus 4 tablespoons melted butter
- 1 large Persian flatbread (*lavash*), to serve (optional)
- 2 tablespoons sumac
- Parsley sprigs, radishes, and grilled peppers, tomatoes, and pearl onions to serve

This traditional Persian kebab dish is made with ground (minced) lamb or beef, onions, and spices. The kebabs are broiled over coals and typically served over steamed rice and Persian flatbread (*lavash*), so that the meat juices flavor the rice and bread. When served with Beef Kebabs (page 126), rice, and sumac, it becomes *Chelow Kebab* (page 131). This dish is also delicious the next day, wrapped in lavash or pita as a sandwich with sliced pickles and sprinkle of sumac.

Try to use wide metal skewers, which will prevent the meat from spinning around. These can be purchased at a Persian grocery store or online.

In a small bowl, bloom the saffron in 3 tablespoons of hot water, if using.

In a large bowl, combine the ground (minced) lamb, onions, garlic, baking soda (bicarbonate of soda), salt, pepper, egg yolk, and bloomed saffron water, if using. Using your hands, knead until it forms a smooth, homogeneous, and sticky paste that will hold its form when on the skewers. Dip your hands in warm water occasionally to help with the stickiness of the mixture.

Preheat a grill over high heat until hot. (See Note.) (If using charcoal, the hot charcoals should be smoldering.) Take a handful of meat, about 3 inches (7.5 cm) in diameter, and place it in the center of a 1-inch (2.5-cm)-wide metal skewer. Spread the meat toward each end of the skewer and shape it with your hands until the kebab is 8 inches (20 cm) long. The thickness of the meat should be about a ½ inch (1 cm) all around the skewer. (Leave a few inches clear from the tip and handle of the skewer.) Repeat with the remaining mixture.

Lightly brush the kebabs with melted butter to keep the meat moist. Place the skewers on the grill and turn them continuously for 8–12 minutes, until grilled on the outside and no longer pink on the inside. Turning the kebabs frequently ensures even grilling and prevents the meat from firming up too quickly on one side and falling off the skewer.

Serve on top of Persian bread (*lavash*) with sumac, parsley, radishes, and grilled vegetable kebabs.

Notes: You can broil the kebabs instead of grilling them. Preheat the broiler over high heat. Place the meat skewers in a roasting pan, spacing them ½ inch (1 cm) apart. Brush the meat with melted butter to keep it moist. Place the pan 3 inches (7.5 cm) below the broiler. Broil for 4–5 minutes, until nicely colored, then turn the skewers and cook for another 5 minutes, until fully cooked.

You may use a food processor to grate the onions.

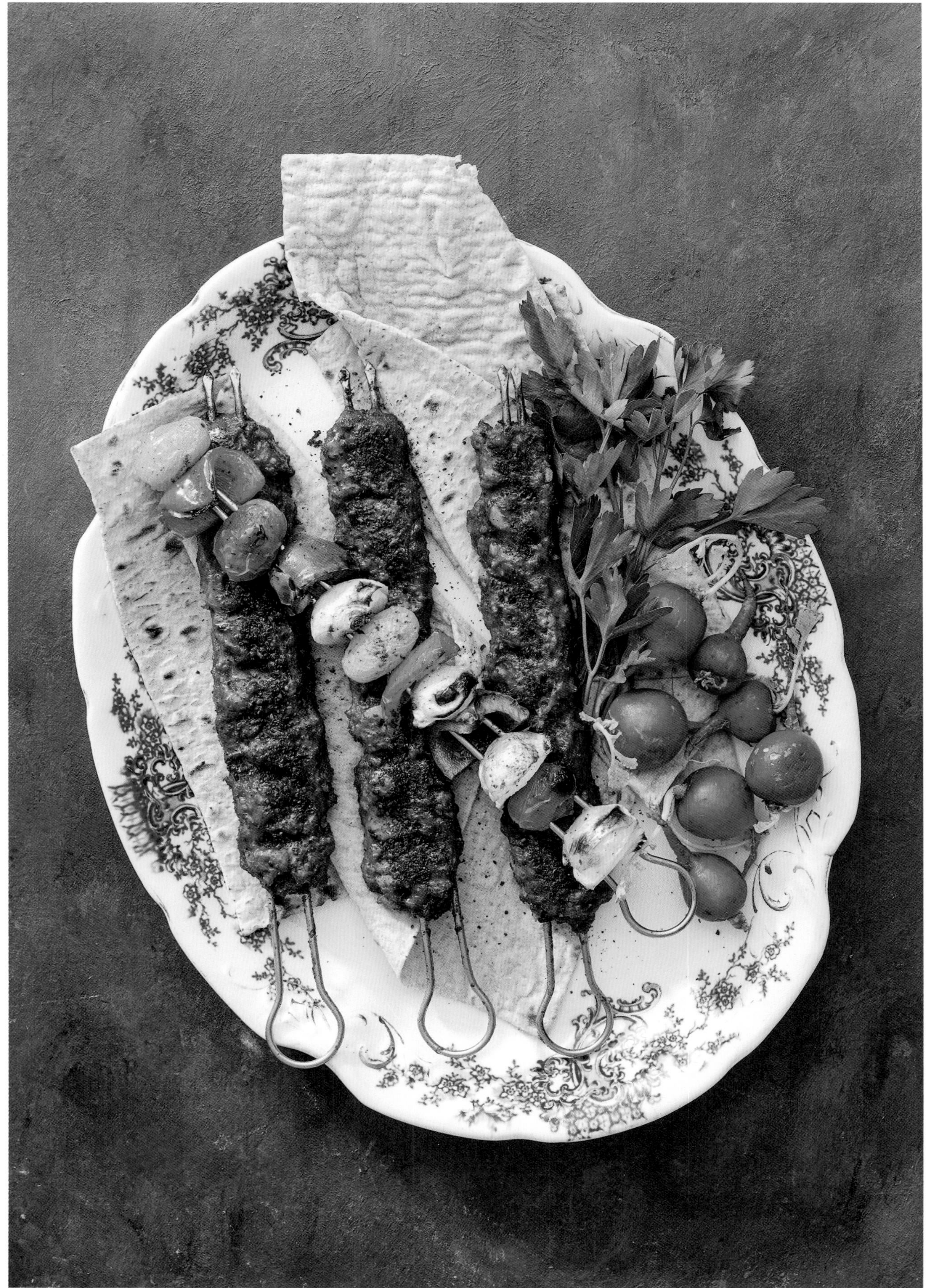

KEBABS WITH RICE

Chelow Kebab + چلوکباب

Serves 8–10

Preparation time: 10 minutes

Cooking time: 10 minutes

- ½ teaspoon ground saffron (optional)
- 8 medium-small tomatoes
- 2 cups (1 lb 2 oz/500 g) Chelow (page 248)
- 1 tablespoon butter (optional)
- 1 egg yolk (optional)
- Large Persian flatbread (*lavash*)
- Beef Kebabs (page 126) or Ground Lamb or Beef Kebabs (page 128)

For the accompaniments:
- Onions, quartered
- Your favorite chutneys (pages 204–9)
- Herb Platter (page 24)
- Yogurt Drink with Mint (page 223)
- Ground sumac, for sprinkling
- Cucumber-Mint Yogurt (optional)

Chelow kebab transcends regional boundaries and culinary traditions across Iran. It is a meal served in kebab houses, fancy restaurants in metropolitan centers, and modest eateries in villages across the country. And it is often the sole offering at restaurants known as *chelow kebabi*. Families who rarely venture outside their homes for Persian meals make special outings (and queue) for *chelow kebab*.

It's an exquisite dish of skewered charcoal-grilled beef (page 126) or ground (minced) lamb kebabs (page 128), sprinkled with sumac and served with saffron rice, grilled tomatoes, raw onions, fresh herbs, and Persian chutneys (*torshi*).

In a small bowl, bloom the saffron in 3 tablespoons of hot water, if using. Set aside.

Preheat a grill over high heat. Thread the tomatoes onto a skewer and grill for 6 minutes, turning halfway through cooking time.

Place the rice in a bowl. Sprinkle the bloomed saffron water on top and gently mix, until the rice absorbs the saffron and takes on a deep golden color. Traditionalists will mix butter and egg yolk into the rice. Set aside.

Place the Persian flatbread (*lavash*) on a platter, then add the kebab pieces on top. Place the grilled tomatoes around the kebabs. Serve the accompaniments and the rice on a separate platter.

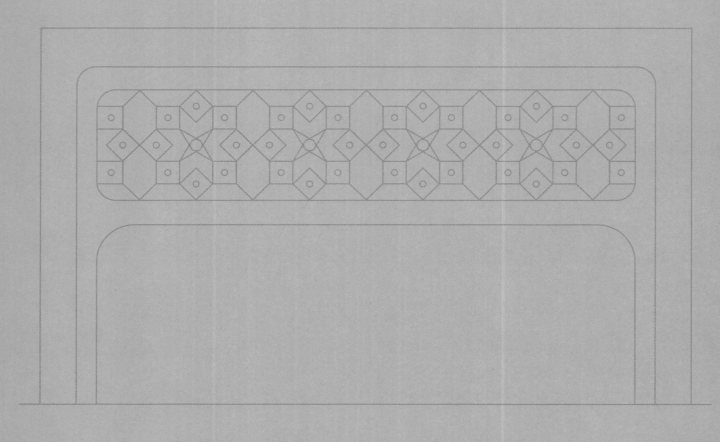

STEWS AND BRAISES

Khoresht (or *khoresh*) is an essential part of Persian cuisine. In fact, the word originates from the verb *khordan*, meaning "to eat." This sophisticated stew combines meats with fresh, preserved, or dried vegetables, legumes, fruits, nuts, herbs, and spices. Seasonal ingredients and regionality play a large part in its many variations.

A full-bodied khoresht starts with sautéed onions (*piaz dagh*) and finishes with a slow, steady simmer over low heat. As a versatile meal, it can be served with white rice, such as *Chelow* (page 248) or *Kateh* (page 247), or a crispy rice dish (*tahchin*).

Khorak, from the same origin as khordan, refers to braises. It has a similar composition and look to khoresht, but with more meat and less vegetables, fruit, and liquid. While it can be served with white rice, most Iranians enjoy it alongside bread (pita or *lavash*).

Like most Persian dishes, a khoresht or khorak will taste as good, if not better, the next day—and it is consumed with equal appetite. That is, if you're lucky enough to have leftovers.

EGGPLANT, WALNUT & POMEGRANATE STEW

Serves 4–6

Preparation time:
30–40 minutes, plus overnight soaking

Cooking time:
35 minutes

Khoresht Fesenjan e Bademjan + خورشت فسنجان با بادمجان

- 2 cups (9 oz/250 g) walnuts, covered in boiling water and soaked overnight
- 3 firm eggplants (aubergines) (about 2 lb/900 g), peeled and cut into ¾-inch (2-cm)-thick slices
- 4 teaspoons salt
- 1 cup (8 fl oz/250 ml) extra-virgin olive oil
- ½ teaspoon black pepper
- 1 cup (8 fl oz/250 ml) pomegranate paste or molasses
- ⅓ cup (2½ fl oz/75 ml) honey, plus extra to taste
- 1 cup (8 fl oz/250 ml) pomegranate juice
- ½ cup (3¼ oz/90 g) pomegranate seeds
- Chelow (page 248), to serve

Fesenjan is a sweet and sour winter dish from the Caspian region. It is traditionally made with duck, cooked in a walnut-pomegranate sauce, and served over rice.

Here is Nazzy Beglari's vegetarian version of that dish, prepared with eggplant (aubergine) rather than duck. Nahid Joon was so impressed, she began preparing it for her vegetarian and vegan friends.

Drain the walnuts, then transfer them into a food processor. Process until grainy. (Take care not to over-process or it will turn into a paste.)

In a strainer, sprinkle the eggplants (aubergines) with 1 tablespoon of salt and set aside for 20–30 minutes to remove the bitterness and water. Pat dry with paper towels.

Heat the oil in a large skillet over medium heat. Add the eggplants in a single layer and fry for 10 minutes, turning halfway, until golden on both sides. If needed, work in batches. Set aside.

Place the ground walnuts in a saucepan and toast over medium heat, stirring continuously, for 5 minutes, until the walnuts feel warm to the touch. Add the remaining 1 teaspoon of salt and the pepper. Reduce the heat to low and sauté for 1 minute. Remove from the heat and set aside.

In a bowl, combine the pomegranate paste and honey. (Add more honey if you prefer it sweeter.) Pour the mixture into the pan of toasted walnuts. Slowly stir in half the pomegranate juice. Cover and cook over very low heat for 20 minutes, stirring occasionally, until the sauce has thickened. If it's too thick, thin out with the remaining pomegranate juice. Remove from the heat.

To serve, pour a third of the pomegranate sauce onto a serving platter. Add a layer of eggplants. Repeat two more times until you have 3 layers of eggplants. Scatter pomegranate seeds over the eggplants. Serve with rice.

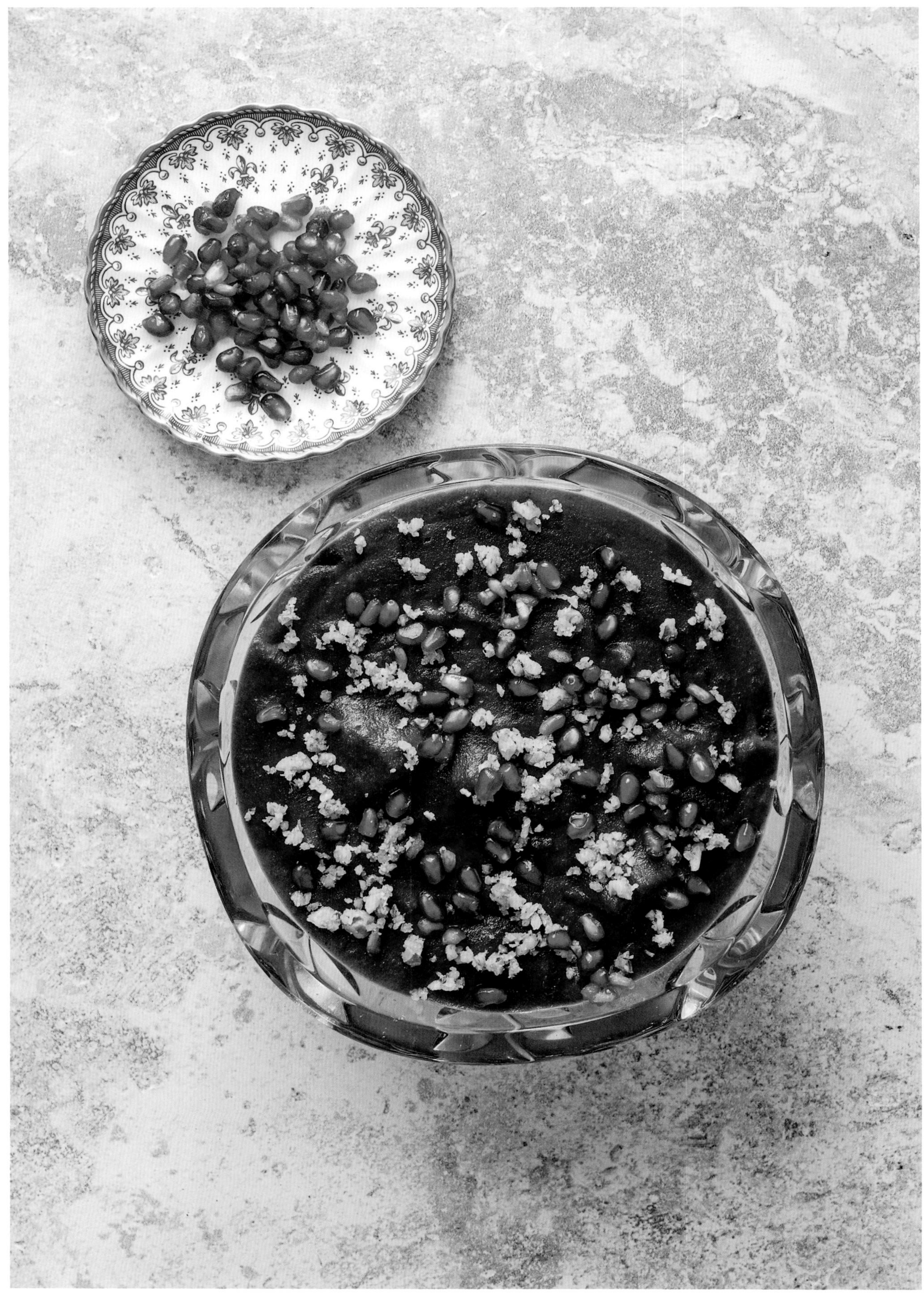

FISH & HERB STEW

Ghaliyeh Mahi + قلیه ماهی

Serves 4–6

Preparation time:
20 minutes

Cooking time:
1 hour 40 minutes

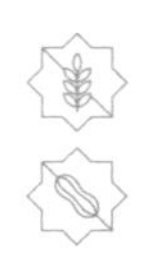

- ⅓ cup (2¾ fl oz/80 ml) virgin olive oil or butter
- 2 yellow onions, finely chopped
- 5 cloves garlic, finely chopped
- 8 cups (1 lb/450 g) finely chopped cilantro (coriander)
- 2 jalapeño peppers, finely chopped
- 1 tomato, seeded and finely chopped
- 4 tablespoons dried fenugreek
- 2 teaspoons salt
- 1 teaspoon black pepper
- 1 teaspoon ground turmeric
- 1 teaspoon grated ginger
- ⅛ teaspoon cayenne pepper
- ¾ cup (6 fl oz/175 ml) tamarind sauce (see Note)
- 2 tablespoons rice flour
- 2 lb (900 g) cod or halibut, cut into 3-inch (7.5-cm) pieces
- 4 tablespoons finely chopped chives

This dish originates from the south of Iran, but Nahid Joon discovered it in Dubai. Bastakis are Iranians who migrated to the Gulf and brought their own spicy and tangy food to the United Arab Emirates.

A Bastaki friend gave her the recipe, and Nahid Joon adapted it with more tamarind, lemon juice, and ginger. She was fascinated by its sour tamarind flavor. In Dubai, this dish is prepared with grouper (hamour) fillets, but Nahid would use other firm white fish such as halibut or cod when she prepared it in New York.

Heat the oil in a medium saucepan over medium heat. Add the onions and sauté for 7–10 minutes, until golden. Add the garlic, then reduce the heat to low and cook for another minute. Add the cilantro (coriander), jalapeños, tomato, fenugreek, 1 teaspoon of salt, ½ teaspoon of pepper, turmeric, ginger, and cayenne pepper. Cook for 5 minutes, or until the jalapeños and tomatoes are softened. Add 1 cup (8 fl oz/250 ml) of water and cook for 45 minutes.

Whisk in the tamarind sauce and rice flour, then cook for another 30 minutes.

Season the fish with the remaining 1 teaspoon of salt and ½ teaspoon of pepper. Add the fish to the pan and cook for another 10 minutes, until the fish is cooked through. Garnish with the chives and serve.

Note: Tamarind sauce can be bought at a Persian, Asian, or Indian specialty store. Alternatively, you can replace it with 3 tablespoons of tamarind paste diluted in ¾ cup (6 fl oz/180 ml) of water.

GREEN HERB CURRY

Curry Sabz + کاری سبز

Serves 8–10

Preparation time:
25 minutes

Cooking time:
1 hour 50 minutes

- 1½ cups (12 fl oz/350 ml) virgin olive oil or butter
- 2 large onions, finely chopped
- 6 cloves garlic, finely grated
- 2 cups (1 lb/450 g) grated ginger
- 7 tablespoons (1½ oz/40 g) curry powder
- 4 tablespoons garam masala
- 2 tablespoons Persian Spice Blend (page 246)
- 2 teaspoons cumin seeds
- 1 teaspoon ground turmeric
- 12 cups (1 lb 8 oz/675 g) finely chopped cilantro (coriander), plus extra for garnish
- 10 cups (1 lb 4 oz/550 g) finely chopped basil
- 6 cups (12 oz/350 g) finely chopped mint
- 6 cups (12 oz/350 g) finely chopped parsley
- 6 cups (1 lb 8 oz/675 g) finely chopped chives
- 6 mild green chilies, finely chopped, or ½ teaspoon cayenne pepper
- 2 teaspoons salt
- 1 teaspoon black pepper
- 3 lb (1.3 kg) lamb shoulder or boneless, skinless chicken thighs, cut into 2-inch (5-cm) pieces
- 8 mangos, coarsely chopped
- White Rice, to serve
- Cilantro Chutney (page 209), to serve

I once made a chicken curry with the herbs in my refrigerator since I'd be traveling the following day. Nahid Joon loved the flavors, but she adapted the recipe for this book.

She had a unique relationship in the 1980s and 1990s with a Korean greengrocer near her home. The grocer wore chic suits and played classical music in his store. He had tremendous taste and created great displays of produce, preserves, spices, and dry goods. One day, my mother ordered an enormous amount of fresh herbs, fruits, and vegetables. When he asked her where her restaurant was located, he was shocked to discover that she was simply hosting a dinner party. They developed a great friendship. She was devastated when he closed his shop a decade later, due to the high rents on Madison Avenue. He told her that the shop would have survived if everyone in the neighborhood shopped like her.

Heat ½ cup (4 fl oz/120 ml) of oil in a deep saucepan over medium heat. Add a third of the onions and sauté for 7–10 minutes, until softened and golden brown. Add the garlic, ginger, curry powder, garam masala, Persian spice blend, cumin seeds, and turmeric. Cook for 2–4 minutes, until fragrant. Add the cilantro (coriander), basil, mint, parsley, chives, chilies, 1 teaspoon of salt, and ½ teaspoon of pepper. Sauté for 15–20 minutes, then set aside.

Heat the remaining 1 cup (8 fl oz/250 ml) of oil in a large saucepan over medium heat. Add the remaining two-thirds of the onion and sauté for 7–10 minutes, until golden brown. Add the lamb and sear for 3 minutes on each side, until browned.

Add 2 cups (16 fl oz/475 ml) of water, the remaining 1 teaspoon of salt, and ½ teaspoon of pepper. Cover, reduce the heat to low, and braise for 30 minutes.

Add the onion-herb mixture and cook for another 30 minutes, or until the curry is saucy and the lamb is tender. If the curry seems dry, add more water. Turn off the heat and stir in three-quarters of the chopped mangos.

Transfer the curry to a large serving bowl, garnish with the remaining 4 tablespoons of cilantro (coriander) and mangos. Serve with white rice and cilantro chutney.

YOGURT STEW WITH TARRAGON

Serves 4–6

Preparation time: 30 minutes

Cooking time: 1½–2 hours

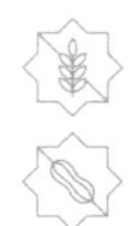

Khoresht Mast va Tarkhan + خورشت ماست با ترخان

- 1 teaspoon ground saffron
- 4 tablespoons virgin olive oil
- 3 large onions, thinly sliced
- 6 cloves garlic, finely chopped
- 1 tablespoon salt
- 2 teaspoons ground turmeric
- 1 teaspoon black pepper
- 4–5 veal shanks or 2 lb (900 g) veal stew, cut into 2-inch (5-cm) cubes
- 2 cups (16 fl oz/475 ml) chicken stock, plus extra if needed
- 2 cups (12 oz/350 g) Greek yogurt
- 2 cups (4 oz/115 g) coarsely chopped tarragon
- 1 tablespoon grated ginger
- 2 teaspoons cornstarch (cornflour)
- ½ teaspoon cayenne pepper (optional)
- 4 tablespoons butter, cubed
- Zest of 1 orange, for garnish (optional)
- White rice, to serve

Nahid Joon always made her own yogurt when we lived in Iran. Because she believed yogurt was so nutritious, my mother often added it to soups and stews, both hot and cold. She always spoke of the mountainous tribal people in Iran and Afghanistan who lived to be over a hundred years old because their diets consist mainly of fresh sheep yogurt and almonds.

In a small bowl, bloom the saffron in 4 tablespoons of hot water.

Heat the oil in a heavy saucepan over medium-high heat. Add the onions and garlic and sauté for 15 minutes, until soft and golden.

Combine the salt, turmeric, and pepper in a small bowl. Season the veal shanks with the seasoning. Place the shanks in the hot pan and sear for 4 minutes on each side, until evenly browned. Pour in the stock and cover. Gently simmer over medium-low heat for 1½ hours, until the meat is tender and the sauce has thickened. If the liquid has reduced by more than a half, add another ½ cup (4 fl oz/120 ml) of stock. Set aside to cool slightly.

Reserve 2 tablespoons of tarragon for garnish. In a medium bowl, combine the yogurt, bloomed saffron water, tarragon, ginger, cornstarch (cornflour), and cayenne pepper, if using. (The cornstarch acts as a thickening agent and prevents the yogurt from curdling.) Whisk until fully combined. Add the mixture to the stew, stirring gently until mixed through. Stir in the butter and cook over low heat until warmed through.

Ladle the stew into a shallow serving platter. Garnish with the reserved tarragon and orange zest, if using. Serve with rice.

CHICKEN & PEACH STEW

Serves 6–8

Preparation time:
35 minutes

Cooking time:
2 hours

Khoresht Hooloo + خورشت هلو

- 1 teaspoon ground saffron
- ¾ cup (6 fl oz/175 ml) extra-virgin olive oil
- 12 cups (1 lb 8 oz/675 g) coarsely chopped basil (see Note)
- 9½ cups (1 lb 3 oz/525 g) coarsely chopped mint, plus ½ cup (1 oz/30 g) for garnish
- 10 cups (1 lb 4 oz/550 g) coarsely chopped cilantro (coriander)
- 3 large onions, finely chopped
- 8 boneless, skinless chicken thighs
- 5 boneless, skinless chicken breasts, cut in half
- 2 teaspoons salt
- 1 teaspoon black pepper
- 1 teaspoon ground turmeric
- 2 cups (16 fl oz/475 ml) chicken or vegetable stock, plus extra if needed
- ½ cup (4 fl oz/120 ml) lemon juice (about 2 lemons)
- 4 teaspoons sugar
- 4 tablespoons butter
- 10 firm peaches, skin removed, pitted, and quartered (see Note)
- White rice or Chelow (page 248), to serve

In the summers, when we lived in Tehran, we would climb up the peach trees in our garden and pluck the ripe fruit from the branches. Sometimes, we would enjoy them on the spot; and other times, we'd gather them for our mom to make us this dish. The sweet peaches combine perfectly with sour lemon juice and fresh herbs. Be sure the peaches are firm. If they're too ripe, they'll disintegrate in the stew.

In a small bowl, bloom the saffron in 4 tablespoons of hot water.

Heat ½ cup (4 fl oz/120 ml) oil in a large skillet over medium heat. Add the basil, mint, and cilantro (coriander) and sauté for 6–8 minutes, until the herbs are wilted and aromatic. Set aside.

Heat the remaining 4 tablespoons of oil in a medium heavy saucepan over medium heat. Add the onions and sauté for 7–10 minutes, until golden brown.

Season the chicken on both sides with salt, pepper, and turmeric. Add the chicken to the pan and cook for 10 minutes, or until lightly brown on all sides. Pour in the stock and bloomed saffron water and cook for 15 minutes. The chicken should be fully submerged in the liquid. If needed, add another 1 cup (8 fl oz/250 ml) of stock or water.

Add the fried herbs, then reduce the heat to medium-low and cook for another 10 minutes. Add the lemon juice and sugar. Adjust the sweetness and sourness to your taste by adding more sugar or lemon juice. Cover and reduce the heat to low. Simmer for 45 minutes, or until the chicken is cooked through and the sauce has slightly thickened.

Meanwhile, melt the butter in a medium skillet over medium-high heat. Add the peach quarters and fry for 10–15 minutes, until soft and golden. Reserve some peaches for the garnish. Gently add the fried peaches to the top of the stew and cook over low heat for 5–10 minutes. Do not stir. Season to taste with salt and pepper. Gently mix in the peaches in the stew, taking care not to crush them.

Transfer the stew to a shallow serving platter. Garnish with mint and peaches, and serve with rice.

Notes: You can use a food processor to chop the herbs.

Fresh peaches may be substituted with frozen peaches, thawed and drained.

EGGPLANT & MUSHROOM STEW IN TOMATO SAUCE

Serves 8

Preparation time: 2 hours

Cooking time: 2 hours 30 minutes

Khoresht Bademjan ba Gharch ✢
خورشت بادمجان با قارچ

- 2 teaspoons ground saffron
- 28 baby eggplants (aubergines) or 12 Japanese eggplants
- 2 tablespoons and 1 teaspoon salt
- 6 tablespoons extra-virgin olive oil
- 2½ lb (1.2 kg) king oyster mushrooms
- 4 onions, thinly sliced
- ¼ teaspoon ground turmeric
- 1 × (1 lb 8-oz/675-g) jar puréed tomatoes (passata)
- Juice of 2 lemons
- 1 teaspoon dried Persian lime powder (see Note)
- ½ teaspoon Persian Spice Blend (page 246)
- 1 teaspoon black pepper
- 3 tomatoes, thinly sliced
- Chelow (page 248), to serve (optional)

This recipe is Lila Charif's vegetarian rendition of *khoresht gheimeh bademjan*, a traditional Persian stew known for its succulent meat and golden-hued split peas. Its creation was inspired by a sojourn to New York City's Chinatown, where she picked up a few pounds of earthy king oyster mushrooms and slender Japanese eggplants (aubergines). She had a canvas awaiting experimentation.

One evening, Lila unveiled the dish at a dinner gathering. Her eyes were drawn, like a moth to a flame, to Nahid's plate, awaiting that pivotal first bite. In that fleeting moment when their gazes met, Nahid, ever the inquisitive epicure, asked for the dish's composition. For Lila, it was the ultimate acknowledgment.

In a small bowl, bloom the saffron in 1 tablespoon of hot water. Set aside.

Using a peeler, peel the eggplants (aubergines) and leave the stem intact so the eggplants remain whole during the cooking process. (As eggplants can stain hands, we recommend wearing gloves.)

Place the eggplants in a colander and evenly sprinkle them with 2 tablespoons of salt. Set aside for 1½ hours to drain excess water and remove some of the bitterness.

Preheat the oven to 400°F (200°C/Gas Mark 6). Remove the eggplants from the colander, one by one. Transfer to a paper towel–lined plate to drain. Gently brush 2 tablespoons of the oil over both sides of the eggplants, then lay them flat on a baking sheet. Roast for 30 minutes. Carefully flip them over and roast for another 15 minutes, until golden brown. Transfer the eggplants to a plate.

Cut the king oyster mushrooms into disks. Heat 2 tablespoons of oil in a large saucepan over medium-low heat. Add the mushrooms and sauté for 40 minutes. (King oyster mushrooms are meaty and require a longer cooking time than most mushrooms.)

Meanwhile, heat the remaining 2 tablespoons of oil in a large heavy saucepan over medium heat. Add the onions and sauté for 12–15 minutes, until golden brown. Add the turmeric and sauté for 2–3 minutes, until fragrant. Add the puréed tomatoes (passata), bloomed saffron water, lemon juice, dried Persian lime, Persian spice blend, 1 teaspoon of salt, and the pepper and bring to boil. Reduce the heat to medium-low and simmer for 5 minutes. Season to taste with salt or lemon juice.

Reduce the oven temperature to 300°F (150°C/Gas Mark 2). Gently place a layer of eggplants in a large ovenproof dish with the stems facing the same direction. Add a layer of king oyster mushrooms, then continue to alternate the layers, switching the direction of the eggplant stems each time. Pour the tomato sauce on top. Layer the tomatoes, cut side up, over the sauce. Cover with aluminum foil and tightly wrap it around the edges. Bake for 1¼ hours. Serve with warm chelow, if desired.

Note: If you can't find dried Persian lime powder, substitute with an additional 6 Persian limes.

TOMATO & CELERY STEW WITH CHICKEN

Serves 4–6

Preparation time:
1 hour 30 minutes

Cooking time:
2 hours

Khoresht Karafs va Gojeh +
خورشت کرفس وگوجه

- 2 teaspoons ground saffron
- Generous ½ cup (4½ fl oz/130 ml) virgin olive oil
- 4 bunches celery (about 30 stalks), cut into 1-inch (2.5-cm) segments
- 3 onions, thinly sliced
- ¼ teaspoon ground turmeric
- 4 boneless, skinless chicken breasts, cut in half
- 4 skinless chicken thighs
- 1 × (28-oz/800-g) can crushed Italian tomatoes
- 1 cup (3 oz/85 g) Blanched Orange Peels (page 246)
- ½ cup (3¼ oz/95 g) sour grapes (*ghoureh*) (optional)
- 2 teaspoons Persian Spice Blend (page 246)
- 2 cups (16 fl oz/475 ml) chicken stock
- ½ cup (4 fl oz/120 ml) lemon juice, plus extra to taste
- 2 teaspoons salt, plus extra to taste
- 1 teaspoon black pepper
- 1 cup (5½ oz/150 g) cherry tomatoes
- Chopped parsley, for garnish (optional)
- Chelow (page 248), to serve

When my son Alexander was attending university in Scotland, he so missed *Khoresht Karafs* and would call his Nana for help with the recipe. Thanks to all those phone calls with her across the Atlantic, Alexander Mamady has now perfected the recipe. When Nahid Joon passed away, he wrote of this dish at her memorial:

"Nahid Joon would prepare Khoresht Karafs for the most elaborate of dinner parties or for her grandchildren on any given evening. The ingredients might project something more elegant, but in reality, this is a feel-good bowl of food over a mountain of white rice. Maybe it is the autumnal colors of the dish that remind me of her warmth inside and out, but there is something about this dish that was just so her. It was a staple at meals and parties with dignitaries, at a Persian Thanksgiving, or an evening after a big dinner at her home (along with a recap of the happenings of the evening before). Her dinners always culminated with storytelling, engaging discussions, and recounting the travels and adventures of her colorful life."

In a small bowl, bloom the saffron in 4 tablespoons of hot water. Set aside.

Heat 3 tablespoons of oil in a large skillet over medium heat. Add the celery and sauté for 5 minutes, until softened.

Heat 5 tablespoons of oil in a large heavy saucepan over medium heat. Add the onions and sauté for 12–15 minutes, until golden brown. Add the turmeric and chicken. Cook for 5 minutes on each side, until golden brown.

Add the crushed tomatoes, orange peels, sautéed celery, sour grapes, if using, and Persian spice blend. Pour in the stock, lemon juice, and bloomed saffron water. Season with salt and pepper. Cover and simmer over low heat for 1 hour, or until the chicken is tender. Increase the heat to medium and cook, uncovered, for another 10–15 minutes, until the sauce has thickened.

Meanwhile, heat the remaining 1 tablespoon of oil in a small saucepan over medium heat. Add the cherry tomatoes and sauté for 3 minutes, until slightly softened. Season to taste with salt or lemon juice.

Transfer the chicken and celery to a large serving dish, then pour the sauce on top and around the stew. Top with the sautéed cherry tomatoes. Garnish with parsley, if using. Serve warm with chelow.

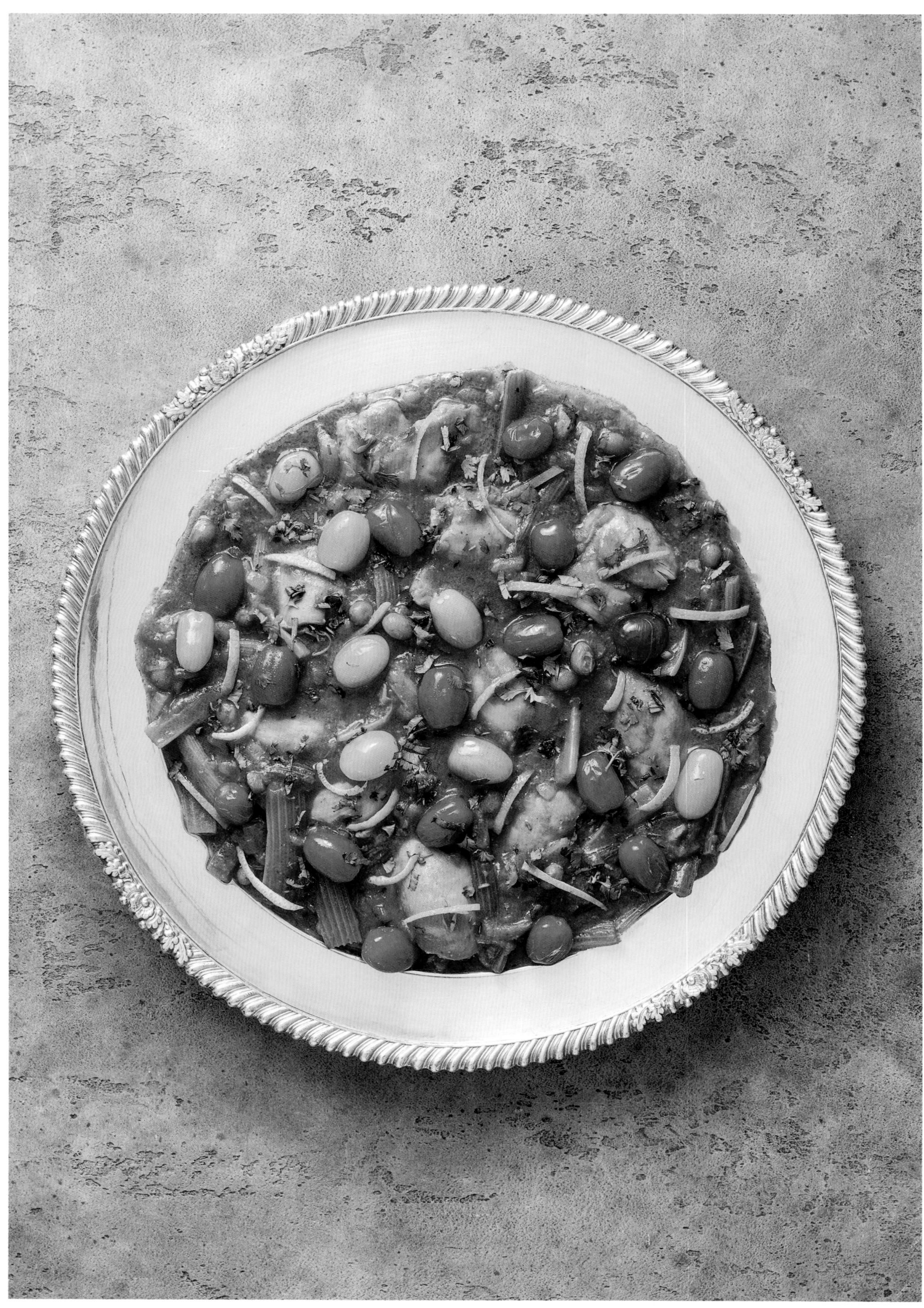

WALNUT, CHICKEN & POMEGRANATE STEW

Serves 6-8

Preparation time:
30 minutes

Cooking time:
3 hours

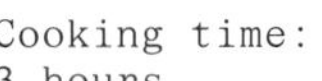

Khoresht Fesenjan + خورشت فسنجان

- ½ teaspoon ground saffron
- 2 lb (900 g) walnuts, covered in boiling water and soaked overnight
- 2 cups (16 fl oz/475 ml) pomegranate juice
- 2⅓ cups (17½ fl oz/525 ml) pomegranate molasses
- Zest and juice of 2 oranges
- 2 tablespoons tomato paste (purée)
- 2 teaspoons salt
- 1 teaspoon black pepper
- 2 tablespoons superfine (caster) sugar (optional)
- 2 tablespoons lemon juice (optional)
- 2 tablespoons virgin olive oil
- 2 onions, finely chopped
- 4 boneless, skinless chicken breasts, cut in half
- 8 boneless, skinless chicken thighs
- ½ teaspoon ground turmeric
- 2 cups (16 fl oz/475 ml) chicken or vegetable stock
- 4 tablespoons pomegranate seeds, for garnish
- Chelow (page 248), to serve

Fesenjan has been my all-time favorite recipe for as long as I can remember. My mother would serve this stew and, as kids, my brother and I would fight to lick the bowl.

My own children called it chocolate chicken since the walnuts, combined with pomegranate juice and pomegranate molasses, gave the dish a dark chocolate color. It is full of earthiness and exotic flavors.

This dish originates from the Caspian Sea region, where pomegranates grow in abundance. It is also very healthy, as pomegranates are full of antioxidants and provide energy. My mother's version was more sour than sweet, which very much appeals to us Persians. For those who prefer the latter, you can add superfine (caster) sugar.

This dish is commonly prepared with chicken, but it can be prepared with duck breast or game meat for a true delicacy.

In a small bowl, bloom the saffron in ½ cup (4 fl oz/120 ml) of hot water.

Drain the walnuts, then reserve 4 tablespoons for garnish. Transfer the walnuts into a food processor and process until grainy. (Take care not to over-process or it will turn into a paste.)

Add the ground walnuts to a nonstick stockpot. Toast over medium heat for 10–12 minutes, stirring frequently, until aromatic and slightly brown. (Keep a close eye on the walnuts, as they can burn quickly.) Pour in the pomegranate juice and 2 cups (16 fl oz/475 ml) of water. Cook for 1 hour, or until the oil has risen to the surface. Using a ladle, skim off the excess oil. Stir frequently, as the mixture can easily burn.

Add the pomegranate molasses, orange zest and juice, tomato paste (purée), bloomed saffron water, 1 teaspoon of salt, and ½ teaspoon of pepper. If the sauce tastes too sour, add superfine (caster) sugar. If you prefer it more sour, add the lemon juice. Simmer for 30 minutes, stirring frequently to avoid burning, until the sauce is creamy. (Use a splatter screen if desired to protect against splatters). Remove from the heat and set aside.

Heat the olive oil in a large saucepan over medium heat. Add the onions and sauté for 7–10 minutes, until soft and golden. Add the chicken and season with the turmeric and the remaining 1 teaspoon of salt and ½ teaspoon of pepper. Slightly brown the chicken until golden.

Pour in the stock and 1 cup (8 fl oz/250 ml) of water. Cook for 1 hour, until the chicken is cooked through and the sauce has slightly thickened. Skim any excess oil from the sauce or blot it with paper towels.

Transfer the onion and meat mixture, with the liquid, to the walnut sauce. Cook over medium heat for another 10–15 minutes, stirring occasionally.

To serve, place the chicken in a shallow serving platter and pour the sauce on top. Garnish with the pomegranate seeds and reserved walnuts.

SOUR CHICKEN STEW WITH HERBS

Serves 8–10

Preparation time: 30 minutes

Cooking time: 1 hour 30 minutes

Khoresht Morghe Torsh ✣
خورشت مرغ ترش

- 2 teaspoons ground saffron
- ½ cup (4 oz/115 g) butter
- 8 cups (1 lb/450 g) finely chopped cilantro (coriander) (see Note)
- 5 cups (10 oz/280 g) finely chopped parsley
- ½ cup (2 oz/55 g) finely chopped chives or 2 bunches of scallions (spring onions), green part only
- ½ cup (4 fl oz/120 ml) extra-virgin olive oil
- 3 onions, finely chopped
- 5 boneless, skinless chicken thighs
- 3 boneless, skinless chicken breasts, cut in half
- 2 teaspoons ground turmeric
- 2 teaspoons salt
- 1 teaspoon black pepper
- 1 cup (8 fl oz/250 ml) chicken stock
- 3 tablespoons yellow split peas
- 2½ cups (18 fl oz/550 ml) lemon juice
- 1 head garlic, crushed
- 4 eggs (optional)
- Chelow (page 248), to serve

Persians love tanginess in their meals. This dish hails from the northern province of Gilan, where it was traditionally made with sour orange (*narenj*) juice, a common Persian ingredient to add sourness to dishes. As it is not readily available in the Western world, it's been substituted here with lemon juice—and lots of it.

In a small bowl, bloom the saffron in ½ cup (4 fl oz/120 ml) of hot water.

Melt the butter in a large saucepan over medium-high heat. Add the cilantro (coriander), parsley, and chives and sauté for 10–15 minutes, or until the herbs are wilted, dark green, and very aromatic. Stir the herbs frequently to prevent burning. Remove from the heat and set aside.

Heat the oil in a nonstick stockpot. Add the onions and fry for 15–20 minutes, until crispy and golden brown. Add the chicken, turmeric, bloomed saffron water, salt, and pepper. Pour in the stock and 2 cups (16 fl oz/475 ml) of water. Cover and cook for 20–25 minutes, until the chicken is half cooked.

Meanwhile, combine the yellow split peas and 1 cup (8 fl oz/250 ml) of water in a small saucepan. Cook for 15 minutes, until nearly cooked and slightly al dente. Drain, then add the split peas to the stew.

Add the fried herbs, lemon juice, and crushed garlic. Reduce the heat to low and cook for 30 minutes, stirring occasionally, until the chicken is cooked through and the sauce has thickened.

If using, beat the eggs in a small bowl. Add the eggs into the hot stew, stirring until the eggs are fully cooked.

Transfer the stew to a shallow serving platter and serve with rice.

Note: You can use a food processor to finely chop the cilantro and parsley, but finely chop the chives or scallions (spring onions) by hand, as they bruise easily.

CURRY STEW WITH FRUITS

Serves 8–10

Preparation time:
25 minutes

Cooking time:
1 hour 30 minutes

Khoresht Curry va Miveh + خورشت کاری و میوه

- ½ cup (4 fl oz/120 ml) virgin olive oil
- 3 onions, finely chopped
- 6 boneless, skinless chicken breasts, cut in half
- 2 teaspoons salt
- 1 teaspoon black pepper
- 1½ cups (12 fl oz/350 ml) chicken stock
- 6 tablespoons curry powder
- 3 tablespoons all-purpose (plain) flour
- ¼ teaspoon cayenne pepper (optional)
- 3 Golden Delicious apples, cored, peeled, and cut into 1-inch (2.5-cm) cubes
- 3 mangos, cut into 1-inch (2.5-cm) cubes
- Chopped cilantro (coriander), for garnish
- Your favorite chutneys (pages 204–9), to serve
- Chelow (page 248), to serve

Nahid Joon made curries with complete originality. She would taste so many different dishes through her travels and return to Tehran to create concoctions from memory—à la Nahid Joon.

You can use any fruit in this curry, but the ones used here were Nahid Joon's favorites. If we couldn't find mangos, we would replace them with plums or peaches. She would always serve it with her homemade chutneys (*torshis*) and *chelow*.

Heat 4 tablespoons of oil in a Dutch oven (casserole) or heavy saucepan over medium heat. Add the onions and sauté for 10–15 minutes, until soft and golden. Add the chicken and fry for 10 minutes, until slightly golden on both sides. If necessary, work in batches to avoid over-crowding. Season the chicken with salt and pepper. Pour in 1 cup (8 fl oz/250 ml) of stock and cook for 20 minutes.

Meanwhile, in a shallow saucepan, combine the curry powder, flour, and cayenne pepper. Cook over low heat for 2–3 minutes, until fragrant. Add the remaining ½ cup (4 fl oz/120 ml) of stock and stir to form a paste. Add the paste to the Dutch oven and whisk to combine. Cook for another 20 minutes.

Meanwhile, heat the remaining 4 tablespoons of oil in a large saucepan over medium-high heat. Add the apples and mangos and sauté for 4–6 minutes, until the fruit has slightly softened. Add the fruit to the chicken mixture and mix in gently to keep the fruit intact. Cook for another 15–20 minutes, until the sauce has thickened. Season to taste.

Transfer the stew to a shallow serving platter, garnish with cilantro (coriander), and serve with chutneys and chelow.

BEEF & BASIL STEW

Khoresht Reyhan + خورشت ریحان

Serves 6

Preparation time:
1 hour

Cooking time:
2 hours

- 6 tablespoons virgin olive oil
- 2 large onions, thinly sliced
- 2 tablespoons ground turmeric
- 3 cloves garlic, coarsely chopped
- 2 lb (900 g) beef stew meat, cut into 1-inch (2.5-cm) cubes
- 4 cups (32 fl oz/950 ml) tomato juice, plus extra if needed
- 2 teaspoons salt
- 1 teaspoon black pepper
- 6 cups (12 oz/350 g) coarsely chopped basil, plus extra leaves for garnish
- 3 cups (6 oz/180 g) coarsely chopped parsley
- 3 cups (6 oz/180 g) coarsely chopped cilantro (coriander)
- 3 cups (9 oz/250 g) coarsely chopped spinach
- 1 teaspoon Persian Spice Blend (page 246)
- ½ cup (4 fl oz/120 ml) lemon juice (about 2 lemons)
- Sautéed cherry tomatoes, for garnish
- White, saffron, or herb rice, to serve

Our beloved family friend Mina Atabai is truly one of our own. She and her husband Kambiz spent every Thanksgiving with us and joined us for many weekends in Southampton.

Mina is an amazing cook, and she and Nahid Joon exchanged recipes daily. Mina had never heard of (or tasted) this dish until a friend brought it to her attention. Upon Mina's request, she obtained the recipe from her dear friend Nasrine Adle and perfected it in her own way. Nahid Joon, who was served this dish at Mina's home, added this aromatic and herbaceous *khoresh* to her own repertoire and gave it her own special touches as well.

Heat 4 tablespoons of oil in a large Dutch oven (casserole) over medium heat. Add the onions and sauté for 7–10 minutes, until soft and golden. Add the turmeric and garlic and sauté for another 3 minutes, until aromatic. Add the beef and cook for 10 minutes, or until browned on all sides. Add the tomato juice, salt, and pepper and cook for 30 minutes.

Meanwhile, heat the remaining 2 tablespoons of oil in a medium skillet over medium heat. Add the basil, parsley, cilantro (coriander), spinach, and Persian spice blend. Gently sauté for 3 minutes, until slightly golden and aromatic. Add this to the Dutch oven, then pour in the lemon juice. Cover and simmer over medium heat for 1 hour, or until thick and soupy. If the soup is too thick, thin it out with tomato juice. Season to taste with salt and pepper.

Transfer the stew to a shallow serving platter. Garnish with the tomatoes and basil. Serve with rice.

VEAL & APPLE STEW

Khoresht Sib + خورشت سیب

Serves 4–6

Preparation time:
45 minutes

Cooking time:
2 hours

- ½ cup (4 fl oz/120 ml) virgin olive oil
- 2–3 large onions, thinly sliced
- 2 teaspoons ground turmeric
- 2 lb (900 g) veal stew meat, cut into 1-inch (2.5-cm) cubes
- 2 teaspoons salt
- ½ teaspoon black pepper
- 1½ cups (12 fl oz/350 ml) chicken stock
- ½ teaspoon ground saffron
- ½ cup (4 oz/115 g) dried yellow split peas, rinsed
- 5 tablespoons butter
- 1 tablespoon tomato paste (purée)
- 5 tart cooking apples (preferably Red Delicious), peeled, cored, and sliced into 8 wedges
- ½ tablespoon sugar
- 4 tablespoons white wine vinegar
- Mint leaves, for garnish
- White rice, to serve

When we lived in Tehran, we had a bounty of apples in our garden in the summers. This is one of the first recipes I learned from Nahid Joon—it is light, easy to make, and deliciously sweet and sour. The veal can be replaced with lamb, beef, or chicken.

Heat the oil in a Dutch oven (casserole) or heavy saucepan over medium heat. Add the onions and sauté for 10–15 minutes, until golden brown. Add the turmeric and sauté for 3 minutes. Add the veal and sear each side for 3 minutes, until evenly browned. Season with the salt and pepper.

Pour in the stock and bring it to a simmer. Cover, then reduce the heat to low and gently simmer for 45–60 minutes, until the meat is tender and the liquid has thickened. If the liquid has reduced by more than half, add 4 tablespoons of water.

In a small bowl, bloom the saffron in 3 tablespoons of hot water.

In a separate saucepan, combine the yellow split peas and 2 tablespoons of butter. Sauté over medium-high heat for 3–5 minutes to coat the peas. Add to the meat mixture. Stir in the tomato paste (purée), 1 tablespoon of bloomed saffron water, and ¾ cup (6 fl oz/175 ml) of water.

Melt the remaining 3 tablespoons of butter in a separate saucepan over medium heat. Add the apples and lightly sauté for 7–10 minutes, until golden. Add to the meat mixture.

In a small bowl, combine the sugar, vinegar, and the remaining 2 tablespoons of saffron water. Add it to the stew and cook over low heat for 30–40 minutes, until everything is cooked through but the apples still retain their shape. The stew should be sweet and sour. If you prefer it sweeter, add more sugar; for a more sour taste, add more vinegar. Place the stew in a shallow serving platter. Garnish with the mint and serve with rice.

VEAL & QUINCE STEW

Khoresht Beh + خورشت به

Serves 6–8

Preparation time:
30–45 minutes

Cooking time:
1½–2 hours

- 1 teaspoon ground saffron
- ¾ cup (6 fl oz/175 ml) virgin olive oil
- 3 onions, coarsely chopped
- 3 lb (1.3 kg) veal stew meat, cut into 1-inch (2.5-cm) cubes
- 2 teaspoons salt
- 1 teaspoon black pepper
- 1 cup (8 fl oz/250 ml) chicken stock
- 2 dried Persian limes, pierced
- 1 cup (8 oz/225 g) dried yellow split peas, rinsed
- 1 × (14-oz/400-g) can crushed tomatoes
- 3 quinces, peeled and chopped into ½-inch (1-cm) cubes
- ½ cup (4 oz/115 g) butter
- Juice of 4 oranges
- 2 tablespoons chopped cilantro (coriander), for garnish
- White rice, to serve

One of our favorite stews originates from the Isfahan region of Iran. Nahid Joon's autumnal specialty made great use of the quinces that grew in our garden. We would watch them turn from green to yellow as they ripened. Raw quince is firm and tart with an unpleasant taste, but the fruit turns soft and sweet with notes of citrus and pear once cooked.

My mother would always dry the seeds in a glass jar. When we were ill, she would mix the seeds with hot water, which would turn gelatinous. She would then give us spoonfuls to alleviate a cough or sore throat.

In a small bowl, bloom the saffron in ½ cup (4 fl oz/120 ml) of hot water.

Heat ½ cup (4 fl oz/120 ml) of oil in a deep, large skillet over medium heat. Add the onions and sauté for 7–10 minutes, until crispy and golden brown. Transfer the fried onions to a paper towel–lined plate to drain and set aside for later.

Season the veal with salt and pepper. Add the veal to the skillet and sauté over medium heat for 10 minutes, or until the veal is browned on all sides. Add 2 cups (16 fl oz/475 ml) of water, stock, and the fried onions and bring to a boil. Add the dried Persian limes, split peas, and crushed tomatoes.

Reduce the heat to medium and simmer for 45 minutes, until tender and cooked through.

Meanwhile, heat the remaining 4 tablespoons of oil in a large skillet over medium heat. Add the quince and fry for 3–4 minutes. Flip over and fry for another 3–4 minutes, until slightly golden.

To the veal mixture, add the quinces, butter, orange juice, and bloomed saffron water. Simmer over low heat for 20 minutes, until the sauce has thickened.

Transfer the stew to a shallow serving platter, garnish with cilantro (coriander), and serve with rice.

MEAT & YELLOW SPLIT PEA STEW

Serves 4–6

Preparation time: 20 minutes

Cooking time: 2 hours

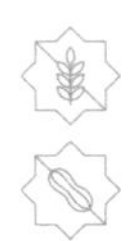

Khoresht Gheimeh + خورشت قیمه

- ¾ teaspoon ground saffron
- 1½ cups (12 fl oz/350 ml) virgin olive oil or butter
- 3 onions, finely chopped
- 2 lb (900 g) veal or lamb stew meat, cut into ¼-inch (5-mm) lengths
- 2½ teaspoons salt
- 1 teaspoon black pepper
- 3 cups (25 fl oz/750 ml) chicken stock
- ¾ cup (6 oz/180 g) dried yellow split peas, rinsed
- 5 dried Persian limes or 1 teaspoon dried Persian lime powder
- ½ cup (1½ oz/45 g) Blanched Orange Peels (page 246)
- 3 tablespoons tomato paste (purée)
- 1 teaspoon Persian Spice Blend (page 246)
- Juice of 4 oranges
- 4 large potatoes
- Chelow (page 248), to serve

As my father was born in Samarkand, Russia, he loved Russian food and we frequented two very good Russian restaurants in Tehran. Our favorite meal was beef Stroganoff served with French fries on top. At home, we would make a meat and split pea stew, topped with thin, crispy potatoes. We called this our Persian Stroganoff.

In a small bowl, bloom the saffron in ½ cup (4 fl oz/120 ml) of hot water. Set aside.

Heat ½ cup (4 fl oz/120 ml) of oil in a large heavy saucepan over medium heat. Add the onions and sauté for 8–12 minutes, until soft and golden. Transfer the onions to a plate and set aside.

Season the veal with 1 teaspoon of salt and the pepper. Add to the same pan and cook over medium heat for 10 minutes, until browned on all sides. Add the onions, the bloomed saffron water, and 2 cups (16 fl oz/475 ml) of stock. Reduce the heat to low and cover. Cook for 30 minutes, or until the meat is half cooked.

Meanwhile, place the split peas in a small saucepan and add enough cold water to cover them by 1 inch (2.5 cm). Add a ½ teaspoon of salt and boil over medium heat for 6 minutes, until the split peas are half cooked. (If the split peas are fully cooked, they will turn to mush once cooked in the stew.) Drain, then rinse under cold running water. Add the split peas to the veal mixture.

Using a sharp knife, make a few small holes in the Persian limes, then add them to the mixture. Add the orange peels, tomato paste (purée), Persian spice blend, and orange juice. Reduce the heat to medium-low and simmer for 30–45 minutes, stirring occasionally to prevent the stew from burning. The stew is ready once the sauce has slightly thickened and the meat is cooked through.

Meanwhile, peel and slice the potatoes into 2 × ⅛-inch (50 × 3-mm) slivers, like shoestring potatoes or skinny French fries. Place the potatoes in a colander and rinse under cold running water to remove some of the starch. Pat dry with paper towels.

Heat the remaining 1 cup (8 fl oz/250 ml) of oil in a deep skillet over medium heat, until hot. Carefully lower the potatoes into the pan in a single layer and stir a few times to ensure the potatoes are coated with oil. If necessary, work in batches to avoid overcrowding. Fry the potatoes for 15 minutes, or until golden brown and crispy. Using a slotted spoon, transfer the fried potatoes to a paper towel–lined plate to drain. Season the fries with the remaining 1 teaspoon of salt.

Ladle the stew into a shallow serving platter and top with the French fries. Serve with chelow.

Note: If you are short on time, cut 3 potatoes into ¾-inch (2-cm) cubes and add them to the stew with the split peas.

HERB & PERSIAN LIME STEW

Khoresht Ghormeh Sabzi + خورشت قورمه سبزی

Serves 4–6

Preparation time:
30 minutes, plus
overnight soaking

Cooking time:
3 hours

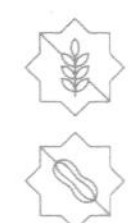

- 1 teaspoon saffron threads
- 2 cups (13 oz/375 g) dried red kidney beans, soaked overnight and drained (see Note)
- 6 cups (47 fl oz/1.4 L) chicken stock
- 1 cup (8 fl oz/250 ml) virgin olive oil or butter
- 3 onions, finely chopped
- 2 lb (900 g) veal shanks, lamb shoulder, chicken thighs, or chicken breasts, cut into 2-inch (5-cm) pieces (see Note)
- 8 bay leaves
- 2 tablespoons dried fenugreek (optional)
- 2 teaspoons ground turmeric
- 1½ teaspoons salt
- 1 teaspoon black pepper
- 2 cups (4 oz/115 g) finely chopped flat-leaf parsley
- 2 cups (4 oz/115 g) finely chopped curly parsley
- 2 cups (4 oz/115 g) coarsely chopped cilantro (coriander)
- 4 cups (12 oz/350 g) coarsely chopped spinach
- 2 cups (7 oz/200 g) finely sliced scallions (spring onions)
- 10 dried Persian limes, pierced
- 1 cup (8 fl oz/250 ml) lemon juice (see Note)

This recipe dates back 5,000 years to northern Iran. *Ghormeh sabzi*, meaning "braised herbs," combines dark, leafy greens such as kale, turnip greens, and spinach with traditional pungent herbs like fenugreek, parsley, cilantro (coriander), scallions (spring onions), and dried lime. It is then braised in spices and sauces, creating a delicious and nutrient-rich stew.

The meat can be replaced with legumes such as kidney beans, lentils, and chickpeas, making the dish easily adaptable to suit gluten-free, low-carb, and vegetarian diets. It is delicious on its own, but Persians love to pair it with white rice and *tahdig*.

Nahid Joon created a curry version of this, which eventually became her Green Herb Curry (page 139). For a traditional *ghormeh sabzi,* Nahid Joon and I both love this version here by Faranak Ghassemieh Amirsaleh, which she learned from her dear mom, Fati Joon.

In a small bowl, bloom the saffron in 4 tablespoons of hot water. Set aside.

In a saucepan, combine the kidney beans and 1 cup (8 fl oz/250 ml) of stock and cook over medium heat for 20 minutes, until halfway cooked. Drain, then set aside.

Heat half the oil in a large saucepan over medium heat. Add the onions and sauté for 7–10 minutes, until golden brown. Add the meat and sear for 15 minutes, until evenly browned on all sides. If necessary, work in batches to avoid overcrowding. Add the bay leaves, fenugreek, if using, turmeric, salt, pepper, bloomed saffron water, and remaining 5 cups (40 fl oz/1.2 L) of stock. Simmer for 1 hour, or until the meat is half cooked.

Heat the remaining half of the oil in a large saucepan over medium heat. Add the parsleys, cilantro (coriander), spinach, and scallions (spring onions) and sauté for 10–15 minutes, until the herbs are wilted, dark green, and very aromatic. Stir frequently to prevent the herbs from burning. Remove from the heat and set aside.

Add the herb mixture, kidney beans, dried Persian limes, and lemon juice to the meat mixture. Reduce the heat to low and cook for another hour, until the meat is fully cooked and the stew is thick. Season to taste.

Serve in a shallow serving bowl. Make sure the red kidney beans are visible to add a dash of red to your presentation.

Notes: For a vegetarian version, replace the meat with ½ cup (3¼ oz/90 g) cooked lentils and ½ cup (3 oz/85 g) cooked chickpeas and use vegetable stock.

If you're short on time, replace dried kidney beans with 3 cups (1 lb 2 oz/ 500 g) canned kidney beans. Drain and rinse, then add with the herb mixture.

If you want this dish more sour, add more lemon juice.

ARTICHOKE HEARTS & GREENS STEW

Serves 6

Preparation time:
1 hour

Cooking time:
2 hours 50 minutes

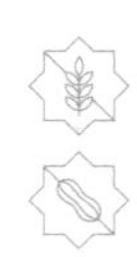

Khoresht Artichow

خورشت آرتیشو +

- ¼ teaspoon ground saffron
- ½ cup (4 fl oz/120 ml) and 2 tablespoons extra-virgin olive oil
- 4 onions, thinly sliced
- ½ teaspoon ground turmeric
- 3 veal shanks (about 2 lb/900 g)
- 2½ teaspoons salt
- 2¼ teaspoons black pepper
- ½ teaspoon Persian Spice Blend (page 246)
- ¼ teaspoon lemon pepper
- 3½ cups (27 fl oz/800 ml) vegetable stock, plus extra if needed
- 8 cups (1 lb/450 g) finely chopped parsley (see Note)
- 3 cups (6 oz/175 g) finely chopped cilantro (coriander)
- 3 cups (6 oz/175 g) finely chopped mint
- 4 tablespoons butter
- Juice of 3 lemons
- 3½ × (14-oz/400-g) cans artichoke hearts, drained
- Chelow (page 248), to serve

Ferechteh Fathi and Nahid Joon's enduring friendship spanned five decades. A bond forged when Ferechteh returned from her Parisian fashion school to Tehran and established her atelier in the late 1960s. Nahid Joon was among her earliest and most fashion-forward clients.

Post-Iranian Revolution, destiny guided Nahid and Ferechteh to southern France, where they became neighbors. Nahid, renowned for her culinary artistry, held a cherished place within the Persian community. Ferechteh's family frequented Nahid's home, where aromatic soups, vibrant rice dishes, and heavenly desserts tantalized their senses.

Ferechteh, a curious cook in her own right, went to the weekly market intent on making a celery stew. However, her quest was thwarted by lackluster celery stalks. She chanced upon artichoke hearts and the spirit of experimentation took hold. That evening, a symphony of artichoke hearts and aromatic herbs was born—a dish that swiftly became a beloved family staple.

In a small bowl, bloom the saffron in 4 tablespoons of hot water. Set aside.

Heat 3 tablespoons of oil in a medium heavy saucepan over medium heat. Add the onions and cook for 10–12 minutes, until golden brown. Stir in the turmeric. Set aside.

Heat 2 tablespoons of oil in a large skillet over medium-high heat. Season the veal shanks with 2 teaspoons of salt and 2 teaspoons of pepper. Add the shanks to the pan and sear for 3–4 minutes on each side, until evenly browned. Transfer the veal shanks to the saucepan of onions.

Add the Persian spice blend, lemon pepper, and bloomed saffron water. Pour in 1½ cups (12 fl oz/350 ml) of stock. Reduce the heat to medium and boil for 5 minutes. Reduce the heat to very low and cover. Gently simmer for 1¼ hours. Occasionally check the sauce and add more stock, if needed, to prevent it from drying out. Set aside.

Heat the remaining 5 tablespoons of oil in a large heavy saucepan over medium heat. Add the parsley, cilantro (coriander), and the remaining 2 cups (16 fl oz/475 ml) of stock and bring to a boil. Stir in the mint and cook for 30 minutes, or until the herbs are wilted and softened. Add the butter and lemon juice and cook for another 10 minutes.

Add the shanks, sauce, and artichoke hearts to the herb mixture. Cook over low heat for 30 minutes, stirring gently to prevent the delicate artichoke hearts from breaking. Season to taste with salt and pepper.

Transfer the stew to a large serving bowl. Serve warm with chelow.

Note: You can use a food processor to coarsely chop the herbs.

BRAISED VEAL SHANKS WITH YOGURT

Serves 6–8

Preparation time:
30 minutes

Cooking time:
1 hour 45 minutes

Khorak Boz Ghormeh +
خوراک بز قورمه

- 5 tablespoons virgin olive oil or butter
- 4 onions, coarsely chopped
- 6 cloves garlic, finely chopped
- 1 teaspoon ground saffron
- 6 veal shanks or lamb shanks
- 4 cups (32 fl oz/950 ml) chicken stock
- 2½ cups (15 oz/425 g) Greek yogurt
- 1 egg
- 1 tablespoon all-purpose (plain) flour
- 1 teaspoon salt
- ½ teaspoon black pepper
- 1½ cups (5½ oz/150 g) finely chopped scallions (spring onions), for garnish
- 2 cups (8 oz/225 g) finely chopped chives, for garnish

Nahid Ahari was our favorite aunt. Her husband, Dr. Hassan Ahari, was my mom's first cousin and our pediatrician. I remember how much I hated getting shots, but the fear soon disappeared as I knew we would be going upstairs to their home, where we played with our cousins Nasser, Narges, and Nader and then were treated by Auntie Nahid to a delicious feast featuring her *boz ghormeh.*

In the days when there were no refrigerators, hot *boz ghormeh* was placed in a freestanding pot and covered with sheep tallow to preserve it for the winter. It was stored in the cold basement or outdoors throughout the winter. Family members from Azerbaijan would bring us large pots of this stew when they visited.

Heat 2 tablespoons of oil in a large saucepan over medium heat. Add the onions and garlic and sauté for 7–10 minutes, until golden. Set aside.

In a small bowl, bloom the saffron in 4 tablespoons of hot water. Set aside.

Heat the remaining 3 tablespoons of oil in a large saucepan over medium-high heat. Add the veal shanks and sear for 5 minutes on each side, or until evenly browned. If necessary, work in batches to avoid overcrowding.

Add three-quarters of the sautéed onions and the stock to the pan, making sure the veal shanks are submerged. If necessary, top it up with water. Cook over medium heat for 1½ hours, until tender and cooked through. Stir occasionally to prevent the shanks from burning. Remove the pan from the heat.

In a separate bowl, whisk the yogurt, bloomed saffron water, egg, flour, salt, and pepper. Add the mixture to the saucepan, whisking continuously to prevent it from splitting. Transfer the shanks and sauce to a serving platter, then garnish with the remaining sautéed onions, scallions (spring onions), and chives. Serve.

BRAISED LAMB SHANKS

Mahicheh Bareh + ماهیچه بره

Serves 6

Preparation time:
30 minutes

Cooking time:
2–3 hours

- 6 tablespoons virgin olive oil or butter
- 4 onions, coarsely chopped
- 6 cloves garlic, finely chopped
- 6 lamb shanks
- 1 tablespoon ground turmeric
- 1½ teaspoons salt
- ½ teaspoon black pepper
- 4 cups (32 fl oz/950 ml) chicken stock, plus extra if needed
- 2 tablespoons chopped cilantro (coriander), for garnish (optional)
- 2 cups (8 oz/225 g) finely chopped chives, for garnish (optional)
- 1½ cups (5½ oz/150 g) finely chopped scallions (spring onions), for garnish (optional)
- Your favorite rice dish and vegetables, to serve

I can't recall a party or feast without Nahid Joon's braised lamb shanks. She would simmer them with onion and turmeric for hours until they were so tender that they fell off the bone. Once we'd eaten all the meat, we'd enjoy the prized bone marrow.

Heat 2 tablespoons of oil in a skillet over high heat. Add the onions and garlic and sauté for 5–10 minutes, until browned. Set aside, reserving 4 tablespoons for garnish.

Heat the remaining 4 tablespoons of oil in a large saucepan over medium-high heat. Add the lamb shanks and cook for 5 minutes on each side, or until browned. If necessary, work in batches to avoid overcrowding. With all lamb shanks in the pan, add the turmeric, salt, pepper, sautéed onions and garlic, and stock. The shanks should be submerged in the liquid. If needed, top up with more stock or water.

Reduce the heat to medium and cover. Simmer for 2–3 hours, until the meat is tender enough to fall off the bone. (The cooking time depends on the size of the lamb shanks.) Stir occasionally to prevent burning.

Transfer shanks to a serving platter or individual plates. Generously scatter cilantro (coriander), scallions (spring onions), and/or chives on top. Serve with rice and vegetables.

RICE DISHES

Rice symbolizes fertility, abundance, and prosperity. (Hence, the tossing of rice at weddings.) Nutrient-rich, it is also the focal point of every Persian meal.

The most common rice variety for these dishes is long-grain basmati. Around the fourth century BCE, rice was brought from Southeast Asia, especially India, to the Caspian region. In present-day Iran, rice cultivation mostly takes place in the provinces of Mazandaran and Gilan, both of which border the Caspian Sea. I recall the shimmering rice paddies and the nutty, fragrant aroma that permeated the humid air on our trips to the region.

Persian rice is traditionally cooked in one of four ways. *Kateh* (page 247), originating from Gilan, is the easiest method of cooking rice. *Dami* is a version of *kateh* mixed with vegetables. *Chelow* involves a more sophisticated process where the rice is presoaked, boiled, and steamed, resulting in fluffy, separated grains. And finally, the elaborate rice dish *polo* features alternating layers of rice, meat, vegetables, fruits, herbs, and spices—or a combination of these—steamed in a saucepan or rice cooker.

EGGPLANT & BARBERRY RICE

Serves 6–8

Preparation time:
30 minutes, plus
15 minutes soaking

Cooking time:
1 hour 10 minutes

Tahchin Bademjan va Zereshk +
ته چین بادمجان و زرشک

- 1 teaspoon ground saffron
- 4 tablespoons and 1 teaspoon salt
- 3 cups (1 lb 5 oz/600 g) basmati rice, well rinsed
- 1 cup (4 oz/115 g) dried barberries, rinsed
- 2 eggplants (aubergines), peeled and cut lengthwise into ¼-inch (5-mm) slices
- ⅓ cup (2¾ fl oz/80 ml) and 2 tablespoons virgin olive oil, plus extra for greasing
- 4 tablespoons butter
- ½ cup (2 oz/55 g) pistachio or almond slivers (optional)
- 2 tablespoons sugar
- 1 egg
- 3 egg yolks
- 1 cup (6 oz/180 g) Greek yogurt
- 3 tablespoons rose water (optional)
- ¼ teaspoon black pepper

My dear friend Bahman Kia is a brilliant cook who makes the most delicious meals. His vegetarian rice dish with saffron, eggplant (aubergine), and barberries brings together the best of Persian cuisine into one dish.

In a small bowl, bloom the saffron in 1 cup (8 fl oz/250 ml) of hot water.

Bring 2 quarts (2 L) of water to a boil in a large saucepan. Add 2 tablespoons of salt. Pour the rice into the boiling water and cook for 6 minutes, until al dente. Stir occasionally to prevent the rice from sticking to the bottom of the pan. Drain the rice, then rinse under cold running water. Toss the rice a few times, then set aside to drain completely.

Put the dried barberries in a bowl of cold water and set aside for 15 minutes.

Place the eggplants (aubergines) on baking sheets, sprinkle with 2 tablespoons of salt, and set aside for 15 minutes. (This helps remove their bitterness.) Rinse the eggplants, then pat dry with paper towels.

Heat 1 tablespoon of oil in a large skillet over medium-high heat. Working in batches, lightly brown the eggplants in a single layer. Transfer the eggplants to a paper towel–lined plate to drain. Make the second batch with more oil.

Drain the barberries. Melt 2 tablespoons of butter in a skillet over medium heat. Add the barberries, pistachios, sugar, and 2 tablespoons of bloomed saffron water. Sauté for 2 minutes, until vibrant.

In a large mixing bowl, combine the egg, egg yolks, yogurt, rose water, if using, 4 tablespoons of saffron water, the remaining 1 teaspoon of salt, pepper, and the remaining ⅓ cup (2¾ fl oz/80 ml) of oil. It should be orange in color; if not, add 1 more tablespoon of saffron water.

Fold in the rice and mix thoroughly. Set aside some barberries and pistachios for garnish. Mix in the rest.

Preheat the oven to 375°F (190°C/Gas Mark 5). Add just enough oil to coat the bottom of a 3-quart (3-L) baking dish. Add 3 spatulas of the rice mixture to the dish, spreading out the rice evenly and pressing it firmly to compact. Add a layer of eggplants, making sure they don't touch the sides of the dish. Add the barberry mixture, then top with the remaining rice. Press down firmly.

Combine 2 tablespoons of melted butter and 4 tablespoons of saffron water and pour it over the rice. Cover with aluminum foil and pierce a few small holes into it so the steam can escape. Bake for 1 hour, or until the sides are golden. Set aside for 10 minutes to cool.

Run a spatula or palette knife along the edges of the dish to release any rice stuck to it. Once cooled, put the bottom of the dish in shallow cold water for 1 minute. (This allows the crispy rice to separate from the dish.) Place a large, flat platter over the dish. Using both hands to hold the dish securely to the platter, carefully invert the rice onto the platter. Garnish with barberries and pistachios.

RICE WITH VEAL AND GREEN BEANS

Serves 8–10

Preparation time: 25 minutes

Cooking time: 2 hours

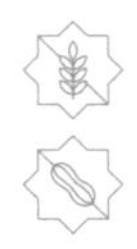

Loubiya Polo + لوبیا پلو

- 1 tablespoon ground saffron
- 1 tablespoon rose water (optional)
- 2 tablespoons and 2 teaspoons salt
- 3 cups (1 lb 5 oz/600 g) basmati rice, well rinsed
- 1 cup (8 fl oz/250 ml) and 3 tablespoons virgin olive oil
- 2 lb (900 g) veal stew meat, cut into 1-inch (2.5-cm) cubes
- 2 large onions, finely chopped
- 4 tablespoons Blanched Orange Peels (page 246)
- 4 tablespoons tomato paste (purée)
- 4 teaspoons Persian Spice Blend (page 246)
- 2 teaspoons ground turmeric
- 1 teaspoon black pepper
- ¾ cup (6 fl oz/175 ml) chicken stock
- ½ cup (4 oz/115 g) and 2 tablespoons butter
- 2 lb (900 g) green beans, trimmed and cut into 1-inch (2.5-cm) lengths
- 2 tablespoons Greek yogurt
- 1 egg
- 1 tablespoon dried rose petals (optional)

When I was a little girl, I had my own kitchen set. Nahid Joon would cook, and I would mimic her actions and pretend to cook for my dolls. *Loubiya polo* was one of the dishes I'd "prepare."

During my freshman year at university, the international house asked me to make an Iranian dish for our food festival. In those days, you couldn't just call your mother on the phone for the recipe, so I visualized the steps in my head. I made this green bean rice dish from memory, and it won a prize.

In a small bowl, combine the saffron, rose water, if using, and ½ cup (4 fl oz/120 ml) of hot water. Set aside.

Bring 2½ quarts (2.3 L) of water to a boil in a large saucepan. Add 2 tablespoons of salt. Pour the rice into the boiling water and cook for 6 minutes, until al dente. Stir occasionally to prevent the rice from sticking to the bottom of the pan. Drain the rice, then rinse under cold running water. Toss the rice, then drain again.

Heat ½ cup (4 fl oz/120 ml) of oil in a large saucepan over medium heat. Add the veal and sear for 8–10 minutes, until evenly browned on all sides. If necessary, work in batches to avoid overcrowding. Set aside.

Heat ½ cup (4 fl oz/120 ml) of oil in a medium skillet over medium heat. Add the onions and sauté for 6–8 minutes, until softened and golden brown.

To the pan of veal, add the onions, orange peels, tomato paste (purée), the remaining 2 teaspoons of salt, 1 teaspoon of Persian spice blend, the turmeric, and pepper. Pour in the stock and 1 tablespoon of bloomed saffron water. Cover and cook over medium-low heat for 20 minutes.

Meanwhile, melt 4 tablespoons of butter in a skillet over medium heat. Add the green beans and sauté for 3–5 minutes, until slightly softened. Add the green beans to the veal mixture and cook for another 15 minutes, or until the sauce has thickened. Set aside to cool.

Place 2 tablespoons of melted butter and 3 tablespoons of oil in a nonstick stockpot or rice cooker. In a small bowl, whisk together the yogurt, egg, and 1 tablespoon of saffron water. Add this mixture to the saucepan. Tilt the pan until the bottom is coated.

Place some of the rice at the bottom of the saucepan, about 2 inches (5 cm) deep. Add a layer of the green beans. Sprinkle over 1 teaspoon each of Persian spice blend and dried rose petals, if using, and 1 tablespoon of saffron water. Repeat alternate layers to form a pyramid until the rice, green beans, and veal sauce are all used up. Top with a layer of rice.

Cover and cook for 10 minutes over medium heat. Drizzle over 3 tablespoons of melted butter. Place a clean dish towel over the top of the pan, then cover the pan and dish towel with the lid to create a tight seal. (This prevents the steam from escaping.) If the dish towel is long, wrap it over the lid to prevent it from dangling. Reduce the heat to low and cook for 45–50 minutes, until the rice is cooked through. Gently mix the layers.

To serve, gently scoop the rice, one spatula at a time, onto a serving platter. Using a wooden spoon, detach the rice crust (*tahdig*) from the bottom of the saucepan.

Break apart the rice crust with your hands or cut it with scissors or a knife. Place the crust pieces on a separate serving platter or around the rice. Garnish the rice with the remaining saffron water and dried rose petals, if using.

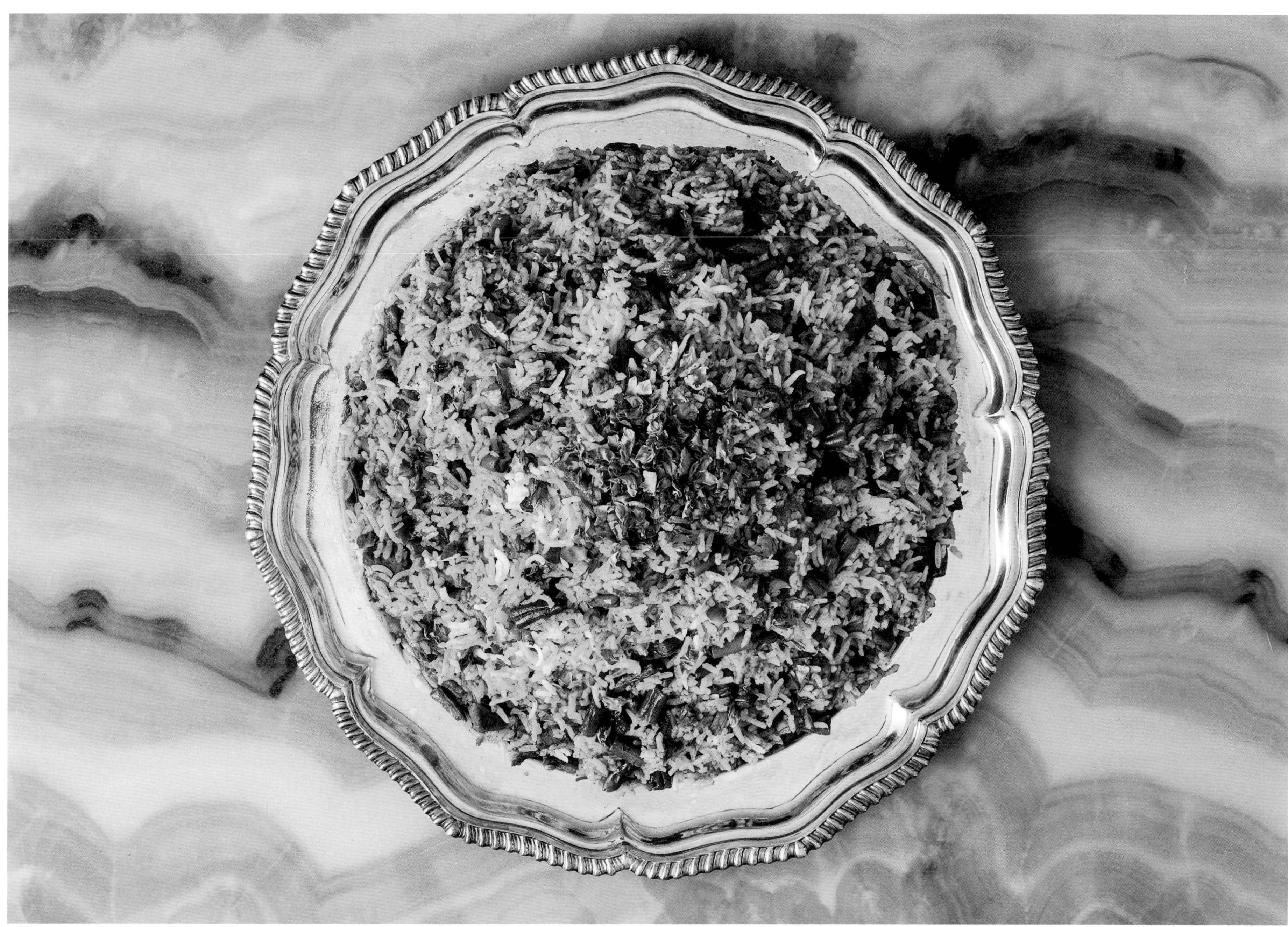

RICE WITH FAVA BEANS & DILL

Baghali Polo + باقالی پلو

Serves 6–8

Preparation time:
30 minutes

Cooking time:
60–75 minutes

- 2 teaspoons ground saffron
- 3 tablespoons salt
- 2½ cups (1 lb 2 oz/500 g) basmati rice, well rinsed
- ½ cup (4 fl oz/120 ml) virgin olive oil
- 2 tablespoons Greek yogurt
- 2 tablespoons rose water
- 2½ lb (1.2 kg) frozen shelled fava (broad) beans, thawed
- 8 cups (14 oz/400 g) coarsely chopped dill
- 2 teaspoons ground cardamom
- ½ cup (4 oz/115 g) melted butter
- Braised Lamb Shanks (page 169), to serve (optional)

Baghali polo is very popular in our home, as we love the combination of basmati rice and fava (broad) beans with fresh dill and saffron. The aroma is intoxicating. Nahid Joon always served this dish with Braised Lamb Shanks (page 169).

In a small bowl, bloom the saffron in 5 tablespoons of hot water. Set aside.

Bring 2½ quarts (2.3 L) of water to a boil in a large saucepan. Add 2 tablespoons of salt. Pour the rice into the boiling water and cook for 6 minutes, until al dente. Stir occasionally to prevent the rice from sticking to the bottom of the pan. Drain the rice, then rinse under cold running water. Toss the rice a few times, then set aside to drain completely.

In a small bowl, combine the oil, yogurt, and 1 tablespoon of rose water and mix well. Spread the mixture in the bottom of a nonstick stockpot or rice cooker. Using a slotted spatula, gently add some rice to the pan, about 2 inches (5 cm) deep. Drizzle with 1 teaspoon of bloomed saffron water. Add 1–2 spatulas of fava (broad) beans on top. Sprinkle a generous handful of dill and ½ teaspoon of cardamom. Repeat steps by alternating layers of rice, bloomed saffron water, fava beans, dill, and cardamom to form a pyramid. Wearing gloves, you may use your hands to very gently turn the rice mixture over a few times. You do not want to break up the rice grains.

In a small bowl, combine the melted butter, the remaining 1 tablespoon of salt, and the remaining 1 tablespoon of rose water. Pour over the rice. Place a clean dish towel over the top of the pan, then cover the pan and dish towel with the lid to create a tight seal. (This prevents the steam from escaping.) If the dish towel is long, wrap it over the lid to prevent it from dangling. Cook over medium-high heat for 10–15 minutes. Reduce the heat to low, then cook for another 45 minutes.

To serve, gently scoop out the rice, one spatula at a time, until all the rice is out of the saucepan. Take 2 large spatulas of the rice and put it in a bowl. Add 1 tablespoon of saffron water. Mix well until the rice has a beautiful golden hue. Spread the golden saffron mixture on top.

Using a wooden spoon, detach the rice crust (*tahdig*) from the bottom of the saucepan.

Break apart the rice crust with your hands or cut it with scissors or a knife. Place the crust pieces on a separate serving platter or around the rice.

Serve with lamb shanks, if desired.

RICE WITH SOUR CHERRIES

Serves 6–8

Preparation time: 15 minutes

Cooking time: 1 hour 30 minutes

Albaloo Polo + آلبالو پلو

- 2 teaspoons ground saffron
- 2 tablespoons salt
- 2½ cups (1 lb 2 oz/500 g) basmati rice or Persian rice, well rinsed
- 4 × (25-oz/700-g) jars of pitted sour cherries in light syrup, pitted
- 1½ tablespoons lemon juice
- 2 cups (14 oz/400 g) sugar
- ½ cup (4 fl oz/120 ml) virgin olive oil
- ½ cup (4 oz/115 g) melted butter
- 6 tablespoons Persian Spice Blend (page 246)
- ½ cup (2 oz/55 g) slivered pistachios
- Braised Turmeric Chicken (page 98), to serve (optional)

Nahid Joon served this side dish at dinner parties and at Thanksgiving. My son Philip Salar wrote these words of the dish:

"*Albaloo polo*, with its flavor-bursting cherries and rich saffron, proudly stands on its own. As we gather around the dinner table, all eyes are on the steam wafting from the dish. Everyone around the table listens as the host breaks into the *tahdig* (the crispy rice crust) and rich scents fill the air. Once your plate is served, most Persians quickly grab the tahdig with their fingers and take a bite, hoping that no one is looking. As your teeth work through the burnt rice and melt-in-your-mouth cherries, flavors run through the taste buds and eyes close to magnify this sensational experience."

In a small bowl, bloom the saffron in 4 tablespoons of hot water. Set aside.

Bring 2 quarts (2 L) of water to a boil in a large saucepan. Add the salt. Pour the rice into the boiling water and cook for 6 minutes, until al dente. Stir occasionally to prevent the rice from sticking to the bottom of the pan. Drain the rice, then rinse under cold running water. Toss the rice a few times, then set aside to drain completely.

Drain the sour cherries, reserving ½ cup (4 fl oz/120 ml) of the syrup for later. In a saucepan, combine the cherries, lemon juice, and sugar. Boil for 5 minutes, stirring continuously, until thick and syrupy. (Take care not to burn or caramelize. Reduce the heat if necessary.) Set aside to cool.

Combine 4 tablespoons each of oil and butter in a nonstick stockpot or rice cooker. Tilt the pan until the bottom is coated. Using a spatula, add some of the rice to the saucepan, about 2 inches (5 cm) deep. Drizzle 2 teaspoons of bloomed saffron water on the rice. Add 2 spatulas of the cherry mixture. Sprinkle 2 tablespoons of the Persian spice blend on top. Repeat the layers until the rice, cherries, Persian spice blend, and saffron water are all used. Cover and cook over medium heat for 10–15 minutes. Add the remaining 4 tablespoons each of oil and butter on top. Place a clean dish towel over the top of the pan, then cover the pan and dish towel with the lid to create a tight seal. (This prevents the steam from escaping.) If the dish towel is long, wrap it over the lid to prevent it from dangling. Cook over low heat for 50–60 minutes.

To serve, gently scoop the rice, one spatula at a time, onto a serving platter.

Using a wooden spoon, detach the rice crust (*tahdig*) from the bottom of the saucepan.

Break apart the rice crust with your hands or cut it with scissors or a knife. Place the crust pieces on a separate serving platter or around the rice.

Heat the reserved sour cherry syrup in a small saucepan, then sprinkle over the rice. Garnish the rice with the remaining saffron water and slivered pistachios. Serve with braised turmeric chicken, if desired.

RICE WITH FRESH HERBS

Serves 6

Preparation time: 1 hour

Cooking time: 1 hour 15 minutes

Sabzi Polo + سبزی پلو

- 1 teaspoon ground saffron
- 2 tablespoons salt
- 3 cups (1 lb 5 oz/600 g) basmati rice or Persian rice, well rinsed
- 3½ cups (7 oz/200 g) coarsely chopped cilantro (coriander)
- 3 cups (6 oz/180 g) coarsely chopped parsley
- 1½ cups (6 oz/180 g) finely chopped chives or scallions (spring onions)
- 1½ cups (2¾ oz/75 g) coarsely chopped dill
- ½ cup (4 fl oz/120 ml) virgin olive oil
- ½ cup (4 oz/115 g) melted butter
- 1 tablespoon Greek yogurt
- 4 scallions, finely chopped
- Whole Roasted Fish with Herbs (page 120), to serve (optional)

Persian New Year (Nowruz) celebrates the beginning of spring, and this festive dish is packed with layers of fresh herbs to symbolize new birth, and rebirth when new life germinates at the beginning of spring. This dish is usually served with white fish for the festivities.

Sabzi means "herbs or vegetables" in Farsi. The herbs impart a beautiful green hue to the dish.

In a small bowl, bloom the saffron in 4 tablespoons of hot water. Set aside.

Bring 2½ quarts (2.3 L) of water to a boil in a large saucepan. Add the salt. Pour the rice into the boiling water and cook for 6 minutes, until al dente. Stir occasionally to prevent the rice from sticking to the bottom of the pan. Drain the rice, then rinse under cold running water. Toss the rice a few times, then set aside to drain completely.

In a large bowl, combine all the herbs and mix well. In a medium mixing bowl, whisk together 3 tablespoons of oil, the melted butter, yogurt, and 2 tablespoons of bloomed saffron water. Pour the mixture into a nonstick stockpot or rice cooker. Tilt the pan until the bottom is coated.

Place two spatulas of the drained rice in the saucepan, then add one spatula of the herb mixture and 1 teaspoon of saffron water. Repeat by alternating layers of rice, herbs, and saffron water and forming a pyramid with a final layer of rice on top. Cover and cook over medium heat for 20 minutes. Pour the remaining 5 tablespoons of oil over the rice and sprinkle the scallions (spring onions) around the rice. Place a clean dish towel over the top of the pan, then cover the pan and dish towel with the lid to create a tight seal. (This prevents the steam from escaping.) If the dish towel is long, wrap it over the lid to prevent it from dangling. Cook over low heat for 50–60 minutes.

To serve, gently scoop the rice, one spatula at a time, onto a serving platter.

Using a wooden spoon, detach the rice crust (*tahdig*) from the bottom of the saucepan and place over the rice. (Alternatively, break apart the rice crust with your hands or cut it with scissors or a knife. Place the crust pieces on a separate serving platter or around the rice.)

Garnish the rice with the remaining saffron water. Serve with whole roasted fish, if desired.

SWEET RICE WITH ORANGE PEELS

Shirin Polo + شیرین پلو

Serves 8–10

Preparation time: 45 minutes

Cooking time: 2 hours

- 1 tablespoon ground saffron
- 4 tablespoons salt
- 3½ cups (1 lb 9 oz/700 g) basmati rice or Persian rice, well rinsed
- 2 cups (1 lb/450 g) slivered almonds
- ½ cup (2 oz/55 g) slivered pistachios
- 4 cups (12 oz/350 g) julienned orange or clementine peels
- 6 cups (1 lb 5 oz/600 g) julienned carrots
- 3 cups (1 lb 5 oz/600 g) sugar
- 1 tablespoon ground cardamom
- 4 tablespoons orange blossom water
- 1 cup (8 oz/225 g) melted butter
- 4 tablespoons extra-virgin olive oil
- 1 tablespoon Greek yogurt
- Braised Turmeric Chicken (page 98), to serve (optional)

Traditionally prepared for weddings and engagement parties, this dish is commonly known as "Persian wedding rice." The sweet taste is meant to symbolize a sweet marriage, and by eating this rice, the couple is guaranteed an enduring life together. It is also referred to as jeweled rice (*javaher polo*), as it is dotted with sweet orange peels, pistachios, and almonds.

The dish originates from Shiraz, known as the gateway to Persepolis. The city is renowned for its rose gardens and Iran's finest poets, Saadi and Hafez.

In a small bowl, bloom the saffron in 5 tablespoons of hot water. Set aside.

Bring 2½ quarts (2.3 L) of water to a boil in a large saucepan. Add the salt. Pour the rice into the boiling water and cook for 6 minutes, until al dente. Stir occasionally to prevent the rice from sticking to the bottom of the pan. Drain the rice, then rinse under cold running water. Toss the rice, then drain.

Preheat the oven to 350°F (180°C/Gas Mark 4). Line a large baking sheet with parchment paper.

Place the almonds and pistachios in a single layer on the prepared baking sheet. Toast them in the oven for 4–6 minutes, stirring occasionally, until golden brown. Set aside.

In a medium saucepan, combine the orange peels and 2½ quarts (2.3 L) of water. Bring to a boil, then reduce the heat to medium-low and simmer for 20 minutes. Drain, then rinse under cold running water. Set aside to drain completely. This process helps to remove the bitterness from the peels.

In a medium heavy saucepan, combine the orange peels, carrots, sugar, cardamom, orange blossom water, and 2 tablespoons of the bloomed saffron water. Pour in 3 cups (25 fl oz/750 ml) of water and cook gently over low heat for 20 minutes, or until thick and syrupy.

Reserve 2 tablespoons each of the almonds and pistachios for garnish. Add the rest to the pan and mix well.

In a medium mixing bowl, whisk together ½ cup (4 oz/115 g) of melted butter, the oil, and yogurt. Pour the mixture into a nonstick stockpot or rice cooker. Tilt the pan until the bottom is coated. Using a spatula, add some of the rice to the pan, about 2 inches (5 cm) deep. Spread 1 teaspoon of saffron water over the rice. Add 3 spatulas of the orange and nut mixture. Repeat with alternating layers of the rice and orange and nut mixture, forming a pyramid shape until you finish with a final layer of rice on top. Pour the remaining ½ cup (4 fl oz/120 ml) of butter over the rice. Cover and cook over medium heat for 10–15 minutes. Place a clean dish towel over the top of the pan, then cover the pan and dish towel with the lid to create a tight seal. (This prevents the steam from escaping.) If the dish towel is long, wrap it over the lid to prevent it from dangling. Cook over low heat for 50–60 minutes.

To serve, gently scoop the rice, one spatula at a time, onto a serving platter. Using a wooden spoon, detach the rice crust (*tahdig*) from the bottom of the saucepan.

Break apart the rice crust with your hands or cut it with scissors or a knife. Place the crust pieces on a separate serving platter or around the rice. Garnish the rice with the remaining slivered almonds and pistachios and 1 tablespoon of saffron water. Serve as is or with turmeric chicken.

SHIRAZI RICE WITH CABBAGE & MEATBALLS

Serves 4–6

Preparation time:
45 minutes

Cooking time:
1 hour 40 minutes

Kalam Polo + کلم پلو

For the rice and cabbage:
- ½ teaspoon ground saffron
- 2 tablespoons salt
- 2 cups (14 oz/400 g) basmati rice or Persian rice, well rinsed
- 6 tablespoons extra-virgin olive oil
- 2 large onions, thinly sliced
- 1 large white cabbage, shredded into 1 × 2-inch (2.5 × 5-cm) strips
- 1¼ cups (7 oz/200 g) tomato paste (purée)
- 3 tablespoons curry powder
- 2 tablespoons Persian Spice Blend (page 246)
- 1 teaspoon salt
- ½ teaspoon black pepper
- ½ teaspoon ground turmeric
- ⅓ teaspoon chili powder

For the meatballs:
- 1½ lb (625 g) ground (minced) sirloin beef, lamb, or veal
- 1 large onion, puréed and drained
- 2 cloves garlic, finely chopped
- 2 eggs
- ⅓ cup (¾ oz/20 g) coarsely chopped parsley
- ½ cup (2¾ oz/80 g) cooked basmati or brown rice
- 2 tablespoons salt
- ½ teaspoon black pepper
- ½ teaspoon dried oregano
- ½ teaspoon ground turmeric
- ⅓ cup (2¾ fl oz/80 ml) extra-virgin olive oil

Assembly:
- 4 tablespoons melted butter
- 2 tablespoons Greek yogurt

This traditional rice dish originates from the city of Shiraz, one of Iran's culinary capitals and producer of delicious wines. Small succulent meatballs are layered into the rice, enhanced with herbs and Nahid Joon's Persian spice blend (*advieh*). You can also omit the meatballs for a delicious vegetarian dish.

Shirazi Salad (page 26) makes for a great cooling accompaniment to this dish.

Make the rice. In a small bowl, bloom the saffron in 4 tablespoons of hot water. Set aside.

Bring 2½ quarts (2.3 L) of water to a boil in a large saucepan. Add the salt. Pour the rice into the boiling water and cook for 6 minutes, until al dente. Stir occasionally to prevent the rice from sticking to the bottom of the pan. Drain the rice, then rinse under cold running water. Toss the rice a few times, then set aside to drain completely.

Make the cabbage. Heat the oil in a large saucepan over medium heat. Add the onions and sauté for 8–10 minutes, until golden brown and softened. Increase the heat to medium-high, then add the cabbage. Sauté for 8–10 minutes, until the cabbage is wilted and the juice is absorbed. Add the tomato paste (purée), curry powder, 1 tablespoon of Persian spice blend, ½ teaspoon of salt, the pepper, turmeric, chili powder, and 3½ tablespoons of bloomed saffron water. Mix well, then set aside to cool. Reserve 2 tablespoons of the cabbage mixture for garnish.

Make the meatballs. In a large bowl, mix all the ingredients together, except for the oil, until just combined. Wet your hands and roll a small portion into a meatball, about ½ inch (1 cm) in diameter. Repeat with the remaining mixture.

Heat the oil in a large skillet over medium-high heat. Working in batches to avoid overcrowding, add the meatballs and sauté for 5 minutes, until golden on all sides. (Do not overcook them, as they will continue to cook in the rice.) Transfer the meatballs to a paper towel–lined plate to drain. Set aside.

To assemble, whisk together 2 tablespoons of the melted butter and yogurt in a small bowl. Pour the mixture into a nonstick stockpot. Divide the rice, meatballs, and cabbage into four equal portions. Add a quarter of the rice to the saucepan using a slotted spatula. Sprinkle 1 tablespoon of Persian spice blend and the remaining saffron water. Add a quarter of the cabbage as the next layer. Add a layer of meatballs as the third layer. Repeat and continue to build the layers, forming a pyramid shape until all are used up. Cover and cook over medium heat for 10–15 minutes. Drizzle the remaining 2 tablespoons of melted butter over the rice. Place a clean dish towel over the top of the pan, then cover the pan and dish towel with the lid to create a tight seal. (This prevents the steam from escaping.) If the dish towel is long, wrap it over the lid to prevent it from dangling. Cook over low heat for 50–60 minutes.

Using a large spatula, gently mix the rice and the cabbage mixture.

To serve, gently scoop the rice, one spatula at a time, onto a serving platter.

Using a wooden spoon, detach the rice crust (*tahdig*) from the bottom of the saucepan.

Break apart the rice crust with your hands or cut it with scissors or a knife. Place the crust pieces on a separate serving platter or around the rice. Decorate the rice with the reserved cabbage.

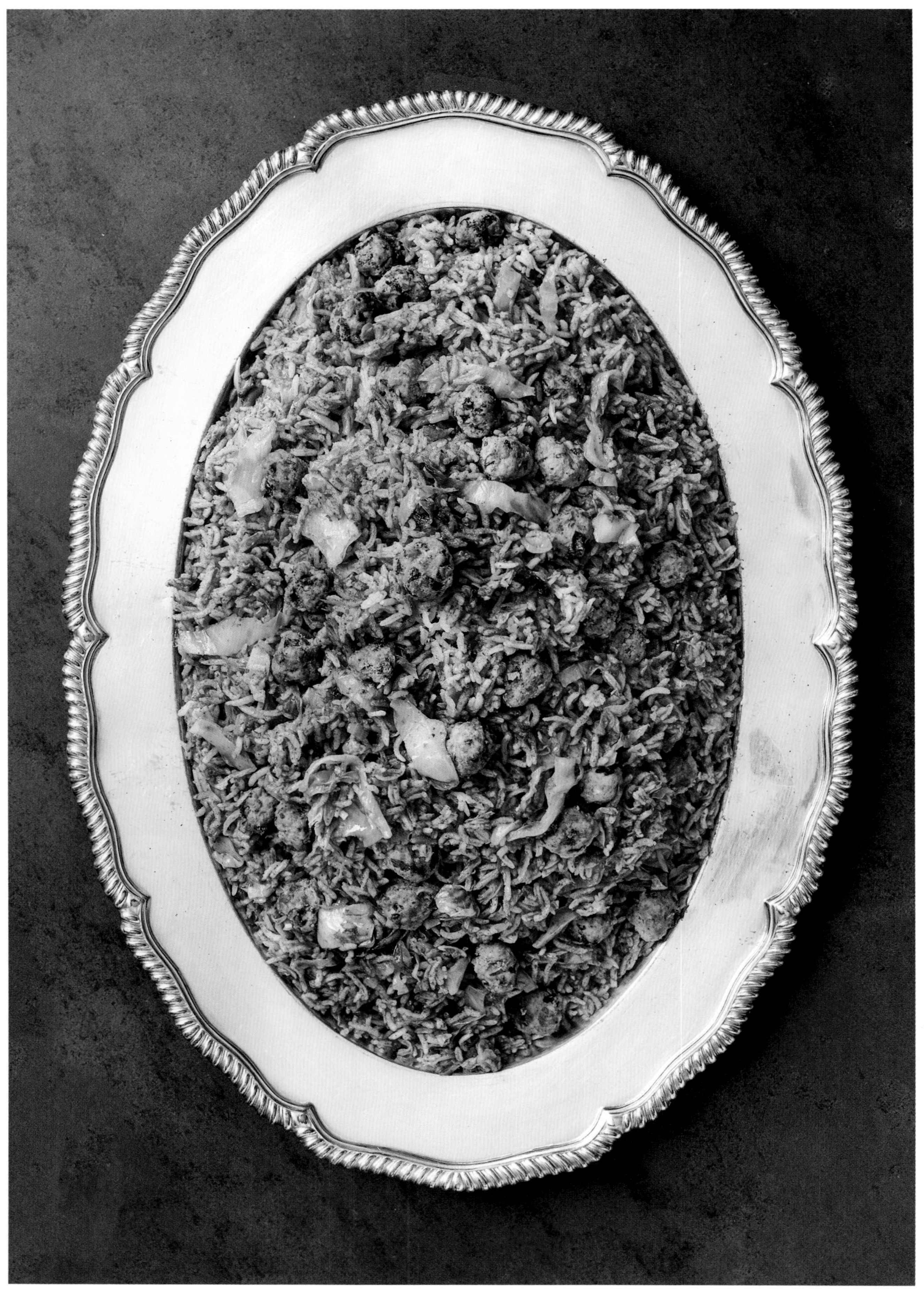

RICE WITH CURRY

Curry Polo + کاری پلو

Serves 8–10

Preparation time: 20 minutes

Cooking time: 3 hours

- 1 tablespoon ground saffron
- 2 tablespoons and 2 teaspoons salt
- 2½ cups (1 lb 2 oz/500 g) basmati or Persian rice, well rinsed
- 1½ cups (12 fl oz/350 ml) extra-virgin olive oil
- 6 onions, finely chopped
- 6 boneless, skinless chicken breasts
- 1 teaspoon black pepper
- ½ teaspoon ground turmeric
- 1½ cups (12 fl oz/350 ml) chicken stock
- 4 large carrots, shredded
- 4 bell peppers (1 each of red, yellow, green, and orange), seeded, deveined, and thinly sliced
- 2 cups (10 oz/280 g) raisins
- 1 cup (4 oz/115 g) slivered almonds
- 3 tablespoons curry powder
- 1 tablespoon grated ginger
- 1½ tablespoons tomato paste (purée)
- ½ cup (4 oz/115 g) melted butter
- 1 tablespoon Greek yogurt
- 2 tablespoons Persian Spice Blend (page 246)
- ½ cup (2 oz/55 g) slivered pistachios
- Mango Chutney (page 204) or Cilantro (Coriander) Chutney (page 209), to serve (optional)

Nahid Joon loved using curry alongside her famous spice blend (*advieh*) in many of her dishes. This flavorful recipe is a variation of Sweet Rice with Orange Peels (page 183), with layers of curry, spices, carrots, and raisins—minus the sweetness. She served it with her favorite chutneys (page 204–9).

In a small bowl, bloom the saffron in ½ cup (4 fl oz/120 ml) of hot water. Set aside.

Bring 2 quarts (2 L) of water to a boil in a large saucepan. Add 2 tablespoons of salt. Pour the rice into the boiling water and cook for 6 minutes, until al dente. Stir occasionally to prevent the rice from sticking to the bottom of the pan. Drain the rice, then rinse under cold running water. Toss the rice a few times, then set aside to drain completely.

Heat 1 cup (8 fl oz/250 ml) of oil in a large skillet over medium heat. Add three-quarters of the chopped onions and sauté for 12–15 minutes, until golden brown. Set aside to cool.

In a medium saucepan, combine the chicken, the remaining quarter of chopped onions, turmeric, 1 teaspoon of salt, and ½ teaspoon of pepper. Add the stock and cover. Cook over medium heat for 1 hour, or until the chicken is cooked through. About 1 cup (8 fl oz/250 ml) of juice should remain. Set aside to cool.

Heat the remaining ½ cup (4 fl oz/120 ml) of oil in a large skillet over medium-high heat. Add the carrots, bell peppers, and raisins and cook, stirring well, until soft and shiny. Add the almonds, curry powder, fried onions, ginger, tomato paste (purée), and the remaining 1 teaspoon of salt, and ½ teaspoon of pepper. Mix until combined. Set aside.

Using your hands, tear the chicken into thin, long strips. Alternatively, cut them into ¾-inch (2-cm) cubes. Add to the vegetable mixture.

In a small bowl, combine 4 tablespoons of melted butter and the yogurt and whisk. Pour the mixture into a nonstick stockpot. Tilt the pan until the bottom is coated.

Ladle the rice on top, about 2 inches (5 cm) deep. Sprinkle 3 tablespoons of bloomed saffron water and ½ teaspoon of Persian spice blend on top. Place a layer of the chicken-vegetable mixture on top. Repeat by alternating the layers and forming a pyramid shape until all the rice, Persian spice blend, saffron water, and chicken-vegetable mixture are used up. Cover and cook over medium heat for 15–20 minutes.

Drizzle the remaining 4 tablespoons melted butter on top. Place a clean dish towel over the top of the pan, then cover the pan and dish towel with the lid to create a tight seal. (This prevents the steam from escaping.) If the dish towel is long, wrap it over the lid to prevent it from dangling. Cook over low heat for 50–60 minutes.

To serve, gently scoop out the rice, one spatula at a time, until all the rice is out of the saucepan. Using a wooden spoon, detach the rice crust (*tahdig*) from the bottom of the saucepan.

Using your hands, break apart the rice crust. (Alternatively, you can cut them with scissors or a knife.) Place the crust pieces in a separate serving platter or around the rice. Garnish with slivered pistachios and serve with chutney, if desired.

RICE WITH LENTILS

Adas Polo + عدس پلو

Serves 8–10

Preparation time: 20 minutes, overnight soaking

Cooking time: 60–75 minutes

- ¼ teaspoon ground saffron
- 3 cups (1 lb 8 oz/675 g) dried Puy lentils, soaked overnight
- 2½ tablespoons salt
- 6 cups (2 lb 6 oz/1.2 kg) basmati rice or Persian rice, well rinsed
- ½ cup (4 fl oz/120 ml) and ½ tablespoon virgin olive oil
- ⅓ cup (2¾ oz/80 g) melted butter
- ½ cup (3 oz/85 g) Greek yogurt
- 2 tablespoons Persian Spice Blend (page 246)
- ½ cup (2¼ oz/60 g) caramelized barberries, raisins, or dates, for garnish
- 4 tablespoons caramelized onions, for garnish (optional)

Nahid Joon always prepared this simple, delicious, and versatile Persian dish with small Puy lentils, but any lentil can be used. Every night before my brother or I had an exam in school, Nahid Joon fed us a big bowl of this rice, using twice the amount of lentils she normally used, as she believed lentils were great for memory. We would also have leftovers for breakfast before rushing to our exams.

Nahid Joon served this dish with Braised Turmeric Chicken (page 98) or Braised Lamb Shanks (page 169).

In a small bowl, bloom the saffron in 2 tablespoons of hot water. Set aside.

Drain the lentils, then rinse under cold running water until the water runs clear. In a saucepan, boil the lentils in 6 cups (47 fl oz/1.4 L) of water and ½ tablespoon of salt for 10 minutes, or until al dente. Drain, then rinse under cold running water. Set aside to cool.

Bring 4¼ quarts (4 L) of water to a boil in a large saucepan. Add 2 tablespoons of salt. Pour the rice into the boiling water and cook for 6 minutes, until al dente. Stir occasionally to prevent the rice from sticking to the bottom of the pan. Drain the rice, then rinse under cold running water. Toss the rice a few times, then set aside to drain completely.

Mix ½ tablespoon of oil and 1 tablespoon of butter in the bottom of a saucepan or rice cooker. Tilt the pan until the bottom is coated.

In a medium bowl, combine 1 cup of the rice and the yogurt and mix well.

In a large bowl, combine the remaining rice and lentils. To the pan, add half of this mixture, 1 tablespoon of Persian spice blend, and 1 tablespoon of bloomed saffron water. Add the remaining half of the rice mixture, forming a pyramid shape. Sprinkle the remaining 1 tablespoon of the Persian spice blend and 1 tablespoon of saffron water on top.

In a bowl, mix 4 tablespoons of butter with ½ cup (4 fl oz/120 ml) of oil. Pour over the rice.

Cover and cook for 10 minutes over medium heat. Place a clean dish towel over the top of the pan, then cover the pan and dish towel with the lid to create a tight seal. (This prevents the steam from escaping.) If the dish towel is long, wrap it over the lid to prevent it from dangling. Cook for 45–50 minutes over low heat.

To serve, gently scoop the rice, one spatula at a time, onto a serving platter.

Using a wooden spoon, detach the rice crust (*tahdig*) from the bottom of the saucepan.

Break apart the rice crust with your hands or cut it with scissors or a knife. Place the crust pieces on a separate serving platter or around the rice.

Garnish with caramelized barberries and onions, if desired.

PERSIAN NOODLE RICE

Reshteh Polo + رشته پلو

Serves 6–8

Preparation time:
35 minutes

Cooking time:
1 hour 15 minutes

For the saffron chicken:
- ½ teaspoon ground saffron
- ⅓ cup (2½ fl oz/75 ml) virgin olive oil
- 1 large onion, finely chopped
- 1 tablespoon ground turmeric
- 18 small chicken tenders (see Note)
- 1 teaspoon salt
- 1 teaspoon black pepper

For the rice:
- ½ tablespoon ground saffron
- 2½ tablespoons salt
- 4 cups (1 lb 12 oz/800 g) basmati rice, well rinsed
- 1 × (8-oz/225-g) package roasted noodles (*reshteh*), cut in half
- 1 cup (6 oz/180 g) Greek yogurt
- ⅓ cup (2½ fl oz/75 ml) olive or avocado oil
- 4 tablespoons butter, cubed
- 1 large onion, finely chopped
- 1 tablespoon ground turmeric
- 14 Medjool dates, quartered lengthwise
- 2 cups (10 oz/280 g) Thompson seedless raisins
- 1 tablespoon ground cinnamon
- 1 tablespoon black pepper

Faraz Joon and Nahid Joon admired each other immensely. They would recount elaborate tales of their past for hours, sharing detailed memories of their large family and vast circles of friends—and our generation would consume all their stories.

Faraz prepared this great dish at one Thanksgiving dinner. Sweet, warm, and autumnal, it has become the most important accompaniment for our Thanksgiving meals, where family and guests savor perfectly cooked rice and noodles with fragrant saffron and turmeric and sweet dates and raisins. This recipe was generously provided by Faraz's daughter, Roya Khadjavi.

Make the saffron chicken. In a small bowl, bloom the saffron in 5 tablespoons of hot water. Set aside.

Heat the oil in a large skillet over medium heat. Add the onion and sauté for 5–7 minutes, until lightly brown. Add the turmeric and sauté for another 2 minutes. Season the chicken with the salt and pepper. Add it to the pan and brown for 3 minutes on each side. Add 2 cups (16 fl oz/475 ml) of water, cover, and gently simmer over low heat for 30 minutes, until cooked through. Stir in the bloomed saffron water.

Make the rice. In a small bowl, bloom the saffron in ⅔ cup (5 fl oz/150 ml) of hot water. Set aside.

Bring 3½ quarts (3.3 L) of water to a boil in a large saucepan. Add 2 tablespoons of salt. Add the rice and noodles and cook for 8 minutes, until al dente. Stir gently to prevent the rice and noodles from sticking together and to the bottom of the pan. Drain the rice and noodles, then rinse under cold running water. Toss a few times to mix, then set aside to drain completely.

In a small bowl, combine the yogurt, 4 tablespoons of oil, 1 cup (8 fl oz/250 ml) of water, and 3 tablespoons of the saffron water. Mix until homogeneous. Spread the mixture on the bottom of a nonstick stockpot or rice cooker. Stir the rice and noodles to evenly mix and add them to the saucepan. Top with the butter. Cover and cook for 10 minutes over high heat.

Reduce the heat to medium and cook for another 35–40 minutes, until a crust (*tahdig*) forms on the bottom.

Heat the olive oil in a large skillet over medium heat. Add the onion and sauté for 8 minutes, until golden brown. Add the turmeric and sauté for another 3 minutes. Add the dates, raisins, the remaining ½ teaspoon of salt, cinnamon, pepper, and 3 tablespoons of the saffron water. Reduce the heat to low and cook for 2–3 minutes. Set aside.

To serve, gently take a quantity of rice and noodles and place it onto a serving platter. Add the remaining saffron water and mix until the rice is bright yellow. The rice and noodles should be well mixed. If needed, use your hands to separate any lumpy noodles. Sprinkle some of the raisin mixture over the rice. Repeat the steps until all the rice and noodles have been dished out of the saucepan.

Using a wooden spoon, detach the rice crust (tahdig) from the bottom of the saucepan.

Break apart the rice crust with your hands or cut it with scissors or a knife. Place the crust pieces on a separate serving platter or around the rice.

Serve the chicken and its sauce in separate dishes to enjoy alongside the rice.

Note: Chicken tenders are made of chicken tenderloin. If unavailable, cut 3 boneless, skinless breasts lengthwise in strips, about 1 inch (2.5 cm) wide.

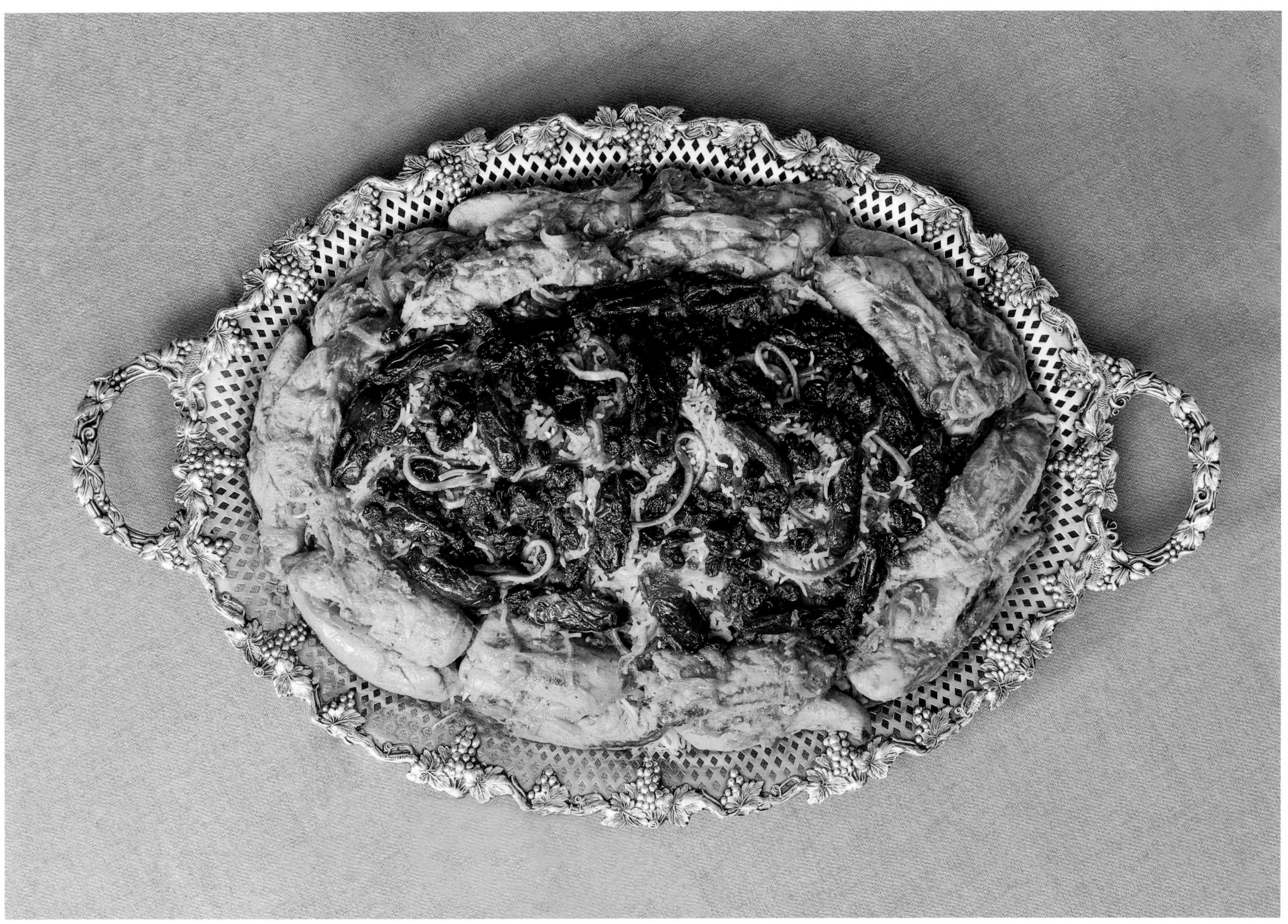

BARBERRY RICE WITH CHICKEN

Serves 8–10

Preparation time: 20 minutes

Cooking time: 75–90 minutes

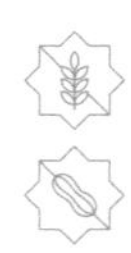

Advieh Polo ba Zereshk + ادویه پلو با زرشک

For the rice:
- 1 tablespoon ground saffron
- 1 tablespoon rose water (optional)
- 6 tablespoons extra-virgin olive oil
- 3 tablespoons salt
- 8 cups (3 lb 8 oz/1.6 kg) basmati rice or Persian rice, well rinsed
- ½ cup (4 oz/60 g) and 2 tablespoons butter
- 2 tablespoons Greek yogurt
- 1 egg
- ⅓ cup (1¼ oz/35 g) Persian Spice Blend (page 246)
- Braised Turmeric Chicken (page 98)

For the garnish:
- 1 tablespoon butter
- ¾ cup (3½ oz/100 g) dried cranberries
- ½ cup (2 oz/55 g) dried barberries, rinsed
- 1 tablespoon superfine (caster) sugar

Nahid and Soraya Tavakolian first met in seventh grade and remained close for decades. Nahid met her husband through the family of Soraya's husband. When they both lived in Tehran, they saw each other regularly at weekly gatherings (*dorehs*) and attended family get-togethers, weddings, and soirees. When Nahid moved to New York in 1978, they didn't see each other for years. Despite the vast distance, they remained close and spoke regularly. When they eventually met up, it was as if they had never been apart.

Advieh polo was a staple of Soraya's childhood home. It was also a staple at Nahid's home, where beautifully cooked rice was infused with her homemade aromatic *advieh*, warm, golden saffron, tart barberries, and tender chicken.

Make the rice. In a small bowl, combine the saffron, rose water, if using, and ½ cup (4 fl oz/120 ml) of hot water. Set aside.

In a large saucepan, combine 2½ quarts (2.3 L) of water, 3 tablespoons of oil, and the salt and bring to a boil. Pour the rice into the boiling water and cook for 6 minutes, until al dente. Stir occasionally to prevent the rice from sticking to the bottom of the pan. Drain the rice, then rinse under cold running water. Toss the rice a few times, then set aside to drain completely.

Place 2 tablespoons of melted butter and 3 tablespoons of oil into a nonstick stockpot. In a small bowl, whisk together the yogurt, egg, and 1 teaspoon of bloomed saffron water and pour into the saucepan. Tilt the pan until the bottom is coated. Using a slotted spatula, gently add some of the rice to a depth of 1 inch (2.5 cm). Using a spoon, sprinkle 2 tablespoons of Persian spice blend on top. Using a teaspoon, sprinkle 2 teaspoons each of the bloomed saffron water on the rice and Persian spice blend. Repeat, alternating the layers of the rice, spice blend, and saffron and forming a pyramid until the rice and spice blend are used up. Place ½ cup (4 oz/60 g) of butter on top of the pyramid.

Place a clean dish towel over the top of the pan, then cover the pan and dish towel with the lid to create a tight seal. (This prevents the steam from escaping.) If the dish towel is long, wrap it over the lid to prevent it from dangling. Cook for 10 minutes over medium-high heat. Reduce the heat and cook for 45–50 minutes over low-medium heat.

Make the garnish. In a separate saucepan, combine the butter, cranberries, barberries, and sugar. Sauté over low heat for 5 minutes, stirring continuously, until the mixture glistens.

Once the rice is ready, turn off the heat and gently mix the layers.

To serve, gently take a spatula full of rice at a time and place it on a serving platter. Place 2 large spatulas of the rice mixture into a bowl and add 2 tablespoons of saffron water to the rice. Using a wooden spoon, detach the rice crust (*tahdig*) from the bottom of the saucepan.

Break apart the rice crust with your hands or cut it with scissors or a knife. Place the crust pieces on a separate serving platter or around the rice. Place the turmeric chicken around the rice. Garnish the rice with the barberry-cranberry mixture.

DILL RICE WITH CRISPY SALMON & LEEKS

Serves 8–10

Preparation time:
20–25 minutes

Cooking time:
50 minutes

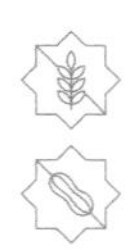

Sabzi Polo ba Mahi Azad + سبزی پلو با ماهی آزاد

- 2 tablespoons ground saffron
- 3½ tablespoons salt
- 1 teaspoon ground turmeric
- 3 cups (1 lb 5 oz/600 g) basmati rice, well rinsed
- 2 tablespoons butter
- 1 leek, tops and bottoms removed and cut in half lengthwise
- 5 lb (2.25 kg) salmon fillets
- 3 cups (5½ oz/150 g) coarsely chopped dill
- 1 lemon, thinly sliced

Nahid Joon loved the *salmon polo* prepared for Nowruz at Marjan Fateh's home in Dubai. Marjan had cooked in her honor that evening. It was an out-of-the-box recipe, as the traditional white fish was replaced with a salmon that became part of the crust (*tahdig*). Nahid was blown away by this recipe and Marjan was so touched.

This delicacy has since become a staple in Marjan's repertoire and continues to delight our family at our gatherings.

In a small bowl, bloom the saffron in 4 tablespoons of water. Set aside.

Bring 2½ quarts (2.3 L) of water to a boil in a large saucepan. Add 3 tablespoons of salt and the turmeric to the boiling water. Pour the rice into the boiling water and cook for 6 minutes, until al dente. Stir occasionally to prevent the rice from sticking to the bottom of the pan. Drain the rice, then rinse under cold running water. Toss the rice a few times, then set aside to drain completely.

Melt the butter in a deep, medium-sized skillet over medium heat and add the bloomed saffron water. Place the leeks, cut side down, into the pan. Sprinkle the remaining ½ tablespoon of salt on both sides of the salmon and place the fillets, skin side down, on top of the leeks. Ensure the entire pan is covered with salmon and leeks.

Reserve ½ cup (1 oz/25 g) of dill for garnish, stir the remainder into the rice. Carefully spread the rice evenly over the salmon and leeks. Cover and cook over high heat for 3–4 minutes. Reduce the heat to low, cover, and cook for 45 minutes. Carefully invert the pan onto a large serving platter. Garnish with the dill and lemon.

RICE WITH LAMB, YOGURT & SAFFRON

Serves 8–10

Preparation time: 30 minutes

Cooking time: 2 hours 45 minutes

Tahchin Goosht + ته چین گوشت

For the rice:

- 2 teaspoons ground saffron
- 4¾ tablespoons salt
- 3½ cups (1 lb 9 oz/700 g) basmati rice or Persian rice, well rinsed
- ½ cup (4 fl oz/120 ml) virgin olive oil
- 1 lb (450 g) boneless leg of lamb or veal stew meat, cubed into 2-inch (5-cm) piece
- ½ tablespoon black pepper
- 2 large onions, coarsely chopped
- 1 tablespoon Persian Spice Blend (page 246)
- ½ tablespoon ground turmeric
- 1 cup (8 fl oz/250 ml) chicken stock
- 1 cup (6 oz/180 g) Greek yogurt
- 1 egg
- 2 egg yolks
- ½ cup (4 oz/115 g) melted butter
- 4 tablespoons slivered pistachios, for garnish

For the barberries:

- 1 tablespoon butter
- 10 tablespoons (2½ oz/70 g) dried barberries, rinsed
- 2 tablespoons sugar

The word *tahchin* means "arranged in the bottom of the pot." Unlike other rice dishes, tahchin is dense with origins in Azerbaijan and Kerman. It generally features layers of rice with meat or vegetables, with a crispy rice crust (*tahdig*). This delicious cake-like version has a beautiful golden crust on the outside and is garnished with tangy barberries.

Make the rice. In a small bowl, bloom the saffron in 4 tablespoons of hot water. Set aside.

Bring 3 quarts (2.8 L) of water to a boil in a large saucepan. Add 4 tablespoons of salt. Pour the rice into the boiling water and cook for 6 minutes, until al dente. Stir occasionally to prevent the rice from sticking to the bottom of the pan. Drain the rice, then rinse under cold running water. Toss the rice a few times, then set aside to drain completely.

Heat 2 tablespoons of oil in a heavy saucepan over medium-high heat. Season the lamb with 1 teaspoon of salt and the pepper. Add the lamb to the pan and sear for 2 minutes on each side, until evenly browned. Transfer the lamb to a plate and set aside.

In the same skillet, combine the onions, Persian spice blend, and turmeric and sauté over medium heat for 10–12 minutes, until softened and golden. Add the lamb to the pan, then pour in the stock and ½ cup (4 fl oz/120 ml) of water. Bring to a boil, then reduce the heat to low. Cover and gently simmer for 1 hour, until the meat is tender and the sauce is sticky. Transfer the lamb to a plate and set aside.

Boil the sauce for 3 minutes, or until it has reduced to less than ½ cup (4 fl oz/120 ml). Mix in the lamb, then set aside to fully cool.

Preheat the oven to 450°F (230°C/Gas Mark 8).

In a medium bowl, combine the yogurt, egg, egg yolks, 2 tablespoons of bloomed saffron water, and 1 teaspoon of salt. Whisk until homogeneous.

Evenly spread 4 tablespoons of melted butter and 4 tablespoons of oil on the bottom of a 10-inch (25-cm) square baking dish. Add the yogurt mixture and spread out evenly. Scoop 4 cups of the rice on top, spreading it out evenly and pressing it down to compact. Place the meat and sauce on top and gently push them into the rice sso that the meat touches the bottom of the pan. Add the rest of the rice and pour in the remaining saffron water, 4 tablespoons of oil, and 4 tablespoons melted butter on top. Cover the dish tightly with aluminum foil and bake for 40 minutes, or until the bottom of the rice forms a crust and turns golden yellow.

Reduce the heat to 350°F (180°C/Gas Mark 4) and bake for another 40 minutes. Set aside for 10 minutes to cool.

Make the barberries. Heat the butter in a small saucepan over low heat. Add the barberries and sugar and sauté for 2–4 minutes. (Take care not to overcook the barberries, as they burn quickly.)

To serve, remove the foil from the rice dish. Run a spatula or palette knife along the edges of the dish to release any rice stuck to the dish. Place a large, flat platter over the dish. Using both hands to hold the dish securely to the platter, carefully invert the rice onto the platter. (Alternatively, cut the rice into sections and place on a serving plate.) Garnish with barberries and slivered pistachios.

FOOD AND HOSPITALITY IN SAFAVID IRAN

Dr. Massumeh Farhad

A house in which no guest enters is not entered by angels.
—Prophetic tradition (*hadith*)

In Iran, hospitality has been a defining characteristic of social and cultural life for millennia.[1] Whether for simple gatherings or elaborate celebrations, meals are meant to be shared to mark both mundane and special occasions. Each meal includes many stages of preparation, from the choice of ingredients, balance, and mixture of dishes to the final presentation. Every step is carefully deliberated as a measure of the host's respect for the guests. As early as the eleventh century, detailed manuals regulated the etiquette of dining for the invitees and how best to express pleasure and gratitude in return, emphasizing the importance of social reciprocity.[2] During the Safavid period (1502–1722), Persian culinary arts reached a new height and became the basis for contemporary cuisine in Iran.

As one of the finest culinary traditions in the world, Persian fare relies fundamentally on cereals, an array of thick vegetable soups (*aash*), a subtle combination of meat, vegetables, and fruits, complemented by dairy products, such as yogurt (*māst*, *kashk*) and cheese. Of course, today, the staple of Persian cuisine is rice. It is unclear when rice was introduced into Iran, but it may have been long before the arrival of Islam in the seventh century. As the word for rice in Persian, *berenj*, is derived from Sanskrit, the cereal was probably introduced from India. Until the fourteenth century, rice was considered a luxury staple and used only by the elite. Based on the recipes in two surviving Safavid cookbooks, rice grew in popularity and eventually became the main staple of modern Persian cuisine.[3]

Before the rise of the Safavid dynasty, descriptions of Persian food and eating habits were relatively rare. With the flourishing trade between Iran and Europe after the sixteenth century and a steady stream of European diplomats, merchants, clerics, and adventurers to the court, who now frequented Iran, interest in Persian life and customs grew. Many of the visitors kept invaluable travel accounts, which included careful observations on Safavid food and eating habits. For example, the French jeweler Jean Chardin, who was in Iran in the late seventeenth century, mentions that Persians would skip breakfast, except for a cup of coffee and, in general, would eat two meals a day. The high cost of firewood, especially on Iran's largely tree-less central plateau, meant that the lower classes did not cook at home and instead ate or bought their meals at shops or stalls in the bazaar. In some regions, families would consume only one meal a day, usually in the late afternoon. Only the wealthy could afford to eat meat (mutton and goat), usually roasted on skewers as kebab and eaten with rice. Beef was rarely eaten. According to Western observers, Persians ate less and healthier than their European counterparts.

Visitors to Safavid Iran unanimously praise the succulent and flavorsome fruit and vegetables. Grapes, apricots, peaches, melons, pomegranates, cucumbers, and apples were considered second to none and were used for a variety of stews and sweet dishes, or they were eaten raw. Missionaries introduced a number of European ingredients, such as parsley, asparagus, artichokes, cauliflower, and potato, some of which gradually entered the Safavid culinary tradition.

With the accession of Shah Abbas I in 1589, and the transformation of Isfahan into a grand Safavid capital, court ceremonies grew more formal and elaborate in both scale and scope. Royal banquets became one of the most important occasions to honor the growing number of foreign visitors as well as local dignitaries. The gatherings served to highlight Safavid sophistication, generosity, and hospitality.

The preparation of food also grew more complex. The royal kitchen, which served the entire court, was supervised by the *tushmal-bashi*, who was also the official royal taster. The *sufrachi-bashi* was responsible for the floor cloth on which the food was served and arranged. Other individuals oversaw the preparation of a rich variety of drinks, pickled vegetables, sweets, coffee, sherbets, and so on. The number of staff and their specific tasks suggest that the work of the royal kitchen was strictly regulated and structured, a necessary requirement to feed a large and bustling court.

Based on European accounts, royal banquets were elaborate affairs and usually took place after foreign dignitaries had presented their gifts to the monarch. Seating was of utmost importance and a clear indication of a guest's rank and status. Safavid palaces did not include specific dining spaces, so royal receptions were staged in different pavilions on the vast palace grounds in Isfahan. These were appropriately prepared and decorated with luxurious carpets, hangings, covers, and cushions and lit with lamps and candles.

Some of the banquets could take as long as four hours, especially if wine was offered, but only at the discretion of the shah to specific guests. If neither wine nor side dishes were served, then the meal could be over in an hour. To the surprise of Western observers, a royal meal would begin with fruits and a series of sweet dishes. The French jeweler Jean Chardin claimed that, following the shah orders, attendants would remove the first set of dishes, and the next course would commence by replacing the floor cloth with a fresh one. Then, each guest would be served a variety of meats and stews in as many as ten to twenty small plates and bowls, accompanied by sherbet. Chardin maintained that these dishes were not the main course and were meant to stimulate the guests' appetites. At this time, cup bearers would also serve wine to attendees selected by the king, who directed both the pace and mood of the event. When everyone had drunk sufficiently, the floor covering would be replaced once again, and the final course was served. It consisted of a variety of soups, boiled meats, stews, and different rice dishes, served on large platters. According to Chardin, a banquet for the Russian ambassador included at least five different rice dishes. Finally, as soon as the shah rose to leave, the banquet came to an end, and guests were expected to depart.

The most popular of Safavid dishes, especially those enjoyed by the court, are described in two important cooking manuals that have survived from the sixteenth and seventeenth centuries.[4] The first one is referred to as

Kārnameh: dar bāb tabbākhi va san'at ān [Book of deeds: on cooking and its craft] by Hajji Muhammad Ali Bāvarchi Baghdādi, composed in 1521 for an unidentified prince. The second work, *Māddat al-hayyat: resāle dar elm-e tabbākhi* [Essence of life: a treatise on the art of cooking] was written in 1598 by Shah Abbas I's chef, Nasrullah, when Isfahan became the official new capital. Both accounts provide information about the ingredients, method of preparation, and the look of various dishes, confirming the importance of both appearance and taste in Persian cuisine.

The *Kārnameh* is divided into twenty-two chapters and begins with a variety of recipes for a sweet bun (*kamacheh*), followed by heavy soup (*aash*), yogurt, rice pudding (*shir-berenj*) stews (*ghalieh*), chicken, meats, kebabs, rice dishes, and ends with the popular dessert *baghlava*. Bāvarchi lists the ingredients for each recipe and its varieties, plus practical advice on how to regulate the heat, thicken and thin stews, and decorate the dish (usually with raisins, almonds, and pistachios). For a recipe for lemon (*limu*) or bitter orange (*aārenj*) rice, for example, he suggests first placing some rice in a ceramic (*chini*) dish, then placing the meat in, and covering it with additional rice. The growing popularity of rice dishes in the early sixteenth century is evident from the thirty-three different recipes that are included in the *Kārnameh*, which are largely organized according to flavor. Rice, which always went through the process of washing, parboiling, and steaming, was combined with meat (usually lamb) and legumes and other ingredients.

Seventy years later, Nasrullah composed his treatise to includes sixty-six rice dishes. They are described at the beginning of the work, emphasizing their importance in later Safavid cuisine. A descendant of a family of chefs, Nasrullah introduced his account by describing the qualities of a master cook. He never neglected his responsibilities and did not depend on others. He kept himself pure both spiritually and physically, just as he needed to ensure that his cooking tools were clean. Nasrullah singled out the importance of washing meat to bring out flavor and taste. A pleasant disposition is also important for a master cook. Nasrullah's instructions are not always as precise as those of Bāvarchi and in the case of a particular type of *kuku*, a dish similar to a frittata, he maintained that describing the recipe would be too troublesome for the reader and writer. Like his predecessor, Bāvarchi, he prescribed how a dish should be served. One of the most complicated dishes in his treatise is *qabuli marseh*, known today as *marseh polo*, which Nasrullah maintains is a must at royal functions. It includes raisins, almonds, dates, as well as cooked chestnuts, peas, lentils, and meat, all of which are artfully arranged in rows on a bed of rice. The dish is topped with meatballs with an egg in the center, cut to show off the egg. Nasrullah maintains that some chefs also set a bowl of thick soup (*aash*) in the middle of the plate.

The variety of dishes in the Safavid period required large number of platters, plates, bowls, and cups of different sizes and shapes. Guests to royal banquets often speak of gold and silver vessels, but few of these objects survived. Less costly ceramic vessels were also used, and today many such examples can be seen in private and public collections around the world. Some of these plates and bowls are inscribed with poems and sayings, which draw attention to their role and function in banquets beyond merely holding food. They remind the hosts and guests of the infinite pleasures of eating and drinking, which should appeal to the senses of taste, sight, smell, and touch, in which the vessels also play an important role. The inscription on a seventeenth-century dish in the Afshar collection reads: "When the sun turns yellow in the dark-blue sky, I am reminded of saffron rice on a lapis-colored dish."

The brilliant colors and designs of vessels, the carefully combined ingredients and complex tastes and aromas, all intermingle in a Persian dish to create memorable culinary experiences to be savored, shared, and celebrated. All these qualities were trademarks of Nahid Taghinia-Milani's (Nahid Joon's) boundless hospitality and memorably delicious cuisine.

—Dr. Massumeh Farhad, Freer Gallery of Art and the Arthur M. Sackler Gallery, National Museum of Asian Art, Smithsonian

CHUTNEYS AND JAMS

Most Persian families make their own chutneys, jams, and preserves using everyday vegetables, fruits, and herbs. They are important components of Persian meals, and their preparation is a tradition that is passed on from generation to generation.

Persians have more than a hundred types of *torshi* (chutney/preserve), reflective of regional tastes, customs, and celebrations (page 17). Torshi has beneficial probiotics to foster good digestion, health, and immunity. Persian chutneys are flavorful condiments made from slow-cooked fruits and vegetables, herbs, spices, and a lot of vinegar.

Nahid Joon came up with her own invention of "torshi chutney," which combines the best of both condiments and tastes like a spicy, sharp, and pungent chutney. (Whereas most chutneys use a cup of vinegar, Nahid Joon used a bottle and a half!) Nahid would make an assortment of fruit and vegetable torshi chutneys, but her mango and eggplant (aubergine) ones were my favorites.

To preserve homemade jams and marmalades, jars must be properly sterilized before use. Wash the jars in warm, soapy water, rinse thoroughly, and dry them with a clean dish towel. Heat the jars in a preheated oven at 275°F (140°C/Gas Mark 1) for 10 minutes. Fill the jars with warm jam. If using a ladle, be sure to sterilize the ladle by dipping its bowl into the jam just after it has finished boiling.

Homemade jams and chutneys should be stored in a cool, dark, and dry place and used within twelve months. It is best to seal them with wax or use a tight-fitting clip-top jar. Once opened, jams should be stored in the refrigerator and used within one month. Discard any jam with mold on the surface.

MANGO CHUTNEY

Torshi Anbe + ترشی انبه

Makes 6 × (24-oz/675-g) jars

Preparation time: 35 minutes, plus overnight soaking

- 8 cups (1 lb/450 g) sun-dried tomatoes
- 1 cup (8 oz/225 g) dried apricots
- ½ cup (2¼ oz/60 g) dried currants
- 2¼ cups (17 fl oz/500 ml) apple cider vinegar
- 2 × (16-oz/450-g) jars smoked red peppers, drained
- 10 ripe mangos, cut into ½-inch (1-cm) cubes, plus extra for garnish
- ½ cup (½ oz/15 g) dried mint
- 2 tablespoons ground cinnamon
- 1 tablespoon ground nutmeg
- 1 tablespoon ground cumin
- 1 tablespoon salt
- 2½ teaspoons ground coriander
- 1½ cups (12 fl oz/350 ml) cassis or sour cherry jam
- 2½ tablespoons harissa paste
- 1 tablespoon curry paste

Nahid Joon made this deliciously sweet and sour concoction after a trip to the Round Hill Hotel and Villas in Jamaica, where she discovered their signature mango chutney. She was obsessed with it and created a tangier version by adding more vinegar. This chutney is a great accompaniment for chicken, lamb, and any curry recipe.

In a large bowl, combine the sun-dried tomatoes, apricots, currants, and vinegar. Soak overnight. Drain the fruit, reserving the strained vinegar.

In a food processor, combine the smoked peppers, sun-dried tomato mixture, and mangos and purée until smooth. Transfer the mixture to a bowl, then add the mint, cinnamon, nutmeg, cumin, salt, and coriander. Stir in the cassis and harissa and curry pastes and mix well to combine. Transfer to sterilized glass jars and seal. For the best taste, allow to sit for 1 day to allow the flavors to meld.

Serve in a small bowl and garnish with the mango. Properly jarred chutney can be stored in a cupboard for up to 1 year. Once opened, it can be refrigerated for a year.

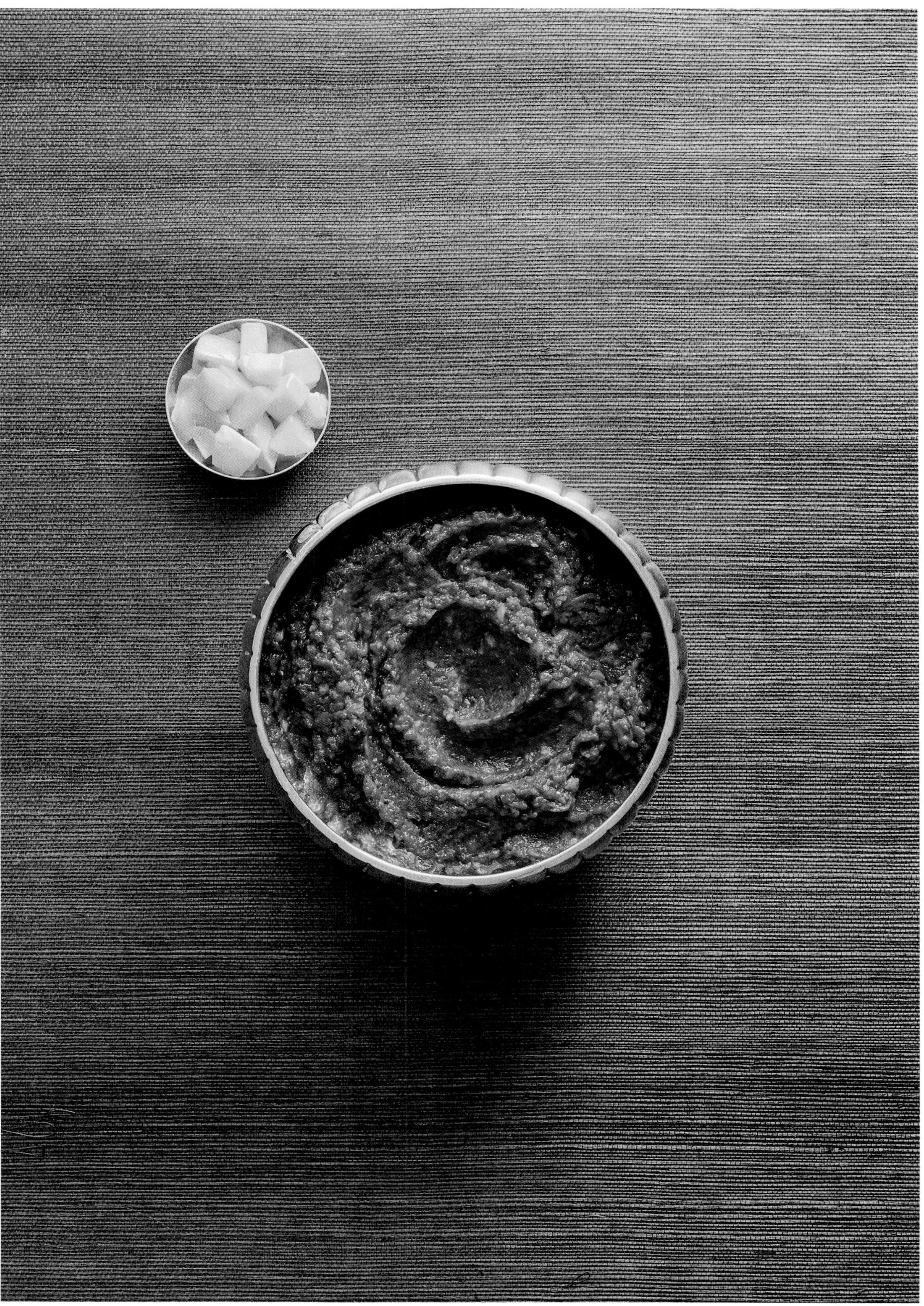

EGGPLANT CHUTNEY

Torshi Liteh Bademjan + ترشی لیته بادمجان

Makes 4 × (24-oz/675-g) jars

Preparation time: 20 minutes

Cooking time: 10–15 minutes

- 6 Japanese eggplants (aubergines), cut into 1-inch (2.5-cm) cubes
- 1 head garlic, cloves finely chopped
- 2 teaspoons salt
- 2 teaspoons black pepper
- 6 cups (47 fl oz/1.4 L) apple cider vinegar, plus extra if needed
- 2 tablespoons grape molasses or honey
- 1 cup (½ oz/15 g) tarragon leaves
- 1 cup (2 oz/55 g) cilantro (coriander) leaves
- 1 cup (¼ oz/10 g) mint leaves
- ½ cup (¼ oz/10 g) marjoram leaves
- 1 teaspoon dried rose petal powder
- 1 teaspoon ground turmeric
- Golden Fried Onions (page 246), for garnish

Persians love their pickled vegetables and Nahid Joon's eggplant (aubergine) chutney makes a tangy complement to many dishes. The best eggplants for this recipe are thin, young Japanese eggplants, which are less bitter than other varieties.

The chutney can be enjoyed with rice dishes, stews, kebabs, chicken, meat, and fish entrees.

In a large saucepan, combine the eggplants (aubergines), garlic, salt, and pepper. Add the apple cider vinegar and grape molasses and bring to a boil. Reduce the heat to medium and simmer for 10–15 minutes, until the eggplant is tender but not overcooked. Remove from the heat, then set aside to cool.

Wash the herbs and separate the leaves from the stems. Rinse the herbs, then pat dry with paper towels. Put them in a food processor and coarsely chop.

Once the eggplant mixture has cooled, add the chopped herbs, rose petal powder, and turmeric. The eggplant should be fully submerged in the vinegar. Top it up with more, if needed.

Use a sterilized ladle to carefully fill sterilized canning jars. Seal the jars tight.

To serve, transfer the chutney to a serving bowl and top with the fried onions.

Chutney can be stored in a cupboard for up to 2 months. Once opened, refrigerate and use within 1 week.

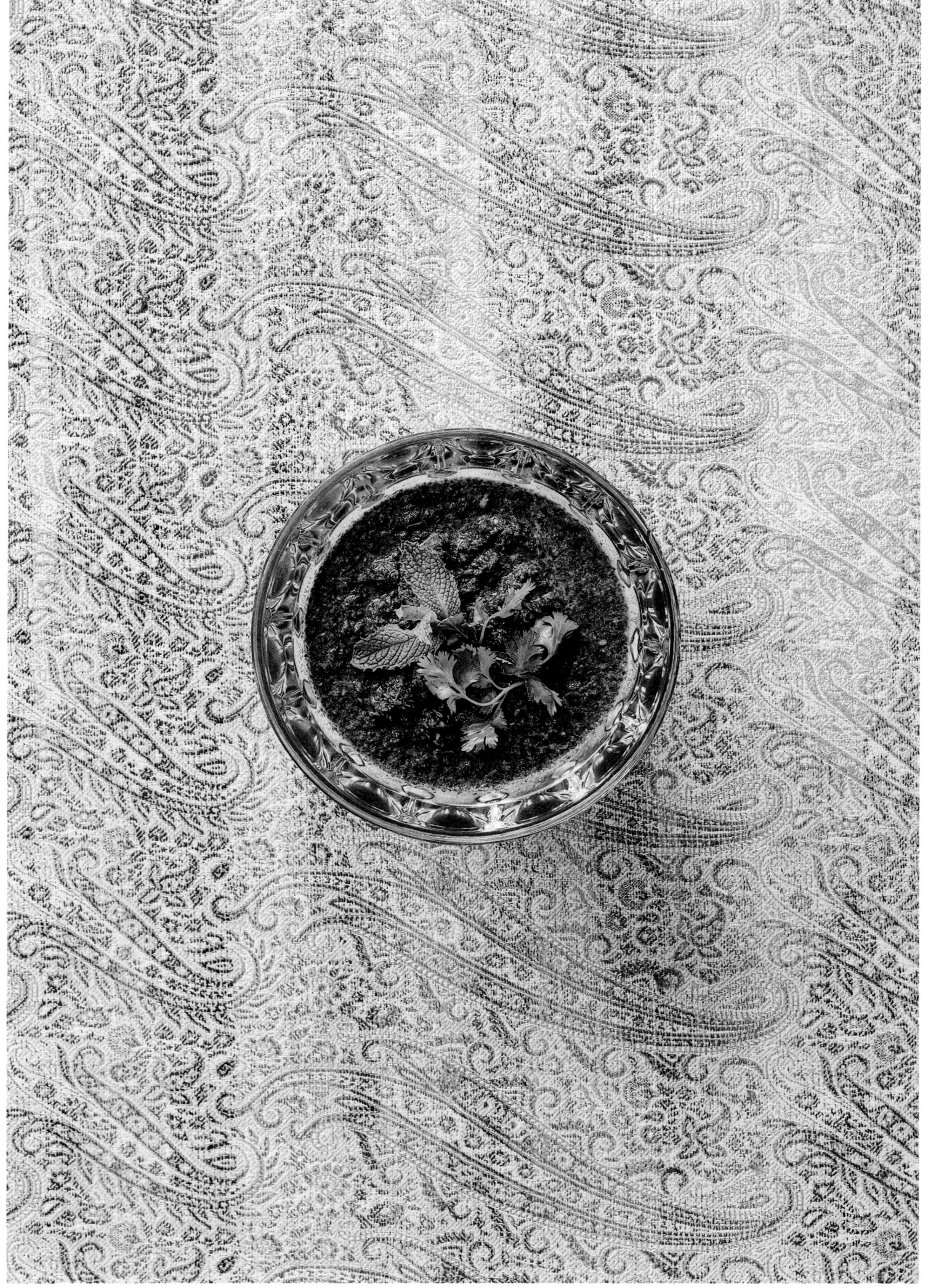

CILANTRO CHUTNEY

Torshi Geshniz + ترشی گشنیز

Makes 2 cups
(1 lb/450 g)

Preparation time:
45 minutes

- 1–2 small jalapeño peppers
- 1 clove garlic
- 6 cups (12 oz/350 g) cilantro (coriander) with the tender stems, plus extra for garnish
- ⅓ cup (¼ oz/10 g) mint leaves, plus extra for garnish
- 2 tablespoons cumin seeds, toasted
- 2 tablespoons grated ginger
- ¾ teaspoon salt
- ½ teaspoon black pepper
- ½ teaspoon sugar
- 5 tablespoons white vinegar or lemon juice

Nahid Joon used this versatile chutney in her Green Herb Curry (page 139), as a paste for fish fillets, an accompaniment to meat dishes, and a spread for sandwiches and hors d'oeuvres. She also added it to her famous Hamburgers (page 104).

Put all the ingredients in a blender and add 4 tablespoons of water. Blend until smooth. Add more water if needed. Set aside to cool, then store in sterilized glass jars.

Serve in a small decorative bowl. Garnish with cilantro (coriander) and mint.

Properly jarred chutney can be stored in a cupboard for up to 1 year. Once opened, refrigerate and use within 1 year.

SOUR CHERRY JAM

Morabaye Albaloo + مربای آلبالو

Makes 3 × (8-oz/225-g) jars

Preparation time: 10 minutes

Cooking time: 40 minutes

- 2 lb (900 g) fresh or frozen pitted sour cherries
- 1½ cups (10½ oz/300 g) sugar
- Juice of 1 lime (optional)

When I was growing up in Tehran, we made big batches of jams with the fruits from our gardens. I so loved climbing up the trees with my brother and shaking their branches until the fruit fell onto the bedsheet my mother would hold below. In the summer, we would use sour cherries, pears, raspberries, apples, peaches, rose petals, and mulberries. In the fall, we preserved persimmons, quinces, oranges, Persian citrons (*balangs*), and grapefruits.

Traditionally, we would have jam at the breakfast table. Once Nahid Joon moved to New York, she would make jams for herself or for friends. When she passed away, everyone told me how they think of her at every breakfast, as they so missed her variety of jams.

Sour cherries, which are indigenous to Iran and Turkey, have very soft flesh and bruise easily, so Nahid Joon would make her jam after my brother and I picked them fresh off the tree. She added lime juice to enhance the cherry flavor.

Combine all the ingredients in a large saucepan. Mash together and cook over high heat, stirring frequently, until the mixture starts to boil. Reduce the heat to medium-low and simmer, uncovered, for 40 minutes. Stir frequently. Set aside to cool, then store in sterilized glass jars.

Sour cherry jam can be stored in a cupboard for up to 2 months. Once opened, refrigerate and use within 1 week.

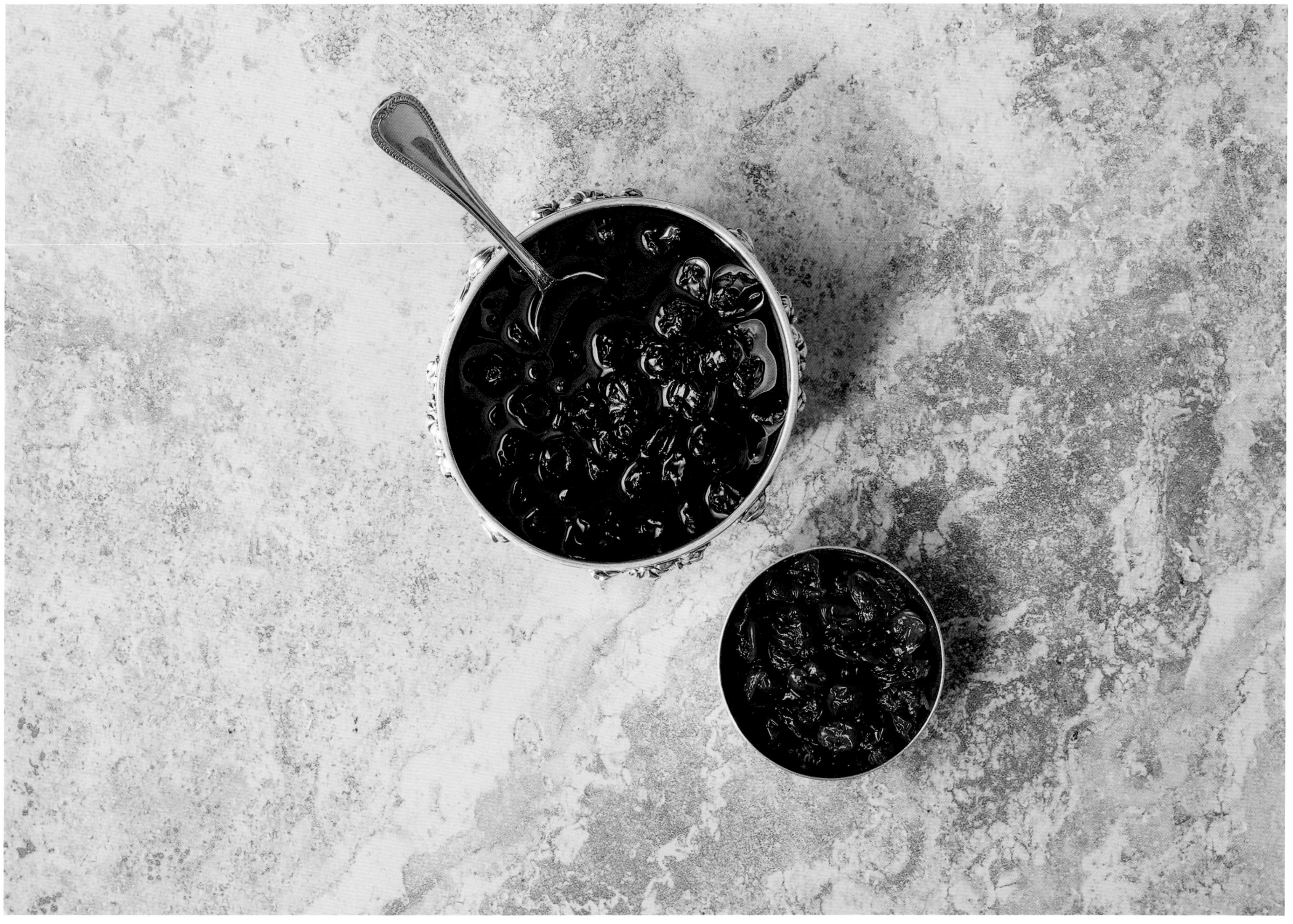

QUINCE JAM

Morabaye Beh + مربای به

Makes 5 × (8-oz/225-g) jars

Preparation time: 10 minutes

Cooking time: 1 hour 50 minutes

- 5 cups (2 lb 4 oz/1 kg) sugar
- 1 tablespoon citric acid
- 6 quinces, cored and sliced into 8 wedges
- Zest and juice of 1 lemon
- ¾ cup (3 oz/85 g) blackberries

Quince jam was Nahid Joon's signature jam. Once cooked, the white flesh of quince changes to a deep pink color with reddish hues. It also thickens naturally because it is so high in pectin.

This jam is delicious with bread and butter for breakfast, but it also makes a tasty accompaniment for lamb and duck dishes. It can also be served with cheeses for a touch of sweetness.

In a large saucepan, add the sugar, citric acid, and 3 cups (25 fl oz/750 ml) of water. Bring to a boil and reduce the heat to medium. Cook for 15 minutes, until the sugar has dissolved and the liquid is syrupy. Add the quinces and the lemon zest and juice. Increase the heat to medium-high and boil for 15–20 minutes, stirring occasionally to prevent the fruit from sticking to the bottom of the saucepan.

Reduce the heat to medium-low and add the blackberries. Cook for 1 hour 15 minutes, or until the quince turns red and the syrup thickens. Set aside to cool, then store in sterilized glass jars.

Quince jam can be stored in a cupboard for up to 1 month. Once opened, refrigerate and use within 1 week.

CITRUS MARMALADE

Marmalade Porteghal va Grapefruit + مارمالاد پرتقال و گریپ فروت

Makes 5 × (8-oz/225-g) jars

Preparation time: 30 minutes

Cooking time: 1 hour

- 12 large Navel oranges
- 6 large Ruby Red grapefruits
- 14 cups (6 lb/2.7 kg) superfine (caster) sugar
- Juice of 2 lemons
- 3 cups (15 oz/425 g) shredded carrots

I'm generally not a fan of orange marmalade, but I love this one so much that I make it all the time. Nahid Joon's secret was to add julienned carrots to balance out the acidity of the grapefruit and orange peels.

Wash the oranges and grapefruits, then pat dry with paper towels. Carefully peel the skins, then cut the peels into quarters. Using a peeler or a sharp knife, separate the peel from the pith. Slice the orange and grapefruit peels into ⅛-inch (3-mm) strips.

Bring a large saucepan of water to a boil. Add the orange and grapefruit strips and boil for 3 minutes. Remove from the heat and set aside to cool for 45 minutes. Drain, then reserve the peels for later. This process removes some of the bitterness from the peels.

Segment the citruses, then chop them and remove all the seeds. In a large saucepan, combine the citrus flesh, citrus peels, sugar, lemon juice, and 7 cups (1¾ quarts/1.7 L) of water. Bring to a boil and boil over medium heat for 30 minutes. Add the carrots and cook over medium heat for another 30 minutes, until thickened and syrupy. Remove from the heat.

Set aside to cool, then store in sterilized glass jars. Properly jarred marmalade can be stored in a cupboard for up to 1 year. Once opened, refrigerate and use within 1 year.

DRINKS AND DESSERTS

While desserts do not figure prominently in Iranian cuisine, there are some world-famous confections that are commonly served in Iranian homes. The most famous may be Persian *baghlava*, which are filled with almonds and pistachios and smaller and lighter than the Turkish or Arab varieties.

Iranian sweets and desserts often include ingredients such as cardamom, saffron, and rose water. The variety of desserts includes Cardamom & Rose Water Pudding (page 229), Saffron Rice Pudding (page 230), and Wheat Flour, Saffron & Carrot Halva (page 235). Typical homes almost always have a bowl of fresh fruit as a dessert, while sweet snacks, such as dried apricots, figs, peaches, and dates, crystallized sugar (*nabaats*), and small saffron-infused candies (*poolakis*) are often enjoyed with afternoon tea.

Our traditional ice cream—deep yellow and speckled with green pistachios—is entirely unique to Iran and will include rose water, saffron, and even morsels of frozen cream.

CUCUMBER & MINT SYRUP

Sharbat Sekanjebin + شربت سکنجبین

Makes 4 cups (32 fl oz/950 ml)

Preparation time: 10 minutes, plus overnight soaking

Cooking time: 30 minutes

- 2 cups (14 oz/400 g) sugar (see Note)
- ½ cup (4 fl oz/120 ml) white vinegar
- 1 cup (¼ oz/10 g) mint leaves, plus extra for garnish
- 3 Persian cucumbers, grated

It might seem impossible to surprise Nahid Joon in the kitchen, considering her wonderfully vast repertoire. One summer day while in graduate school, Tala Gharagozlou made this most refreshing drink. Tala's family were close friends of my family for four generations. Tala's grandmother, Mrs. Malek, was close to Nahid Joon. Her mom, Asiyeh, and her father, Hazi, are very close friends of mine. (I met my husband through Hazi.)

Tala dropped off a bottle of her homemade *sekanjebin* for Nahid Joon during a visit to New York. That evening, she received an excited call from Nahid asking if she had made the sharbat herself. Tala had unwittingly impressed her with a true Iranian classic.

In a medium saucepan, combine the sugar and 2 cups (16 fl oz/475 ml) of water and cook over low heat until the sugar has dissolved. Cook for another 10 minutes, then add the vinegar. Cook for another 10 minutes, or until syrupy. Remove from the heat. (The syrup will thicken further once cooled.)

In a bowl, combine the syrup and mint and refrigerate overnight.

The next day, drain the syrup and discard the mint. Transfer to a bottle.

To serve, pour the syrup into a glass, then top with ice cubes, cucumber, and water to taste. Stir and garnish with mint leaves. Serve.

Alternatively, serve the syrup as a dipping sauce alongside crisp lettuce leaves for a refreshing appetizer.

Note: You can replace the sugar with 1 cup (12 oz/350 g) of honey, if desired.

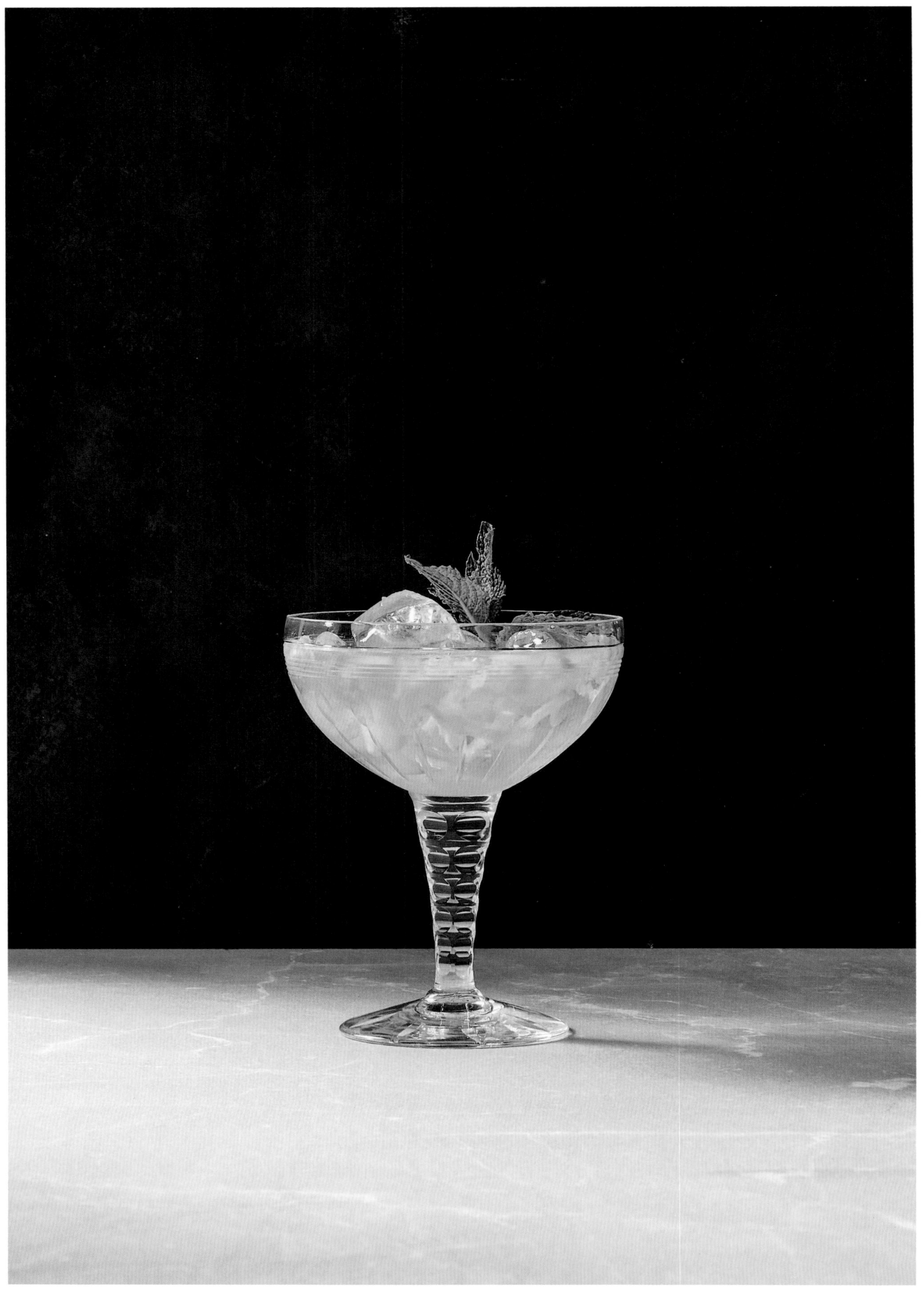

SOUR CHERRY DRINK

Sharbat Albaloo + شربت آلبالو

Serves 6

Preparation time:
5 minutes

Cooking time:
30 minutes

- 3 cups (1 lb 12 oz/800 g) sugar
- 2 cups (14 oz/400 g) sour cherries, stemmed and pitted
- 2 teaspoons lime juice
- 2 teaspoons rose water
- Carbonated water (optional)
- Mint sprigs, for garnish

When I think of hot summers in Iran, I remember this delicious summer drink known as *sharbat albaloo*. In Iran, we had several sour cherry trees in our garden and harvested the fruit for making jams and syrups. I loved the taste and the vibrant ruby red color of the sour cherries. We would mix the syrup with water or sparkling water and drink it with a sprig of mint.

In later years, I would mix the syrup with vodka or tequila and a dash of sparkling water. A true potion indeed.

In a medium saucepan, combine the sugar and 4 cups (32 fl oz/950 ml) of water. Bring to a boil. Lower the heat to a simmer. Add the lime juice and rose water and simmer for 20 minutes, or until thickened. Set aside to cool.

Strain the syrup into a bowl using a colander. (You can top yogurt or ice cream with the cherries.) Transfer the syrup into a jar or bottle using a funnel.

Mix 1 part syrup with 3 parts water or sparkling water and serve over ice. Garnish with mint leaves.

YOGURT DRINK WITH MINT

Doogh + دوغ

Serves 2

Preparation time: 5 minutes

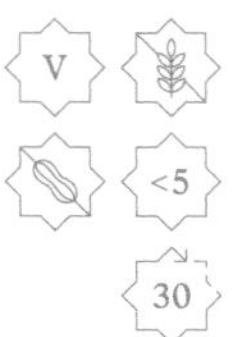

- 2½ cups (15 oz/425 g) Greek yogurt
- ½ teaspoon salt
- 2 sprigs mint, leaves picked and chopped, plus extra for garnish
- 2 cups (16 fl oz/475 ml) carbonated water
- ½ teaspoon dried rose petals, for garnish (optional)

Versions of this drink are known as *airan* in Turkey and *lassi* in India.

This carbonated drink is tangy, refreshing, and full of probiotics, making it the perfect accompaniment to balance out spicy kebabs or rice dishes. The creamier the yogurt, the more delicious the *doogh.*

Serve it plain or mixed with fresh or dried mint. Rose petals make for a beautiful garnish.

In a blender, combine the yogurt, salt, mint, and carbonated water and blend well. Add to a pitcher (jug) and serve over ice. Garnish with a sprig of mint and a few rose petals, if using.

CARAMELIZED PEARS WITH CARDAMOM

Serves 8

Preparation time: 10 minutes

Cooking time: 15 minutes

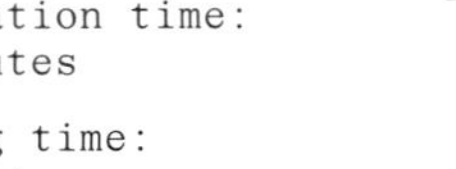

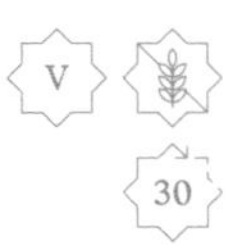

Golabi Caramely Shodeh ba Hel +
گلابی کاراملی شده با هل

- 8 semi-firm pears or peaches, cut in half and cored
- 2 tablespoons butter
- 2 tablespoons honey
- 1 tablespoon ground cardamom
- 1 cup (7 oz/200 g) crème fraîche
- 1 tablespoon cognac
- 1 tablespoon lemon juice
- 2 tablespoons slivered pistachios, for garnish

Growing up in Tehran, we had peach, pear, nectarine, apricot, persimmon, plum, cherry, mulberry, and apple trees in our garden. Depending on the season, Nahid Joon used any one of these fruits to make this dessert. This version was our favorite. The cardamom makes this simple dish so aromatic, flavorful, and special.

Place the pears, cut side down, in a deep skillet and cover with water. Bring to a boil, then add the butter, honey, and cardamom. Reduce the heat to medium-low and cook for 15 minutes, until the liquid has thickened into a heavy syrup. (Stir continuously to prevent the liquid from burning.) Remove from the heat.

In a separate bowl, combine the crème fraîche, cognac, and lemon juice.

Add a generous spoonful of the crème fraîche mixture to individual plates. Add 2 pear halves, then drizzle the sauce on top. Garnish with the pistachios.

POMEGRANATE JELLY

Jeleyeh Anar + ژله انار

Serves 4–6

Preparation time:
10 minutes, plus
4 hours to set

Cooking time:
10 minutes

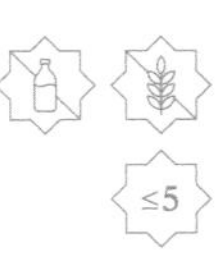

- 6 × (1-oz/25-g) packages unflavored gelatin
- 6 cups (47 fl oz/1.4 L) cold pomegranate juice (such as Pom)
- 1 tablespoon sugar
- 4 tablespoons pomegranates seeds, for garnish
- 1 tablespoon slivered pistachios (optional)

Pomegranates are a symbol of fertility, beauty, love, and vitality in Persian mythology. They appeared in abundance in Persian gardens, known as *pardis*, which is the root word of "paradise." In ancient times, pomegranates were regarded as a medicinal food that cured many digestive and skin disorders due to their high polyphenol levels. They are also an incredible antioxidant.

I loved making this light and refreshing dessert with Nahid Joon when I was growing up—it was so easy and fun to make. We couldn't wait for the pomegranates to ripen in our garden; we would pick them and roll them with our hand to release the juices. We then punctured the pomegranates and squeezed out the juice into a large bowl. Then, all that was left to do was mix the juice with plain gelatin and bring it to a boil with sugar.

In a bowl, whisk the gelatin with 1 cup (8 fl oz/250 ml) of pomegranate juice until combined.

In a saucepan, heat the remaining 5 cups (40 fl oz/1.2 L) of pomegranate juice over medium heat. Add the sugar and bring to a boil, stirring continuously. Slowly add the pomegranate juice–gelatin mixture and stir until the gelatin has completely dissolved. Pour the mixture into a large dish or ramekins. Chill for 4 hours, or until set.

Garnish with pomegranate seeds and pistachios, if using, then serve.

CARDAMOM & ROSE WATER PUDDING

Masghati + مسقطي

Serves 4–6

Preparation time:
5 minutes, plus
1 hour to set

Cooking time:
20 minutes

V

30

- 1 cup (4 oz/115 g) cornstarch (cornflour)
- 1½ cups (10½ oz/300 g) superfine (caster) sugar
- 1 tablespoon ground cardamom
- 2 cups (16 fl oz/475 ml) rose water
- ¾ cup (6 oz/180 g) butter
- ½ cup (2 oz/55 g) slivered almonds, for garnish
- ¾ cup (3 oz/90 g) slivered pistachios, for garnish
- Dried rose petals, for garnish

This refreshing summer dessert is very easy to make (and gluten-free). As a little girl, I would make my own little *masghati* next to my mom. It is light, fluffy, and fragrant with cardamom and rose water, and the slivered pistachios and almonds add textural crunch. The origins of this dessert are from Muscat in Oman, hence its name. The denser and sweeter Omani version is infused with more spices.

In a large nonstick saucepan, combine the cornstarch (cornflour) and 7 cups (1¾ quarts/1.7 L) of cold water and mix until the cornstarch has dissolved. Add the sugar, cardamom, and rose water and mix well over medium heat, until the sugar has dissolved.

Bring to a boil and boil for 20 minutes, stirring constantly, until the mixture is thick enough to coat the back of a spoon. Stir in the butter and slivered almonds, then turn the heat off. Continue to stir until the butter has melted completely.

Transfer the pudding to a large serving bowl or individual ones. Garnish with slivered pistachios and dried rose petals. Chill in the refrigerator for 1 hour, until cool and thick.

SAFFRON RICE PUDDING

Sholeh Zard + شله زرد

Serves 6–8

Preparation time:
20 minutes, plus
2–8 hours soaking

Cooking time:
1 hour 35 minutes

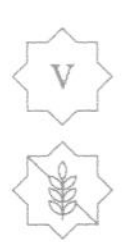

- 1 teaspoon saffron threads
- 2 cups (14 oz/400 g) basmati rice, soaked for 2–8 hours
- 1 teaspoon salt
- 2 cups (14 oz/400 g) sugar
- 4 tablespoons butter
- ½ teaspoon ground cardamom
- ¾ cup (6 fl oz/175 ml) rose water
- ½ cup (2 oz/55 g) slivered almonds, plus 4 tablespoons for garnish
- 4 teaspoons ground cinnamon, for sprinkling
- 4 tablespoons slivered pistachios, for garnish

This traditional dessert from the province of Kermanshah was commonly served during the winter solstice (page 19), the Persian New Year (Nowruz), weddings, and religious holidays.

This light, delicate rice pudding is infused with the fragrant flavors of saffron, rose water, and cardamom. It is often finished with a decorative pattern made from sprinkled cinnamon. Pistachios and rose petals add beautiful color to this delicious canvas.

During religious holidays, Nahid Joon would cook up a large batch over a huge wood fire in her garden and serve it to a hundred people. Friends, neighbors, and construction workers in the vicinity would show up with bowls to scoop out a serving. This dish can be served cold or warm.

In a small bowl, bloom the saffron in 4 tablespoons of hot water. Set aside.

Drain the rice, then rinse under cold running water until it runs clear. In a large saucepan, combine the rice, salt, and 4 quarts (3.8 L) of water. Bring to a boil, skimming the foam off the surface.

Reduce the heat to medium-low and cover. Simmer for 40 minutes, stirring occasionally with a wooden spoon. Add the sugar, butter, cardamom, and bloomed saffron water and stir to combine. Simmer and stir for another 10 minutes. Add the rose water and almonds. Reduce the heat to low and cover the saucepan. Cook for another 45 minutes, stirring occasionally, until the liquid is completely reduced. Remove the pan from the heat.

Ladle the pudding into a large dish or ramekins. Sprinkle cinnamon decoratively on top. Add the pistachios and almonds. Chill in the refrigerator until cooled.

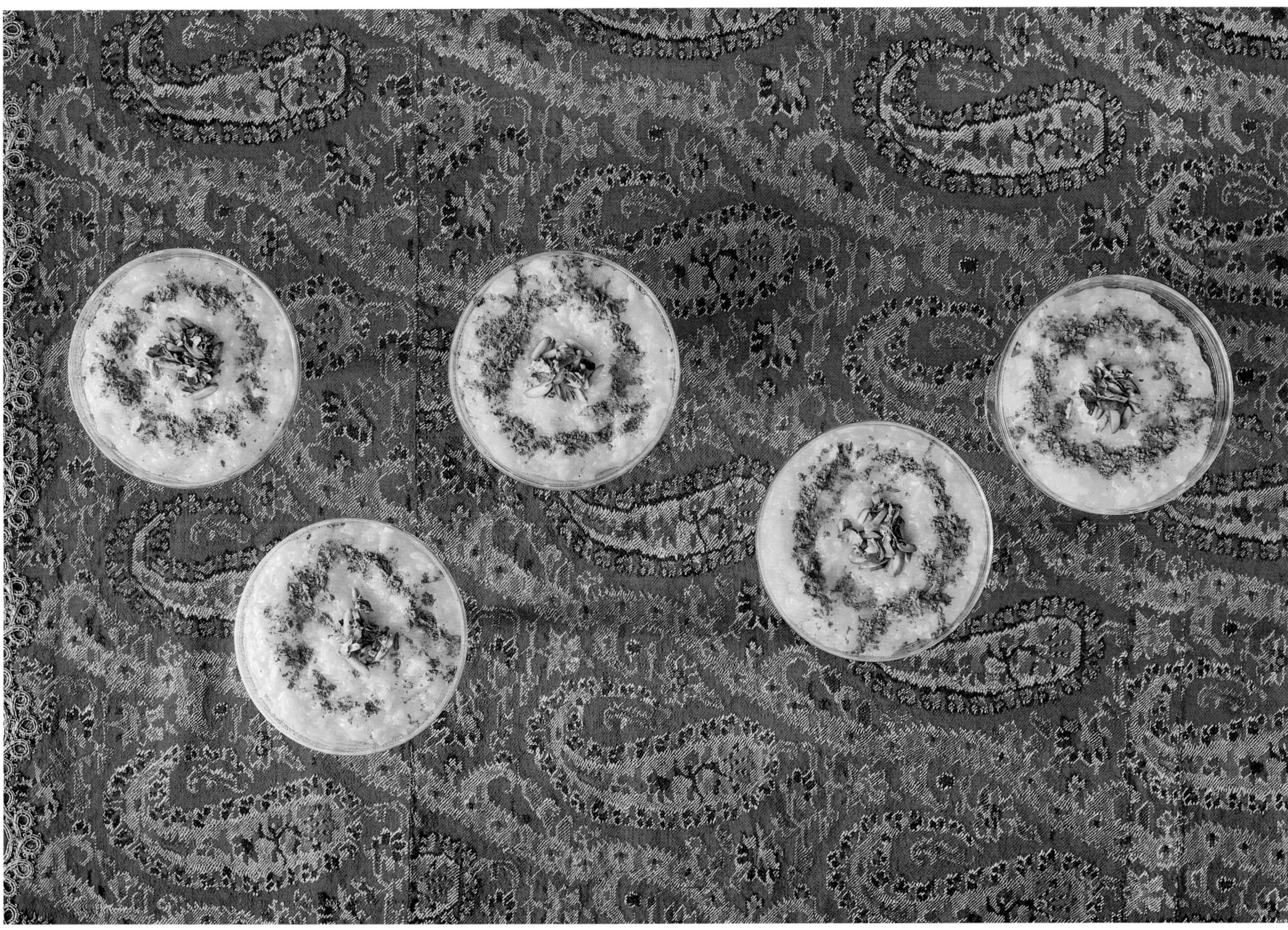

SAFFRON & ROSE WATER FRITTERS

Makes 30 fritters

Preparation time:
15 minutes, plus
2–4 hours to chill

Cooking time:
20 minutes

Zulbia + زولبيا

- ½ teaspoon ground saffron
- 1½ cups (7¼ oz/225 g) all-purpose (plain) flour
- ½ cup (2 oz/55 g) cornstarch (cornflour), plus extra if needed
- 3 × (¼-oz/7-g) packages active dry (fast-action) yeast
- ½ cup (3 oz/85 g) Greek yogurt
- 1 tablespoon rose water
- 2 cups (16 fl oz/475 ml) canola oil, plus extra if needed
- ¾ cup (3 oz/85 g) confectioners' (icing) sugar
- ½ cup (2 oz/55 g) ground pistachios

Growing up, we loved when my mom made this dessert. *Zulbia* is a delicious saffron and rose water fritter with a shape similar to that of a funnel cake. Traditionally, zulbia is soaked in syrup, but this version is much lighter, with only confectioners' (icing) sugar and pistachios on top.

Best eaten fresh out of the fryer, it is crunchy and melts in your mouth. It is an amazing experience.

In a small bowl, bloom the saffron in ½ cup (4 fl oz/120 ml) of hot water.

In the bowl of a stand mixer, combine the flour, cornstarch (cornflour), yeast, yogurt, rose water, bloomed saffron water, and 1½ cups (12 fl oz/350 ml) of warm water. Mix until the batter is smooth and thick like honey. If it's too thin, add more cornstarch. Cover the surface with plastic wrap (cling film) to prevent it from forming a skin. Place in the refrigerator for 2–4 hours.

Pour the batter into a squeeze bottle. Heat the oil in a large, deep saucepan over medium heat until very hot. Squeeze the batter into the oil in a 3-inch (7.5-cm) pretzel shape. (This takes some practice to get the shape right.) Add two more. Fry the fritters for 1 minute, until lightly golden. Gently turn the fritter over and fry for another 1 minute, until crispy and golden brown. Using a slotted spoon or spider, transfer the fritter to a paper towel–lined plate. Repeat with the remaining batter. (If the oil changes color, replace it.)

Arrange on a serving platter and dust with confectioners' (icing) sugar and ground pistachios. Serve warm.

CARROT & SAFFRON HALVA

Serves 10–12

Preparation time:
15 minutes, plus
2 hours to set

Cooking time:
30–40 minutes

Halva ba Zafaran va Havij +
حلوا با زعفران و هویج

- 1 tablespoon ground saffron
- 1 lb (450 g) baby carrots
- 3 cups (1 lb 1 oz/480 g) unbleached all-purpose (plain) flour
- 1 cup (5½ oz/160 g) whole wheat (wholemeal) flour
- 1 cup (8 fl oz/250 ml) extra-virgin olive oil
- 2½ cups (1 lb 4 oz/550 g) butter
- 2 cups (14 oz/400 g) superfine (caster) sugar
- ½ cup (4 fl oz/120 ml) rose water
- ½ cup (2 oz/55 g) skinless slivered pistachios

This Persian delicacy was created in the seventh century and originally made with milk and dates. As time passed, ground wheat and flour were added to the Persian recipe.

While Persians only prepare it with flour, other countries in the Middle East make both a flour-based and seed-based halva. (The Ottomans began preparing it with sesame, which is now prevalent in most Arab countries.)

Iranians commonly serve it at festivities, celebrations, and funerals. When my mother moved to New York, she would make a big platter of halva balls, decorated with slivered pistachios, to deliver to friends in mourning or for the birth of a baby.

In a small bowl, bloom the saffron in ½ cup (4 fl oz/120 ml) of hot water. Set aside.

Place the baby carrots in a medium saucepan and pour in just enough boiling water to cover them by ½ inch (1 cm). Reduce the heat to medium, then cover and simmer for 15–20 minutes, until soft. Drain, then rinse under cold running water. Transfer the cooked carrots to a food processor and purée until smooth. Set aside.

Sift the flours together into a large bowl.

Heat the oil and butter in a deep nonstick skillet over medium heat. Add the flours and stir continuously with a wooden spoon or spatula for 15–20 minutes, until the flour is fried and golden brown. Remove the saucepan from the heat. Stir in the carrot purée and mix until homogeneous.

In a separate medium saucepan, combine the sugar, rose water, bloomed saffron water, and ½ cup (4 fl oz/120 ml) of water. Bring to a boil, stirring continuously. Turn off the heat immediately.

Using a ladle, add the syrup to the carrot mixture, mixing well after each pour. (Be extra careful with the hot syrup—you may want to wear gloves.) Stir until it forms a thick, smooth paste. Hold both sides of the saucepan and rock the paste from side to side for a few minutes to make sure it is even.

Transfer the mixture to a baking sheet, then use a spoon to pack the halva down firmly. Using the side of spoon or fork, create a geometric pattern on the surface. Garnish with pistachios. Cut into small pieces or roll into ¾-inch (2-cm) balls, then place into candy wrappers or wax paper.

Refrigerate the halva for 2 hours, or until cooled. The halva can be stored for up to 1 week in the refrigerator.

ALMOND & PISTACHIO BRITTLE

Makes 30 pieces

Preparation time: 10 minutes

Cooking time: 5–10 minutes

Sohan Asal + سوهان عسل

- ½ teaspoon ground saffron
- 1 cup (7 oz/200 g) sugar
- 2 tablespoons honey
- 2 tablespoons rose water
- 3 tablespoons butter
- ¾ cup (3 oz/90 g) slivered almonds
- ½ cup (2 oz/55 g) slivered pistachios, plus extra for garnish
- Olive oil, for greasing

This crunchy, nutty Persian brittle is commonly served during celebrations, including weddings, Persian New Year (Nowruz), and Winter Solstice (Shab e Yalda) ceremonies. It originates from Isfahan, a region famed for its honey (*asal*).

Nahid Joon taught me to make this brittle when I was six years old. Her version had more slivered almonds and pistachios and less caramel brittle than traditional versions and was infused with saffron and rose water. Nahid Joon always served hers with a cup of Persian tea.

The brittle can be stored in an airtight container at room temperature will last for weeks.

In a small bowl, bloom saffron in 3 tablespoons of hot water. Set aside.

Line two large baking sheets with parchment paper.

Add the sugar to a large saucepan and stir over high heat for 1 minute. Add the honey and rose water and stir vigorously for 2–3 minutes, until golden brown. Stir in the butter, bloomed saffron water, almonds, and pistachios. Mix for another 1–2 minutes, until caramel brown in color and the temperature on a candy thermometer reaches 140°F/60°C.

With 2 oiled tablespoons, immediately scoop the mixture onto the prepared baking sheets. (It hardens quickly.) The candies should be 1½ inches (4 cm) in diameter. While still warm, garnish each with pistachio slivers. Allow to cool, then serve on a platter.

CULINARY DABBLES IN MODERN IRANIAN ART

Dr. Talinn Grigor

The vital role of feasting, hosting, and hospitality in Iran's long history revolved around the plentiful and colorful dining table. From the mighty Achaemenid king of kings in antiquities to the superpower that became the Safavid empire in the early modern period, Iranian global politics was decided around the rituals of food and eating, described as "the political utility of feasting" (Babaie, 224). In the turbulent nineteenth and twentieth centuries, this kind of "food art" came to signal wider political concerns such as fair rule, class struggle, and social justice. Or rather seemingly benign activism against autocratic regimes. The vast empires of the Achaemenids, Parthians, Sassanians, and Safavids—that, at their largest, stretched from the Indus River to the Nile Valley—founded and solidified a tradition of kingship that revolved around the notion of hospitality and gifting, for their own sake and as a strategy of statecraft. Unlike the neighboring Assyrian palaces of Nineveh and Nimrud with walls showcasing the king slaying lions and conquering cities, at Persepolis, the stone walls of Apadana narrate the story of hospitality and gifting. Darius I (r. 522–486 BCE) seated on his throne is receiving his audience who bring him the gastronomic riches from all over the then known world. The low reliefs at Apadana testify to the culinary assembling of the most diverse type on the royal table that remained a practicing tradition of statecraft until modern times. The five-hour dinner feast hosted by Mohammad Reza Shah (r. 1941–79) in October 1971 was recorded by the *Guinness Book of World Records* at the time as the longest and the most lavish dinner party in recent history. The Persian king's gift to his subjects—and the world—was, in return, *Pax Iranica*, which then enabled the making of more art and the cooking of more dishes.

The Perso-Muslim empires that ruled the Iranian Plateau after the Battle of Nahavand in 642, appropriated and transformed the Sassanian court's sophisticated artistic and culinary traditions to maintain the unity of vast and diverse territories, cultures, and peoples under the auspices of a single kingship. Food and art both unified the empire and demarcated the religious boundaries within that empire. "From daily consumption to kingly feasts to artistic representations, feasting and wine became established in the Sasanian period" (Daryaee, 239). Around the royal table, political harmony was secured for a diverse social fabric. By the time Shah Abbas I (r. 1588–1629) sat on the throne—one of the three superpowers of the early modern world—the Perso-Shi'a rituals of eating and diplomacy were honed to perfection in "a particular type of ceremonial space, the *talar* palaces" (Babaie, 225). Here, placed under the vaulted hall, decorated floor-to-ceiling by delicate mirrorwork, the king, his large entourage, his foreign guests, and diplomates consumed food and architecture as an elaborate process of international relations. The Achaemenid kingly tradition of hospitality, of food- and gift-exchange, reached a new level of artistic grace under the Safavids. The splendid architecture of the places of Chehel Sotun (Isfahan,

1647) and later Golestan (Tehran, 19th century) were creative outcomes of the monarchical institution of eating-as-statecraft, as "feasting provided the proper ceremonial format for the receipt of diplomatic missions and for the conduct of imperial affairs" (Babaie, 226).

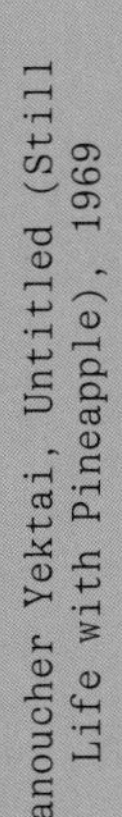

Manoucher Yektai, Untitled (Still Life with Pineapple), 1969

In the story of Iran, the fine arts and fine eating often cross-pollinated and remained, at its most historically visible, in the service of the centralized and absolutist court. The aristocracy was the patron and consumer of both. Certainly, craftsmen and artists expressed the significance of food in Iranian power and identity politics. Throughout the centuries, the king's table was itself a work of art: meticulously orchestrated, colorful, and color-coded, lavish, exclusive, and expensive. As an artwork, it was used as a diplomatic tool, meant to impress, persuade, manipulate, and coerce. Like an art exhibition and unlike later European culinary aesthetics, the different pieces of Iranian dishes were displaced on the table "at once" (Chehabi 2003, 47)—as a grand painterly tableau. The histories of Iranian art and architecture are peppered with culinary references that hint at the nuanced sociopolitical realities of Iranian life. Achaemenid craftsmen lavished the walls of Persepolis with polished low reliefs of dignitaries bearing food and livestock to the king, representing the global power of the emperor who blessed the world with peace and plenty. Sassanian silversmiths produced some of the most outstanding examples of medieval silverware that sat on the royal table and were dispatched to rival rulers as a form of diplomacy. The Safavids painted their palaces with murals of feasts, felicity, and the royal *sofreh*. Iran's rich history of kingship as a foundational institution that organizes society and dictates taste bestowed food a special significance; both the Zoroastrian Achaemenid and Sassanian royal rituals of hosting and hospitality as well as the Islamic "pious act of feeding the poor" (Shirazi, 294) were crucial to the role of both food and art in the modernization of Iranian society.

The Qajar reign (1789–1925) that straddled the most turbulent period of Iran's postcolonial history saw rapid transformations in both eating habits and artistic practices. From the late Qajar until World War II, Iranian cuisine and culinary etiquette ran its course of modernization emblematic of the postcolonial geographies, including among others the introduction of tea, table, and cutlery (Matthee, Shirazi, and Chehabi), under the larger umbrella of "progress." Both the fine arts and fine cuisine became visual tropes of unfolding modernity. The fork and the camera revolutionized the Qajar lifestyle: the young Nasseredin Shah (r. 1848–96) was the first to have taken up both. His court photographer, Antoin Sevruguin, was a pioneer in documenting this transformative every day, where so much of food-making, food-selling, and food consumption happened in the public domain. It is through his skilled photographic eye that we witness the varied culinary practices of a multitiered and complex society; from the sumptuous and meticulously choreographed table of the king to the play of children around a sherbet seller in the dusty Drill Square of Tehran. Sevruguin was also a keen observer of people's lives in their domestic settings: how Kurdish women carried water in large jugs; how Zoroastrian men in Yazd sat around a *sofreh*, set with melons, dates, pomegranates, sweets, pistachios, and a *samovar*; how two Shahsavan tribesmen sell spices while others sell *sangak bread* and *kebab* in the action-packed bazaar (Vorderstrasse 204, 226, 232, 246).

Unknown Artist, Qajar Still Life

Beyond the streets and bazaars and among elite circles, the 1911 opening of a new art academy in Tehran, led by Kamal-al-Molk, trained Iranian art students in "late-nineteenth-century French Academic and Orientalist traditions" (Diba, 48). While others, including Abbas Rassam Arzhangi, returned from abroad to further contribute to this new artistic environment, which engaged food and foodstuffs from the lens of Western canonical painterly tradition: the genre of still-life painting. However, the most underappreciated yet exquisite works of art in the last decade of the Qajar rule and the early period of Reza Shah Pahlavi (r. 1925–41)'s rule were the coffee house paintings. They were unique in that they were enjoyed daily by a wide array of public audiences in the context of food-making and food consumption. By the Constitutional Revolution of 1905, coffee houses—which served tea, not coffee—had become dynamic spaces of political deliberation and intellectual exchange. For marginalized painters and craftsmen whose craft had been replaced by the arrival of European techniques and media as well as the elite taste for these new artworks, coffee houses were not only “centers of artistic debates” (Fays, 8), but also rare public venues which enabled the production, display, and performance of “coffee house” paintings.

Farideh Lashai, Keep Your Interior Empty of Food That You Mayest Behold There in the Light of Interior, 2010

While not focused on the subject matter of feasting or food, with rare exceptions, these paintings were enjoyed by the non-elite classes *while* consuming food. The paintings were usually made with oil on large, movable canvases, contingent on the occasion. Subject matters generally fell into several thematic categories, including the Battle of Karbala (10 October 680), the legends from Ferdowsi’s *Shahnameh* (ca. 977–1010), biblical stories, and scenes from major events in Iran’s recent history. From the extant canvases held at the Reza Abbasi Museum in Tehran, most of which are undated but signed, we can deduce that the sizes varied from as small as 14 inches (35 cm) to as large as 155 inches (4 meters) and the dates ranged from 1909 to 1959. Hossein Qollar-Aqasi and Mohammad Modabber were among the notable “coffee house” artists who died destitute, awaiting art-historical recognition in the 1990s (Fays, 9). During the postwar years, coffee houses were replaced with European-style cafés (Café Firuz, Naderi, Shemiran, and later Chattanooga, Brazilo, and Rivera), restaurants (Palace Hotel, Armenian Club), bars (Bar-e Sepand), and cabarets with live band music (Cabaret Shokufe-ye No, Cabaret Copacabana). In the documentary *The Eye That Hears*, which aired on Iranian National Television in 1974, Bahman Mohassess was shown ardently debating the role of modern art, as well as the unbound surrealist artist in one of these modern cafés. These novel ways of eating and being, impacted the artists’ very engagement with the public and with the metaphor of food itself.

In the aftermath of the coup d’état of 1953, transformation to Iranian culinary culture became even more rapid and radical. “Everything changed,” recently remembered an eyewitness, “the day that Johnnie Walker knocked on our door.” Reacting to these global changes, artists appropriated images of food in their modernist paintings and sculptures to comment on class struggle and social injustice. The more artists were pressured, the more they used local symbols, including culinary images, to voice censure. Some were detached, using fruits and vegetables as abstract allegories, such as Bahman Mohassess' *Untitled* (1969), Vahed Khakdan's *Untitled* (1977), Manuchehr Yektai's *Still Life with Pineapple* (1969), and *Still Life* (1975). Others were poignant. Ahmad Aali's 1964 *Self-portrait* depicted a teapot on kerosene, joined to the artist's mouth (Daftari/Diba, 105). The message—"we are suffocating"—was domestic and culinary, from the home to the nation's lungs. Ardeshir Mohassess' satirical drawing, *Religious Prohibition of the Caviar Fish* (1972), was a morbid social critique of corruption and prohibition, which hinted at how a fish rots from the head down; a food metaphor reused decades later by Siamak Filizadeh in his *Shah and the Russian Ambassador* (2014) (Komaroff 174, 94, and Chehabi 2007).

Marcos Grigorian Abgusht Dizi (Iranian Lunch), executed in 1971 signed and dated "Grigorian 1971"

Marcos Grigorian's interventions into modernism incorporated the very material of food—bread, sugar, ceramic—to replace the traditional medium of paint as a modernist statement. Although he insisted on a cosmopolitan worldview, his *Abgusht Dizi* (1971), *Four Sangak Bread* (1976), and *Dizi Abgusht* (1979) were among the most expressive commentaries on the palpably widening material and cultural gap between the haves and the have-nots throughout the 1970s. He deployed the iconography of the abgusht dizi—a soupy stew made of lamb, chickpeas, white beans, onion, potatoes, tomatoes, turmeric, and dried lime—associated with the working class.

"When I was growing up," remembers another eyewitness, "outside food had class implications." Dizi was a working-class food that was served in coffee houses, while chelow kebab was for the upper classes, served in special *chelow kebabi* restaurants. Grigorian's dizi-assemblage-as-art—in contrast to the Parisian plates and palates of the court and the elite—spoke to the fallacy of high art and how it was adopted by the Pahlavi state as a civilizational trope. The exclusive but well-publicized feast at Persepolis in October 1971 was a case in point. Both the aesthetics of dining and high art were embraced to confirm the already fulfilled promise of progress and modernity.

Similarly, Abbas's photograph, *Car Assembly Plant* (1977) revealed the coming of a revolution, where the lonely elderly worker is not eating an abgusht, but bread, cheese, and cucumber (Gumpert/Balaghi, 105). The Iranian Revolution of 1977–79, shadowed by the establishment of the Islamic Republic in 1980, shifted the meaning of art, its subject matters, and its socio-political purpose. During the brutal Iran-Iraq War (1980–88), the shortage of foods mirrored the unavailability of art supplies—as well as the prohibition on sculptural and figurative works. First, under President Rafsanjani and then during President Khatami's relatively liberal and pro-art policies, there was an expansion of art education, the creation of vibrant artistic circles, and eventually the globalization of the Iranian art market. This period (1988–2005) also witnessed an end to the food embargo, the appearance of fast food, and the opening of restaurants. While most artists stayed away from food-related subject matters as they favored calligraphic art, abstract art, conceptual art, feminist art, figurative art, photocollage and photographic art, martyrdom and war art, a few artists returned to the symbolism of Iranian food and cuisine.

The photographic works of Shadi Ghadirian implanted culinary and domestic items—Pepsi can (*Qajar* series, 1998–99), teapot, teacup, pot, ladle, butcher knife, and saucer (*Like Every Day* series, 2001–2)—on veiled figures as an observation on women's role in contemporary Iranian society, defined by their metaphoric place (back) into the kitchen. Farideh Lashai's *Keep Your Interior Empty of Food* (2010) deployed Safavid-Qajar imagery of the kingly *sofreh* around which are now seated the *ulama*, the work itself conjuring up Judy Chicago's *Dinner Party* (1979). While in Hossein Khosrojerdi's *The Gap* (1993), a red apple symbolized an offering among a drifting couple, it reappeared in Ali Akbar Sadeghi's *Coalitions* series (2001) as a Surrealist trope. Mir Hossein Musavi (*Untitled*, 2005) used the yellow apple decoratively. For female artists like Azadeh Kia (Life, 2014) and Minu Asadi, the apple and the pomegranate seemed to be life-affirming symbols. For Mojtaba Tajik (Untitled, 2013), the fruits and vegetables hanging over a bowl, cynically fall short of their promise. While in the 2000s, Tehran had become "largely a gastronomical wasteland" (Chehabi, 2003, 48), it flourished as a global center of contemporary art production, exhibition, and consumption. The contemporary Iranian art market has since grown, monopolized by auctions houses that opened in the Gulf states to export Iranian art. Likewise, Iranian cuisine—from cheko-kebab to the simple assemblage of bread, cheese, and greens (*nan panir sabzi*)—remains one of the richest, most diverse, and refined traditions in our global and fusion-crazed world.

—Dr. Talinn Grigor, professor of art history in the Department of Art and Art History at the University of California, Davis

APPENDICES

This section features tips, tricks, and secrets to Nahid Joon's beautiful cooking. Every Persian cook should have (and probably will have) these essential spice blends, pantry essentials, and techniques in their repertoire.

The blend of spices is what makes our distinguished cuisine so exquisite, aromatic, and unique. Nahid Joon ground and mixed her own spices and had her own recipe for her Persian Spice Blend (page 246), which was key to many of her delicious and aromatic recipes.

Rice is a staple of Persian cuisine and eaten alongside many dishes. Most recipes are served or prepared with plain steamed rice (*chelow*), where rice is parboiled, drained, and then steamed. In the process, the grains become long and fluffy. *Polos* are rice dishes that include other ingredients—like pilafs. You may wish to experiment preparing rice in a variety of ways, but a common outcome from all of these methods is the *tahdig* (literally meaning "bottom of the pot"). This delicious crispy crust is usually infused with saffron and butter, giving it a vibrant color with the most delicious crunch. This is the tastiest part and one everyone always fights for!

If I were to recommend one cookware as an investment, it would be the electric rice cooker (*polo paz*), ubiquitous in every Persian household. Not to be mistaken for Japanese or Chinese rice cookers, a polo paz can be purchased in any Middle Eastern shop. It will make cooking rice and rice dishes much easier, and creating the perfect, cake-like beauty of tahdig a breeze.

STAPLE RECIPES

PERSIAN SPICE BLEND
ADVIEH ÷ ادویه

I have never tasted other mixtures readily available that have even come close to the sensuous and captivating taste of Nahid Joon's spice mixture. When my children were young, the minute the elevator would open to her floor they would run and say, "Nana has cooked with her magic spices!"

The key to this recipe is to use the best-quality rose petals and spices from India or the Middle East. Nahid Joon only used spices from *Sahadi*, a grocery store in Brooklyn, or Kalustyan's, a specialty shop in Manhattan.

Makes 11½ cups (30 oz/850 g)
Preparation time: 30 minutes

- 3 cups (14 oz/400 g) ground cumin (preferably black Persian cumin)
- 2 cups (9½ oz/265 g) ground cinnamon
- 2 cups (1 oz/30 g) dried rose petals, coarsely ground in the food processor
- 4 cups (2 oz/55 g) dried rose petals, finely ground in the food processor
- ⅓ cup (1½ oz/45 g) madras curry powder
- 4 tablespoons ground turmeric
- 1 tablespoon ground cardamom
- 1 tablespoon ground nutmeg

Mix all the ingredients in a large bowl. Transfer to a glass jar and close tightly to store and preserve freshness. The spice blend will keep for up to 1 year.

BLANCHED ORANGE PEELS
KHALAL PORTEGHAL ÷ خلال پرتقال

Orange rind preparation is something Nahid Joon perfected and used in many of her recipes. The key is to remove the bitterness from the peel. Prepare a large batch and freeze it for future use.

Makes 1 cup (3 oz/85 g)
Preparation time: 20 minutes
Cooking time: 1 hour

- 2 large oranges, washed

Using a peeler or knife, peel the skin, leaving a little pith on it. (Orange pith tends to be chewy and tasteless and adds texture to your rinds.) Cut the peel into thin slivers, about 1 inch (2.5 cm) in length.

Place the slivers in a saucepan and add 5 cups (40 fl oz/1.2 L) of water to cover them. Bring the water to a boil and cook, uncovered, for 15 minutes. Drain, then rinse immediately under cold running water. Add the orange peels back to the pan with another 5 cups (40 fl oz/1.2 L) of water. Bring to a boil, then reduce the heat to medium. Simmer, uncovered, for another 40 minutes. Drain, then rinse the peels under cold running water. Pat dry with paper towels and use immediately. Alternatively, store the peel flat in a freezer bag in the freezer for up to 3 months.

GOLDEN FRIED ONIONS
PIAZ DAGH ÷ پیازداغ

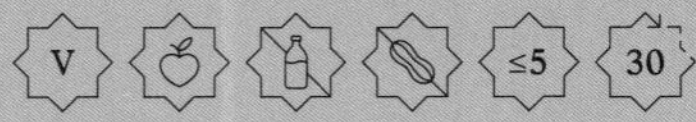

Piaz dagh is an absolute must in Persian cuisine. The natural sugars in the onions are concentrated and take on a glorious sweetness for adding copious flavor to dishes. We always add turmeric to infuse color, enhance flavor, and introduce health benefits. Nahid Joon used more onions than most Persian cooks and she would always say, *ziyad beriz*, meaning "add in abundance" in Farsi.

Makes 1 cup (3½ oz/100 g)
Preparation time: 5 minutes
Cooking time: 25 minutes

- 1 teaspoon extra-virgin olive oil, avocado oil, butter, or ghee (clarified butter)
- 1 onion, thinly sliced or diced
- ¼ teaspoon ground turmeric
- Pinch of salt

Heat the oil in a heavy medium saucepan over high heat. Add the onions and sauté for 5 minutes, until the moisture has evaporated and the onions are softened. Reduce the heat to low and sauté for another 20 minutes, constantly stirring, until golden brown and crispy. Turn off the heat, add the turmeric and salt, and stir for 1 minute.

Transfer the fried onions into a colander set over a plate to drain the excess oil. Cool the onions entirely, then store them in a freezer bag. Using your hands, flatten the bag to a ¾-inch (2-cm) thickness. Remove a portion as needed for your recipe. They can be stored in the freezer for up to 5 months. Remove a portion as needed for your recipe.

Note: You can make larger batches. Multiple the quantities accordingly.

✺

KATEH RICE (WITH A RICE COOKER)
KATEH ⁜ کته - تهیه در پلوپز

Kateh, which originates from the province of Gilan, is a quick and easy way of making Persian rice. It has a sticky, compact consistency, but you can still achieve the crispy *tahdig* at the bottom of the pot. Kateh is mostly served at intimate family gatherings, rather than at elaborate dinner parties and feasts where one opts for the sumptuous chelow or luxurious polo.

There is also a recipe for preparing the rice in a nonstick pot (see *right*).

Serves 6–8
Preparation time: 10 minutes
Cooking time: 1 hour 15 minutes

- 4 cups (1 lb 12 oz/800 g) basmati rice, well rinsed
- ½ cup (3 oz/85 g) Greek yogurt
- 1 tablespoon salt
- ½ cup (4 oz/115 g) melted butter
- 4 tablespoons extra-virgin olive oil

Place the rice in a large container and cover with 2½ quarts (2.3 L) of cold water. Gently stir the rice using your hands to remove the starch. Drain and repeat this process four times, or until the water is completely clear. Place the rice in the rice cooker.

In a bowl, combine the yogurt and 5 cups (40 fl oz/1.2 L) of water and mix well. Add the diluted yogurt, salt, butter, and oil to the rice and stir gently. Place the lid and turn on the rice cooker. Cook the rice for 45 minutes, stirring gently once or twice while it still has liquid.

Remove the rice cooker lid. Place a clean dish towel over the pot to cover, then place the lid on top. If the dish towel is long, wrap it over the lid to prevent it from dangling. (This prevents steam from escaping.) Cook for another 30 minutes, until cooked.

✺

KATEH RICE (IN A POT)
KATEH ⁜ کته - تهیه در دیگ

Serves 6–8
Preparation time: 10 minutes
Cooking time: 1 hour

- 4 cups (1 lb 12 oz/800 g) basmati rice, well rinsed
- 1 cup (6 oz/180 g) Greek yogurt
- 1 tablespoon salt
- ¾ cup (6 oz/180 g) butter
- 4 tablespoons extra-virgin olive oil

Place the rice in a large container and cover with 2½ quarts (2.3 L) of cold water. Gently stir the rice using your hands to remove the starch. Drain and repeat this process four times, or until the water is completely clear.

In a separate bowl, combine the yogurt and 5¼ cups (42 fl oz/1.25 L) of water and mix well. In a nonstick saucepan, combine the drained rice, diluted yogurt, salt, butter, and oil. Mix gently with a spatula, taking care not to break the rice grains. Bring to a boil over high heat and boil for 8 minutes. Reduce the heat to medium and simmer uncovered for 20–25 minutes, gently stirring once or twice to fluff up the rice, until all the liquid is absorbed and the tips of the rice are visible.

Gently make 4–5 holes in the rice with the handle of a wooden spatula to release the steam. Place a clean dish towel over the pot to cover, then place a lid on top. If the dish towel is long, wrap it over the lid to prevent it from dangling. (This prevents steam from escaping.) Cook the rice for another 40 minutes on low heat, until it forms a golden crust known as *tahdig*.

To serve, place a round serving platter over the pot. Carefully invert the pot of rice onto the platter. The rice will be in the shape of a cake, with the tahdig on top.

✳

CHELOW
CHELOW ÷ چلو

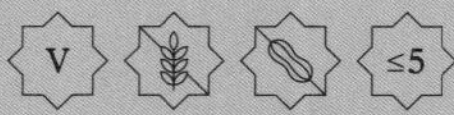

This humble national dish is the ultimate way to prepare Persian rice—and a labor of love. The best rice for chelow is extra-long-grain basmati rice (*dom siah*), regarded as the best Iranian-grown basmati rice and grown in the Caspian Sea region.

The rice is rinsed, then soaked in water and salt and parboiled. It is then mixed with butter and bloomed saffron water in a pot and cooked until silky and fluffy. Chelow is served with grilled meat, stews, and braises.

Serves 6–8
Preparation time: 10 minutes, plus at least 2 hours of soaking
Cooking time: 1 hour 10 minutes

- 4 cups (1 lb 12 oz/800 g) basmati rice
- 1 cup (8 oz/225 g) salt
- ¾ cup (6 fl oz/175 ml) and 1 tablespoon extra-virgin olive oil
- ½ cup (4 oz/115 g) melted butter

Place the rice in a large container and cover with 2½ quarts (2.3 L) of cold water. Gently stir the rice using your hands to remove the starch. Drain and repeat this process four times, or until the water is completely clear.

Add enough cold water to cover the rice by 1½ inches (4 cm). Add the salt and gently stir. Set aside for 2 hours or up to 24 hours. Drain.

Bring 4½ quarts (4.25 L) of water to a boil in a large nonstick saucepan. Gently add the rice and 1 tablespoon of oil to the boiling water. Boil over high heat for 6–8 minutes. The rice should be soft on the outside but firm in the center (al dente). Drain the rice in a large fine-mesh sieve and rinse under cold running water. Shake until drained, then set aside to cool.

Place the remaining ¾ cup (6 fl oz/175 ml) of oil in a large nonstick saucepan. Using a slotted spatula, start adding the rice to the pan, forming a pyramid shape. Cover and cook for 10 minutes over medium heat. Pour the melted butter on top.

Gently make 4–5 holes in the rice with the handle of a wooden spatula to release the steam. Place a clean dish towel over the pot to cover, then place a lid on top. If the dish towel is long, wrap it over the lid to prevent it from dangling. (This prevents steam from escaping.) Cook for 45–50 minutes over low heat.

To serve, transfer the rice to a serving platter, gently scooping a spatula full of rice at a time until all the rice is out of the saucepan. Using a wooden spoon, detach the rice crust (*tahdig*) from the bottom of the saucepan. Using your hands, break apart the rice crust. (Alternatively, you can cut it with scissors or a knife.) Place the crust pieces in a separate serving platter or around the rice.

✳

BONE BROTH
AB GHALAM OSTEKHAN ÷ آب قلم استخوان

Full of flavor and deeply nourishing, bone broth (or stock) made from chicken, meat, or fish bones is used across cultures to remedy minor ailments. In the tenth century, the Persian physician Avicenna referenced the healing powers of chicken soup.

Simple to make, this powerful and soothing elixir has an exquisite umami taste and provides the body with myriad health benefits. Bonus: it's also a hyaluronic acid, which is helpful in retaining moisture for connective tissues, joints, and skin health.

Note: Any of the fresh herbs can be replaced with 1 tablespoon of dried herbs.

Makes 3 quarts (2.8 L)
Preparation time: 20 minutes
Cooking time: 7¾–10 hours

- 2 tablespoons extra-virgin olive oil
- 5 lb (2.25 kg) beef bone marrow
- 8 chicken thighs
- 5 stalks celery, coarsely chopped
- 3 leeks, coarsely chopped

- 2 large carrots, coarsely chopped
- 1 large onion, coarsely chopped
- 1 cup (2 oz/55 g) coarsely chopped cilantro (coriander)
- 1 cup (4 oz/115 g) coarsely chopped chives
- 1 cup (2 oz/55 g) coarsely chopped parsley
- ½ cup (1½ oz/40 g) chopped rosemary
- ½ cup (1½ oz/40 g) coarsely chopped thyme
- ½ cup (1½ oz/40 g) coarsely chopped sage
- Salt and black pepper, to taste
- 4 cloves garlic, finely chopped
- 4 tablespoons finely chopped ginger
- 1 teaspoon coriander seeds, crushed
- 2 tablespoons apple cider vinegar (see Note)

Heat the oil in large stockpot over medium-high heat. Add the bone marrow and cook for 10 minutes, until golden brown. Transfer the marrow to a plate and set aside.

In the same pot, brown the chicken over medium-high heat for 5 minutes. Flip, then brown for another 5 minutes, until golden. Transfer to a plate and set aside.

Add the celery, leeks, carrots, and onion to the same pot. Sauté over medium-high heat for 15 minutes, until soft and browned. Add the chicken, herbs, and salt and pepper. Mix well, then cook over medium heat for 10 minutes.

Add the marrow bone and 4 cups (32 fl oz/ 950 ml) of water. (The water should cover the bones.) Bring to a boil over high heat, then reduce the heat to medium-low. Partially cover and simmer for 7–10 hours. If needed, top up with enough water to just cover the bones. Occasionally, skim the surface of the stock with a slotted spoon to remove the foam. (Take care not to disturb the ingredients at the bottom of the pot.)

Transfer the marrow to a cutting board and set aside to cool slightly. Scoop out the marrow from the bone.

Strain the broth through a fine-mesh sieve and discard the solids. Pour the broth into a blender and blend with the bone marrow. Set aside to cool.

Skim off any congealed fat from the surface. Pour the broth into jars and store in the refrigerator for up to 5 days or for up to 1 month in the freezer.

Notes: An acidic ingredient like apple cider vinegar helps break down the connective tissue and collagen to produce a gelatinous, protein-rich stock. Simmering your stock for too long may cause the gelatin to break down and release histamines to which some people experience sensitivity. A long cooking time also causes the fat in the bone stock to become rancid. You'll still get plenty of protein and loads of flavors with a shorter simmer.

MENUS

Feasting, banqueting, and gracious hospitality are major parts of Persian culture—and were integral elements of Nahid Joon's elaborate entertaining. This was especially the case during Persian holidays, when Nahid Joon would prepare lavish meals with a unique menu for each occasion. Here are some examples of menus she would often use.

PERSIAN NEW YEAR
NOWRUZ

Herb Platter (page 24)
Yogurt & Beets (page 41)
Herb Frittata (page 50)
Whole Roasted Fish with Herbs (page 120)
Rice with Fresh Herbs (page 180)
Eggplant Chutney (page 206)
Cardamom & Rose Water Pudding (page 229)

PERSIAN NEW YEAR PICNIC
SIZDAH BEDAR

Herb Platter (page 24)
Beef Patties (page 59)
Persian Chicken Salad (page 35)
Smoked Eggplant with Tomato (page 42)
Cucumber-Herb Yogurt (page 38)
Stuffed Grape Leaves (page 47)
Shirazi Salad (page 26)
Saffron & Rose Water Fritters (page 232)

SUMMER FESTIVAL
TIRGAN

Herb Platter (page 24)
Beef Patties with Tomato Sauce (page 60)
Rice with Sour Cherries (page 178)
Braised Turmeric Chicken (page 98)
Caramelized Pears with Cardamom (page 224)

FALL FESTIVAL APPETIZERS
MEHREGAN

Herb Platter (page 24)
Pomegranate & Herb Potage (page 78)
Stuffed Eggplants (page 48)
Braised Lamb Shanks (page 169)
Rice with Fava Beans & Dill (page 177)
Cilantro Chutney (page 209)
Pomegranate Jelly (page 226)

THANKSGIVING

Roasted turkey with herb butter
Persian Noodle Rice (page 190)
Chestnut stuffing
Mashed potatoes
Celery Root, Leek & Fennel Purée (page 44)
Cranberry sauce
Mango Chutney (page 204)
Pomegranate Jelly (page 226)
Your favorite Thanksgiving pies

WINTER FESTIVAL
YALDA

Herb Platter (page 24)
Herb Potage (page 72)
Leg of Lamb (page 114)
Rice with Lentils (page 189)
Eggplant Chutney (page 206)
Mango Chutney (page 204)
Saffron Rice Pudding (page 230)

THANKSGIVING

My younger son, Philip, would wake up early every Thanksgiving Day to go to Nahid Joon's and help her with the preparations. He has done this since he was five. Philip Salar and Nahid Joon shared the ultimate love of Thanksgiving and prepared elaborate meals together. Thanks to Nahid Joon, Philip is a fantastic cook with a curiosity to try different cuisines and recipes. He wrote this as a tribute to their favorite menu:

Nahid treasured Thanksgiving as much as her beloved Nowruz, and she used it to bring family and friends together in her home for a night of celebration. Like every part of her life, she put her twist on the celebration, with guests dubbing it the "famous Persian Thanksgiving."

Preparations for Persian Thanksgiving began a month in advance, with the special order of a 28-lb (12.5-kg) turkey. Organization of the fifteen to twenty dishes commenced at least a week before the feast—no small feat. On Thanksgiving Day, the kitchen would be filled with the perplexing yet tantalizing aromas of roasted turkey and Persian rices steaming in their pots.

At the start of the night, guests would fill the room and enjoy hors d'oeuvres such as foie gras, smoked salmon, and Persian cucumbers with dips. After an hour of mingling, guests would take their seats. A traditional American pumpkin soup was served in bowls in the shape of pomegranates, a subtle homage to Persia and the dishes to come. While guests enjoyed warm soup, the buffet table began to fill with a seemingly continuous delivery of dishes.

Thus began the main event, with the size of the buffet table the only thing preventing Nahid from adding more dishes. Friends and family started with a perfectly roasted and succulent turkey. Next came the accompaniments: a bread-crumb stuffing, green beans with roasted garlic, creamy gravy, and her famous Persian-spiced cranberry sauce. Next came the Persian rices, with Rice with Sour Cherries (page 178) and its delicious *tahdig*. If you still had room on your plate, you moved to the warm accompaniments of chestnut purée, cooked pears, and roasted vegetables with Persian spices. A selection of salads at the end of the table suggested that this meal was not about eating your greens.

Nahid smiled as guests would return again and again for third and often fourth helpings. She would eat little during her parties, taking more satisfaction in watching others enjoy the delicious food—for her, this was the greatest pleasure. After a short period to allow the stomach to rest, the buffet table was filled with an array of desserts: pumpkin pie, a bûche de Noël, her favorite fresh persimmons with cream, and Persian-spiced fruit compote. Family members gave speeches, expressing gratitude for health and happiness, everyone's attendance, and Nahid's ultimate feast.

As the night drew to a close, we would settle in the living room with traditional glasses of chai and trade stories old and new.

COOKING OILS

The range of oils found in grocery stores has expanded significantly in the past decade, introducing novel and distinctive options to consumers. People focus on how and what to look for in choosing an oil, yet the healthiness of oil bought off the grocery shelf is only part of the story.

Determining the best cooking oil to use in your dishes can be a nuanced task and isn't always as simple as it appears. While many share similar nutritional and caloric characteristics, they can differ significantly in aroma, taste, health benefits, and cooking properties. Certain oils are more suited for frying, while others are better for baking, sautéing, or lightly drizzling over finished dishes. A key principle to remember is that the level of refinement from the oil's natural or "virgin" state directly impacts its smoke point (the temperature at which the oil starts to degrade). Hence, as oils perform differently under heat, selecting the right oil for your culinary pursuits is paramount to preserve nutritional integrity. (Generally, oils with lower smoke points are of higher quality, making them ideal for dressings and drizzling purposes, rather than for high-heat cooking methods.)

For the recipes in this cookbook, we recommend using organic or grass-fed butter, ghee (clarified butter), widely used olive oil, and even avocado oil.

You'll find three main types of olive oil in stores. Extra-virgin olive oil (EVOO) is the highest quality and least processed, extracted solely by mechanical means. It retains a rich flavor, vibrant green color, and is abundant in heart-healthy monounsaturated fats, antioxidants, and anti-inflammatory compounds. EVOO has a lower smoke point, between 325–375°F (165–190°C), making it suitable for light sautéing, drizzling over salads, or as a finishing oil. Virgin olive oil undergoes minimal processing and has a slightly higher smoke point. It offers similar health benefits to EVOO but with a milder flavor. Refined olive oil has a higher smoke point and a more neutral taste, as it undergoes further processing, including refining and filtering. While it loses some of the antioxidants and flavors of extra-virgin olive oil, it remains a healthier option compared with many other oils. Overall, olive oils provide a range of health benefits by supporting heart health, reducing inflammation, and contributing to a healthy diet when consumed in moderation.

- The best oils for high-temperature cooking (maximum 350°F/180°C): butter, ghee, coconut oil, and lard.
- The best oils for low-temperature cooking, marinades, sautéing, roasting, light frying, and baking (not to exceed 325°F/165°C): extra-virgin olive oil, avocado oil, and macadamia nut oil.
- The best oils for dressings, drizzling, dipping, and finishing: extra-virgin olive oil (unrefined, first cold-pressed), flaxseed oil (cold-pressed), and walnut oil (unrefined, cold-pressed).

Avoid refined oils such as canola (rapeseed) oil, safflower oil, corn oil, sunflower oil, cottonseed oil, soybean oil, margarine, and generic vegetable oil.

Oil declines in both its quality and flavor as it ages. Some varieties of oil have the potential to turn rancid when exposed to light, heat, or oxygen. Therefore, it is best to store oils in a cool and dark place. For best quality, aim to purchase oils in dark glass bottles, as micro-particles from plastic bottles can leech into the oils and allow light in, which can degrade even the beneficial components. To preserve its flavor, an oil should be utilized within one year from the date of purchase. Certain oils may require even swifter consumption.

TYPE OF OIL	SMOKE POINT TEMPERATURES	
Almond oil	440°F	225°C
Avocado oil	375–400°F	190–205°C
Butter	350°F	175°C
Canola (rapeseed) oil	400°F	205°C
Coconut oil	350°F	175°C
Corn oil	450°F	230°C
Extra-virgin olive oil	325–375°F	165–190°C
Flaxseed oil	225°F	110°C
Ghee	450°F	230°C
Grapeseed oil	390°F	195°C
Light/refined olive oil	465°F	240°C
Macadamia nut oil	430°F	220°C
Peanut (groundnut) oil	450°F	230°C
Rice bran oil	490°F	260°C
Safflower oil	510°F	265°C
Sesame oil	350–410°F	175–210°C
Soybean oil	450°F	230°C
Sunflower oil	440°F	225°C
Vegetable oil	400–450°F	205–230°C
Walnut oil (unrefined)	320°F	160°C

HERBS, SPICES & SEEDS

HERBS

Persians have a love affair with fresh and dried herbs, which are used in abundance. Use fresh herbs as much as possible, but dried herbs are acceptable. If using dried herbs, the general rule of thumb is to scale down the measurement to a third of the required amount. For example, if a recipe calls for one tablespoon of chopped fresh tarragon, you should use about one teaspoon. The reverse also applies: if a recipe calls for one teaspoon of dried tarragon, you can substitute one tablespoon of fresh instead.

Just like ground spices, dried herbs lose efficacy when stored improperly. Keep them away from light, heat, air, and moisture. When stored well, dried herbs will be optimal for about six months.

BASIL

Basil comes in many varieties in the Western world. Sweet basil, an aromatic tender herb, is well known to Mediterranean cooks; Thai basil has a spicy fragrance and flavor; and cinnamon basil is the closest relative of the reyhan, grown in Iran. With narrower and smaller leaves and an almost sage green color, reyhan is often eaten raw and included as part of a fresh Herb Platter (page 24). It is also used in Beef & Basil Stew (page 154). Basil can be a tonic for the nervous system and help ease digestive complaints.

CHIVE AND SCALLION (SPRING ONION)

Flavorful and aromatic chives and scallions (spring onions) are key elements in a healthy Persian diet. They are rich in naturally occurring plant chemicals that help feed the gut with antibacterial, antiviral, antifungal, and diuretic properties. Finely chopped chives are an essential ingredient in Herb Frittata (page 50).

CILANTRO (CORIANDER)

This pungent herb can be used raw or dried in cooking. Rich in antioxidants, the leaves have antibiotic properties and can help treat digestive problems. Some people find its leaves have a distinct soapy flavor. The leaves can be added to salads and used in various Persian appetizers, rice dishes, stews, braises, and meat dishes.

DILL

Grassy and flavorful with a hint of anise, dill is used abundantly in Persian cuisine to diversify flavor in soups, stews, braises, and rice dishes. It also adds vibrancy to an otherwise muted-looking dish. Their digestive, antimicrobial, anti-inflammatory, and detoxifying compounds have been used for centuries to treat a host of health and skin conditions, manage halitosis, promote lactation, and reduce cholesterol and blood sugar.

FENUGREEK

Fenugreek leaves and greens are used in Persian curries, stews, and soups. When you roast the raw bitter fenugreek seeds, they become milder and nuttier in flavor. You can either grind the seeds or use them whole to flavor food or to make tea Fenugreek can help support blood sugar control, enhance digestion, and potentially boost milk production in nursing mothers.

MARJORAM AND OREGANO

Marjoram and oregano are different plants, but they can be used interchangeably in cooking and medicine. Marjoram and oregano are potent bactericides, expectorants, and digestive-system stimulants when used in cooking, made into tea, or used in their most common therapeutic form as an essential oil. They add punch to fish and meat dishes.

MINT

Slightly different from that of the common mint variety, bright green Persian mint leaves are long and thin with a delicate flavor. Persian mint is mostly used fresh; however, when fried, it takes on a slightly nutty flavor. Mint has the ability to alleviate digestive discomfort such as indigestion and bloating.

PARSLEY

Parsley brightens flavors and adds balance to dishes. In Persian cuisine, it is commonly added to stews and eaten fresh at almost every meal. The herb is packed with vitamins C and E, folate, and various antioxidants, which can help alleviate inflammation. It also has diuretic properties and serves as a digestive aid, tonic, and laxative.

ROSEMARY

Rosemary has a historical connection dating back to ancient Persian medical texts, where it earned the nickname "the herb of remembrance" thanks to its capacity to enhance memory and mental clarity. A fragrant and versatile culinary herb native to the Mediterranean, rosemary adds flavor and aroma to soups, salads, sauces, fish, and cooked meats and vegetables.

SAGE

A member of the mint family, sage is an aromatic and flavorful herb used sparingly in Persian cuisine. Its abundance in flavonoids, polyphenolic compounds, vitamin K, and vital minerals has made this a popular medicinal herb. In Persian cuisine, it is used to flavor soups and meats.

TARRAGON

Tarragon has a delicate but complex flavor, with predominant notes of aniseed balanced out and hints of vanilla, mint, pepper, and eucalyptus. In Persian cuisine, it is commonly included in the Herb Platter (page 24), a medley of herbs with antispasmodic properties and the ability to improve digestive function.

THYME

Part of the mint family, thyme is often used to add spice and flavor to meats, poultry, and fish. Its essential oil, thymol, displays potent antibacterial qualities and serves as an antiseptic for the throat, lung, and digestive system.

SPICES & SEEDS

Spices are the resplendent gems that adorn our culinary heritage. From sweet cinnamon to perky sumac to luxurious saffron, these spices grace our dishes with aromatic allure, dynamic flavors, and a sensory feast for all.

Persian cuisine is subtly spiced, delicate in taste and appearance, yet not typically hot or spicy. Roasting spices can increase their depth and pungency. For example, turmeric should be toasted and combined with black pepper to release its noble flavors and medicinal virtues, whereas spices like sumac are added just before serving. To maintain their rich flavors, spices must be stored in tightly sealed glass containers in cool, dark, and dry places, as humidity and heat will impact their quality.

ADVIEH

Persian allspice mix is a vital part of our cuisine and an essential culinary ingredient. It is an aromatic blend of warm spices, including cardamom, turmeric, cumin, cinnamon, rose petals, madras curry, and nutmeg. Nahid Joon made large batches of her unique spice blend, with pale Persian dried rose petals (*gol-e-mohamamdi*) or darker ones from Syria—both known to be the best in the world.

ANGELICA OR PERSIAN HOGWEED

Angelica is known in Farsi as *golpar*, meaning "flower feather." Possessing a warm and dry character, the aromatic seeds can be used as a spice, food, dietary supplement, and traditional curative. They can be blended with wild rue seeds and burnt as an incense, which is an ancient Persian tradition passed through generations from Zoroastrianism to avert the evil eye.

BARBERRIES

Barberries come from a shrub that produces tart red berries. Highly nutritious and rich in vitamins and minerals, the fruit, stem, and root bark contain alkaloids (the most prominent being berberine), which are known to have antimicrobial, anti-inflammatory, hypotensive, and sedative effects. They are generally eaten raw, made into jam, or gently fried—adding bursts of color to mounds of fluffy basmati rice like Sweet Rice with Orange Peels (page 183) or garnishing dishes such as Tabrizi Meatballs (page 110). Barberries can also be juiced or used to make tea.

CARDAMOM

Belonging to the ginger family, this aromatic seeds flavor Persian curries, desserts, and teas. Cardamom stimulates appetite and aids digestion. Tip: If you've had a lot of garlic and want to freshen your breath while avoiding heartburn, chew on some cardamom seeds.

CAYENNE PEPPER

Cayenne pepper is over ten times spicier than jalapeño, so a little goes a long way. It adds a kick to Lentil & Quinoa Salad with Herbs (page 30), Yogurt Stew with Tarragon (page 140), and pasta dishes. Both chili powder and cayenne pepper share similar nutrients and health benefits.

CHILI

Chili is used sparingly in Persian cuisine. The essential oil found in chilies, called capsaicin, can be good for your heart and circulatory system. However, it's important to be cautious and moderate consumption, as excessive consumption can lead to chronic inflammation in the stomach and intestines.

CINNAMON

This universal spice is commonly used to flavor a variety of Persian desserts and savory recipes. It is also one of the ingredients in the Persian Spice Blend (page 246). Cinnamon is a natural antibacterial, supporting both your respiratory system and cardiovascular health. Additionally, it is known to soothe muscle spasms and promote healthy digestion.

CLOVES

Used whole or ground, this delicate spice is combined with other spices, such as cardamom and cinnamon, to impart a sweet, warm, and floral flavor to teas. Clove essential oil is a potent germfighter. Cloves also have a little numbing effect and can ease toothaches and mouth sores.

CUMIN

Cumin comes in predominantly two forms—dried seeds or powder. Known for its distinct flavor, it lends earthy, warm, smoky, spicy flavors, and a hint of bitterness to food. Roasted seeds have an enhanced warm, pungent, and citrusy aroma. In powder form, cumin is one of the main ingredients in the Persian Spice Blend (page 246). Cumin seeds are rich in antioxidants, help relieve gas and bloating, and aid in digestion.

FENUGREEK

Fenugreek is a clover-like herb, the seeds fragrant with a deep earthy and grassy aroma. The leaves can be used (see page 254), and their slightly sweet and bitter flavor is intensified upon drying. (It loses some of its bitterness when cooked.) In Persian cooking, it flavors stews and soups such as Herb & Persian Lime Stew (page 163) and Mashed Lamb & Mung Bean with Herbs (page 113). Fenugreek can help support blood sugar control, enhance digestion, and potentially boost milk production in nursing mothers.

GARLIC

Garlic, a root vegetable of the allium family, has been widely used as a flavoring in cooking and medicine throughout history. Both fresh garlic and garlic powder are used abundantly in Persian dishes, including Eggplant Dip (page 36) and Smoked Eggplant with Tomato (page 42). The sulfur compounds in garlic may irritate ulcers, and high doses of garlic can exaggerate the effects of anticoagulants and blood pressure-lowering drugs. Tip: Eat with parsley to avoid garlic on the breath.

GINGER

Ginger is a widely used spice that is warming and fragrant and used in powder form in breads, cookies, sweets, and teas. It helps support overall gastrointestinal health, is a potent anti-inflammatory and antioxidant, and helps alleviates nausea (particularly morning sickness).

HEMP SEED

Despite their small size, these brown seeds are densely packed with protein, fiber, a range of essential minerals, and a variety of vitamins. Used in Iran since ancient times for their unique nutritional profile, they are enjoyed year-round for snacking—notably in a Persian trail mix known as *ajeel*—and traditionally seen around the Persian New Year (Nowruz).

NIGELLA SEEDS

Nigella seeds are tiny, angular black seeds with a robust flavor with notes of onion, oregano, and black pepper. Slightly toasting them in a dry skillet and waiting for them to pop will release their aromatic properties. In Persian cuisine, nigella seeds are commonly sprinkled in a popular traditional Persian flatbread with a crisp crust and light, airy texture (*nan-e-barbari*).

NUTMEG

This spice is made from the inner portion of the seed derived from the nutmeg tree. Available in both ground and whole form, nutmeg enhances sweet and savory dishes and adds complexity to the aromatic Persian Spice Blend (page 246).

(DRIED) PERSIAN LIME

Dried Persian limes, found in Middle Eastern markets, come in varying colors and require a lengthy simmer to soften their hard dry skin and realize flavorful taste in stews; the whole lime is edible, and soaking it in hot water aids in softening the skin for ease of piercing.

ROSE PETALS

Roses have been used as a spice in Persian cuisine for millennia. The queen of all kinds of roses is the delicate, pink Iranian damask rose or “Mohammadi flower.” The flavor can range from floral and sweet to tart to mildly spicy. In this book, you will find it in the Cucumber-Herb Yogurt (page 38), Pistachio Soup (page 68), and Eggplant Chutney (page 206). Store rose petals in an airtight container in a cool, dark place, as the color of the petals can quickly fade.

SAFFRON

Saffron is a valuable spice made from the dried stigma of the autumn crocus flower. This labor-intensive spice is meticulously cultivated and harvested by hand. The flower itself boasts a purple hue, while its stigma is a vibrant red. Interestingly, each crocus bulb yields just one solitary flower, and within each of these flowers, you'll find only three precious stigmas. Given the intensive manual labor required for harvesting, saffron rightfully earns its reputation as one of the world's most expensive spices.

Persian saffron is unique and the most vetted worldwide. When buying saffron, focus on three criteria: the saffron threads should be uniformly red and no other color; they must be dry and brittle to the touch; and they should have a strong and fresh aroma (never musty). (Avoid the powdered version, as it generally disappoints.) Maximize your saffron stigmas (strands) by gently grinding them in a mortar and pestle to a powder, then infusing them in warm liquid for 1–2 minutes to release their color and unique aroma. Blooming saffron is an essential step for all recipes used throughout the book. Once the saffron is bloomed, use the bloomed saffron water as required in the recipe. Saffron has potent antioxidant and anti-inflammatory properties and potential mood enhancing effects.

SUMAC

With its crimson hue and citrus undertones, this exceptional ingredient deserves a prime spot in every spice cabinet. It plays a crucial role in dry rubs, marinades, and dressings, often sprinkled over dishes just before serving to impart its flavor. In the realm of Levantine cuisine, it's a cornerstone of the beloved za'atar spice blend, enhancing everything from succulent kebabs to flavorful lamb chops. Boasting a wealth of polyphenols and flavonoids, it serves as a robust antioxidant with antifungal and antimicrobial properties, potentially aiding in digestion when incorporated into your diet.

TAMARIND

Tamarind is a bean-like pod that contains a sweet, fleshy tangy, and acidic pulp. The flesh is mature when it turns a brown or reddish-brown color. We use it to add an exquisite sweet-sour taste to fish dishes such as Fish & Herb Stew (page 136).

TURMERIC

Belonging to the ginger family, turmeric root bears a striking resemblance to fresh ginger, featuring a papery and knotty outer skin. However, once peeled, its interior reveals a vibrant orange flesh, which transforms into an electrifying shade of yellow upon the drying process. The primary active component of turmeric is curcumin, giving this spice its characteristic yellowish hue.

Pungent, earthy, and mustardy in taste, turmeric is added sparingly to almost all our recipes, from stews to braises to soups, especially in Golden Fried Onions (page 246). It is known for its powerful anti-inflammatory and antioxidant properties, offering potential benefits for joint health and overall well-being.

ESSENCES AND MOLASSES

Food is perceived with three senses—smell, taste, and touch—and Persian cuisine has always been keen to transform and create sensuous-tasting foods. Essences, concentrated and aromatic scents, molasses, and syrups add brilliant taste to meats, sauces, drinks, and desserts. There are a few ingredients we suggest you keep in your Persian pantry to enjoy and use, even if they might not be used in every dish. Most have a long shelf life, so consider having these handy.

GRAPE MOLASSES

This natural sweetener held a significant place in culinary history, recognized as one of the earliest alternatives to cane sugar and honey in the Middle East and Mediterranean regions. It is made by heating grapes in water, then blending them and pressing the mixture through a filter, which results in nutrient-rich nectar. It makes for a good sugar substitute in recipes such as Eggplant Chutney (page 206).

ORANGE BLOSSOM WATER

This sweet and powerful fragrance is commonly used in sweets, cakes, and pastries—and a little goes a long way. It's best kept in opaque glass containers so light doesn't pass through. In savory cooking, this can be used to flavor rices such as Sweet Rice with Orange Peels (page 183). Orange blossom is a natural carminative and antispasmodic.

POMEGRANATE MOLASSES

The thick syrupy juice is extracted from the seeds of the pomegranate fruit, renowned for its jewel tones and tangy flavor. Ideal for both sweet and savory cooking, it is used in many Persian dishes such as Walnut, Chicken & Pomegranate Stew (page 148) and Stuffed Fish with Herbs & Nuts (page 122). Rich in polyphenols, antioxidants, and vitamins B and C, this nutritionally beneficial ingredient will add a new flavor to your food.

ROSE WATER

In Persian literature, roses are a symbol of perfection. During spring, roses can be found blooming all over the country, from small city squares to majestic Persian gardens. Aside from being used as an ornamental plant, roses are widely used in the perfume and food industries.

Rose water, made from distilling rose petals, has a distinctive smell and flavor to enhance Persian desserts, such as Cardamom & Rose Water Pudding (page 229) and Saffron Rice Pudding (page 230). We also use it to add flavor to Rice with Fava Beans & Dill (page 177) and Rice with veal and green beans (page 174). It is hydrating and soothing and has natural antiseptic, anti-inflammatory, and antibacterial properties.

SOUR GRAPE JUICE OR VERJUS

Sour grapes or verjus are the unripened grapes available a few weeks before grape bunches ripen on their vines, where the fruit is ground, dried, pressed, or kept whole as a fresh or frozen ingredient. The tart, sour-tasting, and brownish-hued grape juice (*abghooreh*) has been traditionally used in Persian cuisine as a seasoning or acidifying agent. This remarkable ingredient adds flavor to grilled fish and chicken marinades, hearty soups, fortifying potages, and Stuffed Grape Leaves (page 47).

TEAS

In Tehran, Nahid Joon always served tea in a beautiful samovar (an ornate urn, typically made from metal, iron, brass, copper, or bronze, used to boil water for tea) and brewed her tea mix in an attractive ceramic Persian teapot (*ghouri*) placed on top of the samovar.

Always prepared with loose leaves, tea was consumed from breakfast until sunset and in the afternoons alongside lovely pastries, dates, saffron rock candy, nougat, pistachio brittle, or sugar cubes. Nahid Joon always served her tea in beautiful Russian silver tea sleeve holders with small tea glasses inside them. She then served after-dinner teas in smaller Persian tea glasses (*estekan*) with beautiful ornate saucers. She always told her guests that tea appeals to all five senses, just like wine. You must first touch the cup to feel the heat and see if it is too hot or cold. Use your ears and enjoy the sound of the tea being delicately poured from a high distance and see the tea drops gently filling your glass. You must study the brew's color, ensuring that you are satisfied with the hue. You then use your nose to smell the unique fragrance that she created by blending Persian black teas with Earl Grey, cardamom, and Indian teas. You then taste it with your tongue to get all the tea flavors. For Nahid Joon, tea was a ritual.

BORAGE

This herb grows in northern Iran, where its dried purple flower (echium) is brewed in the same manner as tea leaves. Borage is slightly sour in taste and a diuretic with antimicrobial and antidiarrheal properties. Commonly used to treat coughs and colds, it has calming and soothing effects on the nerves. Borage can make you sleepy and is a good solution for sleep disorders.

CHAMOMILE

Chamomile stands as one of the most ancient, extensively utilized, and comprehensively recorded botanical treasures worldwide. A tablespoon of chamomile flowers and boiling water can be a mild relaxing sleep aid; help treat fevers, colds, stomach ailments, and muscle spasms; and act as an anti-inflammatory.

LEMON VERBENA

Known as the "queen of the aromatic herbs," lemon verbena is traditionally used to aid digestion, alleviate colds, improve stomach function, and boost memory and concentration.

PERSIAN CHAI

Persian tea is brewed in multiple stages and mixed with cardamom and cinnamon for color, fragrance, and flavor. Always use cold water in your kettle, as it plays a significant role in the taste of the tea. Persian chai is usually served with rock candy (*nabat*) and dates.

THYME

Tea made from thyme leaves is a popular cold-weather beverage that has been used to treat many infectious diseases and health conditions because of its antibacterial properties. It is highly recommended for colds and can act as an antiseptic for the throat and lungs. Although thyme is a powerful medical herb, it is not recommended during pregnancy or for people suffering from mint allergies and coagulation disorders.

SAFFRON

The ingredients for saffron tea can vary, but they often encompass a delightful medley of cardamom, cinnamon, fragrant rose petals, invigorating ginger, zesty lemon slices, refreshing mint, and the subtle notes of white or green tea, all harmoniously brought together with the sweet touch of honey. To craft saffron tea, grind dry saffron threads into a fine powder, combined with a dash of sugar, using a mortar and pestle. Following this, steep Persian black tea, adorned with a symphony of spices, along with the infusion of lemon slices, invigorating mint, or aromatic ginger, in hot water for a brief spell. Then, introduce the powdered saffron into the brew. If desired, enhance its sweetness with honey. This elixir can be prepared in generous quantities, ideally in a large pitcher (jug), to be relished either warm or cold.

THE NATURE OF FOOD

Many ancient Eastern culinary cultures have a profound reverence for the medicinal properties of food. According to the traditional medicine of Iran, the "hotness" or "coldness" of food can impact the body. A common misconception of "hot" and "cold" foods occurs when it's taken in its literal sense: that cooked or spicy food is considered hot, and refrigerated food is cold. But the prevailing temperature of food has little impact on its potency.

To redress the equilibrium of metabolic humors and safeguard against digestive tribulations, the "cold" constituents must harmoniously consort with their "hot" counterparts. In essence, "hot" foods, such as meat, fats, wheat, sugars, select spices, and certain fruits, nuts, and vegetables, kindle the fires of vitality, fostering the robust circulation of life's essence. "Hot" foods are also easily digested, resulting in efficient nutrient absorption and restoring vitality.

In contrast, "cold" foods, an elixir of nourishment and hydration, contribute to the gentle fortification of bodily humors. It is noteworthy that the body labors twice as hard when confronted with a frosty repast, expending its energy to restore it to the warmth of its core. Overindulgence in cold foods may usher discomfort, manifesting in joint and muscle discord, frigid extremities, excessive salivation, abdominal distress, and fatigue.

In the mosaic of Persian gastronomy, side dishes emerge as the artisanal architects of balance. For instance, in Walnut, Chicken & Pomegranate Stew (page 148), the "warmth" of chicken finds its counterpoint in the "chill" of walnuts and pomegranate molasses. In Rice with Fava Beans & Dill (page 177), dill corrects the "cold" nature of rice and fava (broad) beans. Fish, inherently "cool," finds solace alongside the "fiery" accompaniment of dill, pickled garlic, or the tangy essence of *torshi*. Yogurt, a "cold" food by nature, will not be served with fish at a Persian table. Instead, it finds its place as an accompaniment, enriching the textures and flavors of dishes such as the Meat & Yellow Split Pea Stew (page 160).

The recipes shared here embody a subtle alchemy, deftly combining the realms of "hot" and "cold." As Persians have known for ages, when we savor food with intention, it transmutes into the very essence of healing artistry. Thus, let us dine in the Persian way, embracing the wisdom that proclaims food as our most potent elixir.

FOOD PROPERTIES

FRUITS

Cooling
Apple
Apricot (neutral)
Avocado (neutral)
Banana (unripe)
Barberry
Cranberry
Fig (neutral)
Grapefruit
Grape (red, purple, black)
Green apple
Honeydew
Kiwi
Lemon
Lime
Melon
Nectarine
Olive (neutral)
Papaya (neutral)
Peach
Pear (neutral)
Persian lime
Persimmon
Pomegranate
Prune
Raspberry
Sour cherry
Strawberry
Tomato
Watermelon

Heating
Banana (ripe)
Blackberry (neutral)
Blueberry (neutral)
Cantaloupe
Cherry
Coconut
Date
Grape (green)
Mango
Orange
Pineapple
Plum
Quince
Raisin
Sweet melon
Tamarind
Tangerine

VEGETABLES

Cooling
Alfalfa sprouts
Asparagus
Beet
Bok choi
Broccoli
Cabbage
Cauliflower
Celery
Chestnut
Corn (neutral)

Cucumber
Eggplant (aubergine)
Grape leaves
Green bean
Green leafy vegetables
Green peas
Kale (and most bitter greens)
Lettuce
Mushroom
Okra
Parsnip
Potato
Pumpkin
Rutabaga
Seaweed
Spinach (raw)
Sprouts
Squash (summer and winter)
White corn
Zucchini (courgette)

Heating
Artichoke
Bell pepper
Brussels sprout
Carrot (neutral)
Chili
Dandelion greens
Garlic
Ginger
Hot pepper
Leek
Mustard green
Onion
Radish
Scallion (spring onion)
Shallot
Spinach (cooked)
Sweet potato (neutral)
Turnip
Yam
Yellow corn

<u>NUTS AND SEEDS</u>

Cooling
Almond, soaked and peeled
Fennel seeds
Pumpkin seeds
Sunflower seeds (neutral)

Heating
Almond (with skin)
Angelica (*golpar*)
Brazil nut
Cashew
Macadamia nut
Peanut
Pecan
Pine nut
Pistachio
Sesame seeds
Walnut

<u>GRAINS</u>

Cooling
Barley
Bran
Brown rice
Millet
Wheat bran
Wheat germ
White rice

Heating
Oats
Quinoa
Spelt

<u>HERBS</u>

Cooling
Cilantro (coriander)
Peppermint
Persian lime, fresh or dried

Heating
Basil
Bay leaf
Chive
Dill
Fenugreek
Marjoram
Mint
Oregano
Parsley
Rosemary
Tarragon

<u>LEGUMES</u>

Cooling
Barley
Bean sprouts
Black-eyed pea (neutral)
Chickpea (neutral)
Kidney bean
Lentil (neutral)
Lima (butter) bean
Mung bean
Peas (neutral)
Pinto bean
Soybean
Tofu
Yellow fava (broad) Beans

Heating
Black bean
Yellow split pea (neutral)

<u>MEAT</u>

Cooling
All fish except red snapper
Rabbit
Turkey

Heating
Beef
Chicken
Duck
Hen
Goat
Lamb
Red snapper
Shrimp (prawn)
Veal
Venison

<u>SPICES</u>

Cooling
Sumac

Heating
Cardamom
Chili
Cinnamon
Cloves
Cumin seeds
Curry powder
Fennel
Ginger
Mustard
Nutmeg
Pepper
Saffron
Salt
Turmeric

<u>DAIRY</u>

Cooling
Buttermilk
Cheese
Cow's milk
Cream
Crème fraîche
Feta cheese (neutral)
Ghee
Goat's milk
Yogurt

Heating
Butter
Sour cream

<u>OTHER</u>

Cooling
Coffee
Green tea
Lemon juice
Milk
Pomegranate paste
Sour grape juice (*ab ghureh*)
Soy milk
Sugar
Tamarind
Tea (neutral)
Tofu
Tomato paste (purée)
Tomato sauce
Water

Heating
Chocolate
Cornstarch (cornflour)
Eggs
Honey
Persian pickles
Rose water
Vinegar
Wheat flour
Whey

INDEX

Page numbers in *italics* refer to photos.

H

J

K

L

M

N

O

P

Q

R

✻ V ✻

✻ W ✻

✻ Y ✻

✻ Z ✻

SOURCES

Pages 198–201:
1 This essay draws on the following works: "Sussan Babai, Feasting and the Perso-Shi'i Etiquette of Kingship," in Isfahan and Its Palaces: Statecraft, Shi'ism, and the Architecture of Conviviality in Early Modern Iran. Edinburgh: Edinburgh University Press, 2008; ibid., "Cookery and Urbanity in Early Modern Isfahan," in Journal for Early Modern Cultural Studies, vol. 18, no. 3 (Summer 2018): pp. 129–153. DOI: https://doi.org/10.1353/jem.2018.0026; Bert G. Fragner, "Zur Erforschung der kulinarishen Kultur Irans," in Der Welt der Islams, new series, vols. 23–24 (1984): 320–360; Rudolph Matthee, "Matbak, 3. In Persia," in Encyclopedia of Islam II, supplement vols. 9–10, 2004: 608–612; ibid., "Patterns of Food Consumption in Early Modern Iran," in Oxford Handbooks Online (February 2016): 1–28. DOI: 10.1093/oxfordhb/9780199935369.013.13.

2 Al-Ghazali on the Manners Relating to Eating: Book XI to the Revival of Religious Sciences Cambridge: The Islamic Text Society, 2000).

3 Iradj Afshar, Ashpazi-ye dore-ye Safavi [Cooking of the Safavid period]. Tehran: SEDA and Sima Publishers, 1981.

4 See Afshar, Ashpazi-ye dore-ye Safavi.

5 Babaie, Sussan. *Isfahan and Its Palaces: Statecraft, Shi'ism and the Architecture of Conviviality in Early Modern Iran*. Edinburgh: Edinburgh University Press, 2018. 228.

Pages 238–243:
Balaghi, Shiva, and Lynn Gumpert, eds. *Picturing Iran: Art, Society and Revolution*. London: I.B. Tauris, 2003.

Chehabi, Houshang. "How Caviar Turned Out to Be Halal." *Gastronomica* 7, no. 2 (2007): 17–23.

———. "The Westernization of Iranian Culinary Culture." *Iranian Studies* 36, no. 1 (2003): 43–61.

Daftari, Fereshteh and Layla S. Diba, *Iran Modern*. New Haven and London: Asia Society Museum and Yale University Press, 2014.

Daryaee, Touraj. "Food, Purity and Pollution: Zoroastrian Views on the Eating Habits of Others." *Iranian Studies* 45, no. 2 (2012): 229–42.

Diba, Layla S. "The Formation of Modern Iranian Art: From Kamal-al-Molk to Zenderoudi." In *Iran Modern*, edited by Fereshteh Daftari and Layla S. Diba, 45–65. New Haven and London: Yale University Press, 2014.

Fays, Hadi. *Coffee-house Painting*. Tehran: Reza Abbasi Museum, 1990.

Komaroff, Linda, ed. *In the Fields of Empty Days*. Munich: Prestel, 2018.

Matthee, Rudi. "From Coffee to Tea: Shifting Patterns of Consumption in Qajar Iran." *Journal of World History* 7, no. 2 (1996): 199–230.

Shirazi, Faegheh. "The *Sofreh*: Comfort and Community among Women in Iran." *Iranian Studies* 38, no. 2 (2005): 293–309.

Vorderstrasse, Tasha. *Antoin Sevruguin: Past and Present*. Chicago: Oriental Institute of the University of Chicago, 2020.

AUTHOR AND CONTRIBUTORS

LEILA TAGHINIA-MILANI HELLER

Leila Taghinia-Milani Heller was born in Tehran, Iran. She is the founder and president of Leila Heller Gallery, a contemporary art gallery in New York and Dubai. Leila received her bachelor of arts degree in art history and French literature from Brown University and her master's degree in art from Sotheby's Institute in London, as well as a second master's degree in art history and museum management from George Washington University. She has published numerous articles and has given talks on the topic of Middle Eastern art. Leila is an accomplished home cook, who learned the art of cooking from her grandmother Nostrat Khanom Bayat Maku and her mother, Nahid Joon. She lives in New York City and Dubai. She is married to Henry Heller and together they have two sons, Alexander Mamady and Philip Salar.

LILA CHARIF

Lila Charif was born in Tehran, Iran, and raised in France. With a degree from the College of Naturopathic Medicine in London, she is currently a practicing naturopathic nutritional therapist. Lila strongly believes that food is medicine, and her mission is to educate people about healthy lifestyle choices. Her love and interest in Persian food began from her early childhood in the south of France, growing up with authentic home-cooked Persian dishes prepared by her mother and her neighbor Nahid Joon. She resides in London with her husband, Behdad, and they have two children, Nina and Lara.

LAYA KHADJAVI

Laya Khadjavi was most recently Head of Strategic Partnerships and Client Relations at Menai Financial Group. She holds a bachelor of science in applied mathematics-economics from Brown University and a master of business administration from Columbia University. She serves on many boards and committees, including Brown's Center for Middle East Studies' Advisory Council and the Iranian American Women Foundation's Board of Advisors. She is a member of the Metropolitan Museum of Art's Ancient Near East Art's Visiting Committee and, in 2008, she received The Ellis Island Medal of Honor Award. Laya met Nahid Joon in Tehran in 1975 and creating this book is the most important homage Laya could give to Nahid Joon. She lives in New York City with her husband and two daughters.

BAHAR TAVAKOLIAN

Bahar Tavakolian was born in Iran and moved to the U.S. as a teenager. Holding a Ph.D. in Materials Science and Engineering from Cornell University, Bahar has had a diverse professional journey with roles in the biotech and aerospace industries, as well as serving as an adjunct professor at the University of California. Bahar currently excels as a residential broker, consistently ranked among the nation's top real estate professionals.

In 1996, Bahar encouraged Nahid Joon to write a cookbook, offering to document the recipes—an offer that Nahid Joon embraced. Living in New York with her husband Majid, Bahar is a proud parent to Sara and Kourosh.

ACKNOWLEDGMENTS

Her Majesty Empress Farah Pahlavi, thank you for empowering me as a woman in Iran to be brave and fight for my rights.

I am forever thankful to my co-authors Lila Charif, Laya Khadjavi, and Bahar Tavakolian for their friendship and helping make Nahid Joon's dream come true.

Debra Black, a million thanks for this opportunity and putting your trust in me. You are an inspiring friend and a great mentor.

Susan and John Hess, I so cherish your friendship. Thank you for the rave review of my albaloo polo and planting the seed for this project.

Ella Schwartz, your presence was an essential element of this cookbook. I would have fallen apart without you. Thank you also to your father Michael Schwartz, celebrated chef and restaurateur, for his guidance.

My sincere thank you to Phaidon's team: Emilia Terragni, Emily Takoudes, and Michelle Meade.

Nader Ahari, you are the rock in my life and were a son to Nahid Joon. Your guidance was essential in this cookbook.

Dr. Massumeh Farhad, my childhood friend and colleague, your essay on the art of feasting in the court of Shah Abbas and the Safavid Court is magnificent

Thank you Dr. Talinn Grigor for your essay on food and feasting in the Qajar courts as well as food portrayed in contemporary Iranian art.

Dr. Jake Stavis, thank you for your essay on the role of food and wine in ancient Iran during the Achemenid era. And thank you Dr. Kim Benzell, for your introduction to Jake.

Maria Herrera, you are a member of our family. Thank you for keeping Nahid Joon's Persian method of cooking alive.

My appreciation to the brilliant photography team Nico Schinco and Katie "Tweezerhands" Wayne. Your talent and creativity are palpable in every picture.

My dear friends and devoted recipe testers Faranak Amirsaleh, Neda Rastegar, Nazgol Shahbazi, Mahshid Ehsani, Roya Khadjavi, Bahman Kia, Suzy Azadi, Nancy Sahni, and Sahba Vaziri: You are forces of nature who ensured our recipes were flawless.

Mina Tavakolian, I appreciate all your help in the standardization and expertise in recipe developing.

Fereshteh Fathi Charif, Lila Charif's mother, I am eternally thankful to you. You were a true sister to Nahid Joon and her partner-in-crime in the kitchen.

Soraya Tavakolian, you have always been present in my life and you and Nahid Joon were soulmates. Thank you.

My gratitude to Faraz Khadjavi, whose friendship with Nahid Joon lasted over five decades. You were a true lion lady (shirzan).

My gratitude to Nayer Joon Mojtabai, Nahid Joon's best friend since childhood. The deep friendship of our families knows no boundaries.

My beautiful friend Vida Tahbaz, who was a second daughter to Nahid Joon, the love that bonded you two had no bounds.

Maryam Arjomand, we were joined at the hip since kindergarten. You are our Persian Martha Stewart. Your Aunt Evelyn Alvieh and dear mom Monir Joon are amazing chefs and it is an honor to have their kotlet recipe in this book.

Maryam Panahy Ansary, I am most grateful to for your epic feasts and gatherings.

Maryam Massoudi, one of Nahid Joon's closest friends and a role model in my life, you have an immense knowledge of the culture and history of Iran. Mohammed and Marie Afkhami, you are our family.

Sheikha Paula Al Sabah, my best friend, mentor, and a sister to Nahid Joon, your veganism inspired Nahid Joon to develop adaptations of her recipes that you could enjoy.

Faranak Amirsaleh, your family and mine are connected for three generations. Our kebab marathons in Lake George are unforgettable.

Nazee Batmanghelij Klotz, our moms were best friends since we were in kindergarten. Our legendary trips to Jamaica inspired Nahid Joon's delicious mango chutney.

Leyla Alaton, who introduced Nahid Joon to the Istanbul spice market which opened a new world of tastes and flavors for her, your Turkish breakfasts are legendary.

Roya Khadjavi Heidari, a big thank you for your creative and diverse menus in our cookbook.

Mina Atabai, Nahid Joon loved exchanging recipes with you. You are an amazing chef and your basil khoresht is exemplary.

Nazzy Beglari, the Queen of vegan Persian cuisine. Your gracious hospitality in Abu Dhabi made Nahid Joon and me regular guests. Marjan Fateh, thank you for introducing me to your signature dish, salmon polo.

Tala Gharagozlou Shea, my sincere appreciation. Nahid Joon so cherished your visits, cooking up a storm and then having a feast together.

Bahman Kia, being invited to yours and Gisue Hariri's home for dinner is a real treat. You are a gifted chef who cooks from your heart.

Majid Tavakolian, my childhood friend and the king of kebabs, thank you.

Dana Hammond Stubgen, no words can express my gratitude to you. Your family have been my quintessential testers for the last thirty-two years. Charlotte, you are on your way to being a master chef with your delicious Persian meals.

Pamela Gross, thank you for being my true sister, my maid of honor, and such an inspiration in my life. Our bond is sacred.

Prince Dimitri of Yugoslavia, you have always been at my side in both my happiest and darkest moments. Thank you for holding my hand, lighting my way, and instilling my strong faith.

Cousins Afagh Majdolmolk Rafiy and Nazli Majdolmolk Moezi, many thanks for enlightening me on our family history of Nahid Joon's mother Nosrat Al Moluk Majdolmolk's lineage.

Patrick Bayat Maku, your contributions to the family history of the Bayat clan in this book puts our legacy into perspective. Thank you for your brilliant research and building the family website.

Cousin Farzaneh Vaziri, your introduction to Patrick Bayat Maku was crucial to the research on our family history. Your love for Nahid Joon is priceless.

Cousin Farideh Vaziri, thank you for connecting me to our cousins who expanded on the stories of Nahid Joon's family. And thank you Shirin Banou for the beautiful flower arrangements from your flower shop Banchi.

Cousins Forough Bayat Maku, Amir Ali Bayat Maku, and Nosrat Ghazi Bayat, thank you for sharing so many stories of our family and connecting the dots of the different branches of our family.

Chakameh Habibi, thank you for keeping alive our 5,000-year-old heritage which our Zoroastrian ancestors left us.

My soulmate, Alidad Mahlouji, who has been an inspiration since our youth. Nahid Joon and I were dazzled by your staging of our Persian wedding celebrations.

My Buckley moms, Alice Michaels, Margie Miller, Sarah Senbahar, Harley Raiff, Susan Hess, Julie Minskoff, and Nancy McCartney, I am grateful for your friendship and the memorable evenings with our families.

Shanthi Veigas, the director of Leila Heller Gallery Dubai, thank you for your love and support. You gave me the peace of mind to set aside the time and write this book.

Dr. Fereshteh Daftari, I am grateful for your guidance in exploring the role of food in Iranian art history.

Shirley and Tina Benmorad, your delicious ghalieh mahi inspired me to make my own version. Thank you.

Reem Kassis, author of *The Palestinian Table* and *The Arabesque Table*, your advice in the early days was a guiding light.

Marvin Doctor, thank you for your support and fabulous photos of our family.

Serena Lin, thank you for your research.

I am indebted to all Persian immigrants who adopted a new country and preserved their culture and cuisine. My co-authors and I are grateful to Najmieh Batmanglij for inspiring us with her book, *Food of Life*.

Henry, Alexander, Philip, and Farah, the loves of my life, thank you for your voracious appetites and love. Henry, you are my rock, inspiration, and partner in our journey. This book would never have been finished without your daily support. Alexander and Philip, I am indebted to you both for keeping our family tight and for helping preserve our legacy. You have inherited Nahid Joon's passion for cooking and throwing amazing parties. Farah, it is no surprise you are such a perfect fit into our family.

Phaidon Press Limited
2 Cooperage Yard
London E15 2QR

Phaidon Press Inc.
111 Broadway
New York, NY 10006
phaidon.com

First published 2024
© 2024 Phaidon Press Limited

ISBN 978 1 83866 752 8

A CIP catalogue record for this book is available from the British Library and the Library of Congress. All rights reserved. No part of this publication may be reproduced, stored in a retrieval system or transmitted, in any form or by any means, electronic, mechanical, photocopying, recording or otherwise, without the written permission of Phaidon Press Limited.

Commissioning Editor: Emily Takoudes
Project Editor: Michelle Meade
Production Controller: Andie Trainer
Design: Marwan Kaabour
Design Assistant: Riccardo Righi
Photography: Nico Schinco, except images on pages 6, 18, and 239–42 courtesy of Leila Heller

Printed in China

Publisher's Acknowledgments
Phaidon would like to thank Iva Cheung, Judy Phillips, Ella Schwartz, Ellie Smith, and Kaitlin Wayne.

Recipe Notes

Unless otherwise specified:

- Use organic where possible.
- Butter is always unsalted.
- Spices, such as black pepper, are freshly ground.
- Individual vegetables and fruits, such as carrots and apples, are assumed to be medium.
- Sugar is superfine (white caster) sugar, and brown sugar is cane or demerara (turbinado).
- Cream is 36–40% fat heavy whipping cream.
- Milk is whole (full-fat) at 3% fat, homogenized and lightly pasteurized.
- Salt is kosher salt.
- Parsley is Italian (flat-leaf).
- Bread crumbs are always dried.
- Fish assumed cleaned and gutted.
- Greek yogurt is full-fat (whole).
- Eggs are US large (extra-large)
- Stock is always unsalted.

Cooking times are for guidance only, as individual ovens vary. If using a conventional oven, follow the manufacturer's instructions concerning oven temperatures.

Exercise a high level of caution when following recipes involving any potentially hazardous activity, including the use of high temperatures and open flames and when deep-frying. In particular, when deep-frying, add food carefully to avoid splashing, wear long sleeves, and never leave the pan unattended.

Some recipes include raw or very lightly cooked eggs, meat, or fish, and fermented products. These should be avoided by the elderly, infants, pregnant people, convalescents, and anyone with an impaired immune system.

As some species of mushrooms have been known to cause allergic reaction and illness, do take extra care when cooking and eating mushrooms and do seek immediate medical help if you experience a reaction after preparing or eating them.

Exercise caution when making fermented products, ensuring all equipment is clean, and seek expert advice if in any doubt.

When no quantity is specified, for example of oils, and sugars used for finishing dishes or for deep-frying, quantities are discretionary and flexible.

Both metric and imperial measures are used in this book. Follow one set of measurements throughout, not a mixture, as they are not interchangeable.

All spoon and cup measurements are level. 1 teaspoon = 5 ml; 1 tablespoon = 15 ml.

Australian standard tablespoons are 20 ml, so Australian readers are advised to use 3 teaspoons in place of 1 tablespoon when measuring small quantities.